Table Stakes
A Manual for Getting in the Game of News

DOUGLAS K. SMITH • QUENTIN HOPE • TIM GRIGGS

A Project of the Knight-Lenfest Newsroom Initiative

About the Authors

Doug Smith, a leader of the Knight-Lenfest Newsroom Initiative, is the architect and founding executive director of the Sulzberger Executive Leadership Program at Columbia Journalism School. Together with Jennifer Preston of Knight Foundation, Doug conceived of and guided the effort that began as Table Stakes in 2015.

Quentin Hope is a co-leader of the Knight-Lenfest Newsroom Initiative and works with the newsrooms involved in defining the table stakes and advising them on their performance challenges. He also serves as a coach and faculty member for the Sulzberger Program and works as an independent consultant on organizational strategy, design and effectiveness.

Tim Griggs is one of the Knight-Lenfest coaches and a consultant/advisor to media organizations and others on revenue and audience growth, product development, user experience and digital strategy. He's a former product and strategy executive at The New York Times, the former publisher of the Texas Tribune, and the former editor of the Wilmington (N.C.) StarNews.

All rights reserved
© Douglas K. Smith, Quentin Hope, Tim Griggs, 2017

Designed by Topos Graphics
Typest in Univers Next

No part of this book may be used or reproduced without express permission from the copyright holders.

Table of Contents

p. 5 **Foreword**
David Boardman
Dean, Klein College of Media and Communication
at Temple University
Chair, Lenfest Institute for Journalism

p. 9 **Introduction**

p. 29 **Focus on Performance Results in Using This Manual**

Table Stakes

p. 44 **Number 1**
Serve Targeted Audiences with Targeted Content

p. 98 **Number 2**
Publish on the Platforms Used by Your Target Audiences

p. 142 **Number 3**
Produce and Publish Continuously to Meet Audience Needs

p. 206 **Number 4**
Funnel Occasional Users into Habitual and Paying Loyalists

p. 244 **Number 5**
Diversify and Grow the Ways You Earn Revenue from the Audiences You Build

p. 280 **Number 6**
Partner to Expand Your Capacity and Capabilities at Lower and More Flexible Cost

p. 304 **Number 7**
Drive Audience Growth and Profitability from a "Mini-Publisher" Perspective

p. 347 **Shaping the Right Staff Roles and Skills for Your Newsroom**

p. 375 **Winning: Execution and Innovation**

Foreword
David Boardman
Dean, Klein College of Media and Communication at Temple University
Chair, Lenfest Institute for Journalism

In South Carolina, more than 300 women were murdered by their husbands and boyfriends in a rash of domestic violence enabled by the state's lax legal system.

In Texas, 250,000 disabled children were illegally denied the special education they need by state officials looking to save money and game school-performance scores.

In Washington state, hundreds of patients were funneled into a neurosurgery "factory" that was conducting brain and spinal operations at an astounding rate, producing astounding profits — and seeing an astounding rate of patient complications.

Each of these revelations, all over the past two years, emerged from the investigative reporting of a local newspaper. In each case, these stories would not have been told without the paper — respectively, the Post and Courier of Charleston, S.C., the Houston Chronicle and The Seattle Times.

And in each case, the positive changes that resulted from this journalism — laws changed, culprits confronted, lives saved or salvaged — would not have occurred.

Local journalism — especially the high-impact, public-service journalism that comes from quality regional newspapers — matters as much as it ever has. But it is that level of journalism that is most seriously threatened in the media market disruption of the 21st century. Since 2003, the typical metropolitan paper has lost about two-thirds of its advertising revenue, resulting in news staffs that are less than half their previous size.

While the editors of The Washington Post and The New York Times are being lauded for the digital resurgence of their nationally focused publications — buoyed by the so-called "Trump bump" in interest in national news — their counterparts in Houston, Charleston, Seattle, Philadelphia, Miami, Milwaukee and dozens of other metropolitan areas continue the slog of trying to reinvent their locally focused newsrooms in the face of these declining revenues and changing audience expectations. Rather than laurels, the editors of these papers have caught darts — from labor unions, corporate budget bosses, and angry readers and non-readers.

In that environment, where these regional editors were heads-down focused on finding any nickel hiding on the newsroom floor, it was virtually impossible for them to lift their vision to the deep horizon, to provide the leadership to create the new workflows, new products and new approaches their newsrooms, their organizations and their communities need and deserve.

Enter, in the fall of 2014, the John S. and James L. Knight Foundation. Alberto Ibarguen, its president and himself a former publisher of The Miami Herald, was deeply concerned about the future of these regional papers. He wondered what Knight might do to help them, and dispatched his new vice president for journalism, Jennifer Preston, to investigate.

Preston, put on the journalist's hat she had worn at The New York Times as a writer and editor, and came back to Knight with this finding: Editors of these local papers knew their newsrooms had to change dramatically, but they needed help, guidance, support and new knowledge in leading that change.

Preston had a notion of how to best help them: through the principles and tools she had learned from management guru Douglas Smith in the Punch Sulzberger News Media Executive Leadership Program at Columbia University. She had seen Smith's "Table Stakes" approach — a system of identifying performance challenges and measuring success by outcomes — transform the lives and careers of individuals in the program, including her own.

Could Smith's magic work with whole newsroom leadership teams — and, by extension, whole news organizations — in the same fashion? Preston, and Smith, believed it could. One of its pillars was to create learning cohorts and challenge teams, a paradigm that could be readily transferred. In fact, might the creation of cohorts among otherwise disconnected papers provide a supportive but motivating peer dynamic that would force editors to focus on creative change rather than simply survival?

They tested the notion with someone who had recently run one of those challenged newsrooms — yours truly, who had spent most of the past decade as executive editor of The Seattle Times, before coming to Temple University as dean of the Klein College of Media and Communication in fall of 2013. I was thrilled to hear that Knight was ready to target its largesse to local, metropolitan papers after several years of funding mostly technological experimentation. And I knew a lot about Doug's successful methods from my assistant dean, Arlene Morgan, who had created the Sulzberger Program at Columbia.

I endorsed the idea, and offered the resources of Temple University's Klein College of Communication to organize and coordinate the project. We were off.

The results from the program's first year, 2016, were striking. That first cohort — the Philadelphia Media Network, the Minneapolis Star-Tribune, the Dallas Morning News and the Miami Herald — each made leaps forward in their digital transformation, far more than they had in any previous year.

Now, with additional funding from Philadelphia's new Lenfest Institute for Journalism, the program has been expanded to include more newsrooms over the next three years and new partners, including the American Press Institute, the Poynter Institute and the University of North Carolina. The road remains steep, to be sure, but this initiative is clearly helping local news organizations climb it more quickly and confidently.

The lessons drawn from the program's first year, and from a second cohort midway through the program, are in these pages. They are a treasure trove for editors and executives who will take the time to read and share them. It's an investment that will surely pay dividends for newsrooms, newspaper companies, and — most importantly — for communities who rely on quality local journalism.

Introduction

Teams from Miami, Minneapolis, Dallas and Philadelphia gathered in November 2015 to kick off the Knight Temple Table Stakes[1] effort. Each comprised folks from across their news enterprises — newsroom, marketing, sales, technology, HR, finance and senior management. And each committed to work together to define and put in place what's required for metro newsrooms to be in the game of news.

The four enterprises already had embarked on efforts to move beyond legacy approaches. Knight Temple Table Stakes was not some sort of light switch separating a 'doing nothing before' from a 'doing something after'. Efforts underway at Miami, Dallas, Minneapolis, and Philadelphia — like those going on across the news industry — underpinned the strong hypothesis of the Table Stakes effort; namely that:

Metro, local and regional publishers knew what is required in specific, granular ways to be in the game. It was just that, in late 2015, no one had gathered teams together to write all this down in a rigorous way and then set in motion strategically relevant efforts to make the table stakes happen sooner and more effectively.

We put this hypothesis to work in the November session. We divided folks into groups of two or three who specifically detailed what's required of newsrooms to be in the game in terms of:

- The **core work and workflows** newsrooms must do to support the overall direction and strategy of their enterprises
- The key **roles and skills** demanded to do that work
- The **technology and tools** required by that work
- The organization and culture needed to succeed at the work, the roles and skills, and the technology and tools

For the **work and workflows**: Teams contrasted

---

[1]

Table stakes comes from thinking about strategy as poker. It asks folks in enterprises to distinguish between table stakes (what is required to have a seat at the poker table — that is, to be in the game) versus differentiators (what's required to win the game). You and your colleagues may not like the term table stakes. That's fine. Pick something else. Just make sure that whatever you select conveys the same meaning: *What's needed for your legacy newspaper metro, local or regional news enterprise to even have a chance in 2017 or beyond?*

- **Table stakes** (what's required to be in the game) versus
- **Indicators of not being in the game** versus
- **Differentiators that might win the game**

They did this for major workflows including: *audience service and growth, platform management, business-side coordination, training and developing staff, performance assessment and feedback, technology and tool management, and innovation and partnering.*

Each major workflow contained sub-workflows, sub-sub-workflows and key elements within sub-sub-workflows. To illustrate, here is the breakdown for one of the major workflows: ***audience service and growth*** (each of the other major workflows were similarly detailed):

Coverage and story planning

- Budgeting
  - Schedule/rundown/playlist
  - Story/post submission and updating
- Meetings
  - Schedule
  - Focus
  - Participants
  - Cascade
- Digital shift schedules
- Assignment coordination
- Story format planning
  - Options considered
  - Aggregation targets and assignments
- Audience reach and engagement planning
  - Timing of planned publication
  - Trending tracking
- Calendar/archive based planning
- Watchdog checks
- Follow-on coverage planning
  - Audience response
- Major project planning
  - Project coordination
- Visuals production planning (photo/video, graphics and interactive)
- Print production planning
  - Print curation support

Story content creation and production for audience engagement

- Content creation
  - Text
  - Visuals
  - Embeds
  - Partnerships
  - Social
- Audience engagement (within stories/posts)
  - Headline
  - Summaries (toplines, highlights)
  - Highlines (pull quotes, etc.)
  - Hyperlinks
  - Tags
  - Related content
  - Social
  - Updates
- Production
  - Post building/production
  - Post scheduling
  - Post editing
  - Real-time communication

Digital publishing

- Publishing on own platforms
  - Post publishing (mobile/desktop)
  - Push notification, curation and sending (alerts, recommendations)
  - Newsletter curation and publishing
- Publishing on others' platforms
  - Facebook and Twitter posting
  - Other social platforms (Instagram, etc.)
  - Publishing through news aggregators

Audience monitoring

Story monitoring and updating

- Updating
- Ongoing budgeting

Asset saving for print and archive

- Media archiving

Print curation and production

- Coordination with digital
- Print package (story assets)
- Editing
- Story updating

For the critical roles and skills: Teams defined **table stakes** for key roles and the skills required for content creation and production, digital publishing and platform management, audience engagement and analytics, print production, technology development and management, training and developing staff, and performance leadership, management and assessment.

In addition, the teams specified what signaled **not yet in the game** — and, on the flip side, what went beyond table stakes to **differentiators** (that is, ways to win the game).

For example, for roles such as reporter and editor when it comes to headline writing, the teams specified the following:

- **Not in the game:** Does not know what the most important angles are for a story or how to pitch a story through a headline alone. Doesn't understand SEO. Relies on copy editors or others for headlines.
- **Table Stakes:** Contributes own headlines and knows how to pitch a story through a headline alone. Can correct headlines as needed. Headlines have a sense of voice (conversational or authoritative depending on needs). Understands and is adept at SEO.
- **Differentiators:** Regularly uses A/B testing tools and/or analytics

Some argued that A/B testing and using analytics is table stakes. Which was fine. The point, though, was that, as expected, these folks really did know — *in granular and specific ways* — what's required to be in the game. And the same level of detail emerged for all key roles and skills involved in content planning, story level planning, reporting and storytelling, multimedia content capture, aggregation and curation, partnering for content, editing, publishing and platform management on owned platforms as well as platforms of others, audience engagement and analytics at the story level, the desk level and cross-platform, cross-newsroom level, print production (including how to curate print from digital), technology development and management, shaping, developing and hiring as needed to ensure the right skills in the newsroom and overall performance leadership, management and assessment.

For technology and tools: teams distinguished details for **not in the game** versus **table stakes** versus **differentiators** for technical functionality and capabilities required for:

- Editorial planning, coordination and tracking
- Authoring and editing
- Image editing
- Digital asset management
- Archive, search and replication
- Point of publication
- Digital curation
- Social media management
- Presentation layers (desktop, mobile, apps, print, other)
- Print curation
- Analytics and optimization
- Site taxonomy and information architecture
- User ID-based layers/feeds
- Sign-on/authentication
- User identify management
- Subscription management and paywall
- E-commerce
- Events
- Ad delivery and yield management

For example, here's what teams specified for the point of publication:

NOT IN THE GAME	TABLE STAKES	DIFFERENTIATORS
Manual export of a story sends almost no information other than the text of the story	Related items (photo, galleries, etc.) can be attached to articles before the article is placed on a print page	Everything gets built first on the digital side and the print paper is created from the contents of the website exported to print
Automatic export doesn't happen until a print page is closed late in the evening	Exporting includes related items regardless of whether the article has yet been placed on a page	Can schedule/embargo content per device/platform, based on audience data for each

NOT IN THE GAME	TABLE STAKES	DIFFERENTIATORS
	Newsrooms can choose a workflow that either requires editing or not, and it's easy to see what needs editing/sending online as it's ready	
	Reporters can publish directly online, especially for blogs and breaking news	

In doing this work, none of the folks involved made any claims that the table stakes described were perfect or perfectly complete — either in late 2015 or for all time. Rather, the teams believed the level of comprehensiveness and detail about table stakes was plenty *good enough* to get going with the harder part: putting table stakes in place in their newsrooms.

Same table stakes — same shortfalls and concerns

After describing the table stakes, the teams assessed **gaps** — that is, where their respective newsrooms fell short. They discovered — again without surprise — that they shared similar shortfalls and concerns about the challenges of implementing the table stakes.

Highlights of this shared picture included:

Work and workflow gaps:

- Print — and text — centric planning, choice making and workflow
- Too little content published where and when digital audiences sought it out (for example, Minneapolis discovered a huge gap between when audiences showed up versus when and where the StarTribune posted content for those audiences)

- Digital expertise tapped *after* stories developed instead of at the beginning (as one Miami social editor said with frustration: "It's only after a story is done — including major stories — that the editors and reporters throw it over the wall and say things like, 'put some links in this'.")
- Routine failure to consider — let alone do — aggregation
- Absence of established and disciplined workflows for innovation in response to changing reality ("We're not nimble." "We don't experiment." "Who gives a hoot about the homepage in 2015?")

Skill, behavior, working relationship and attitude gaps:

- All four teams agreed they lacked the skills needed. When asked at the initial November gathering, "How many of your colleagues 'get it and do it,' the most generous answers were 'maybe half.' One copy editor who worked with editors and reporters in her newsroom answered, "15% … *at best*."
- Suboptimal behaviors, attitudes and working relationships described included too many journalists still overly worried about A1 placements and how many inches a story would get; reporters and editors who feared putting something up on digital before print would 'let the competition get it too soon;' some folks only reluctantly attended training/learning efforts, then quickly forgot what was covered without trying it out; a pattern of those with digital expertise 'doing things for others' instead of '*with*' them in ways that encouraged learning ("X is one of our data experts and there's always a line at her desk"); an orientation toward covering institutions instead of what "affects people's lives;" ongoing reluctance and ineffectiveness in partnering with folks beyond the newsroom such as marketing, sales and technology; and, newsroom leaders with antipathies toward managing ("I didn't become a journalist so that I could manage people.")
- All four groups battled with fears of the unknown in the face of a reality replete with unknowns. While recognizing they did in fact know the required table stakes, they also acknowledged anxieties that their colleagues — *and they themselves* — had to find ways of putting the table stakes in place even though no one

in 2015/2016 had solved the big question about *the* new business and revenue model for metro, local and regional news enterprises. (As an aside, one key lesson learned from Knight Temple Table Stakes relates to avoiding a trap of searching for silver bullets — for THE one new business and revenue model. There is not nor ever will be just one new model.)

Technology, tool, data and analytics gaps:

- The complex dilemmas for how best to blend needs for print and digital content management systems
- None of the newsrooms had a single budget view with which to plan, choose and manage journalist resources
- All four used data and analytics — yet none believed they had what they needed — nor had any yet shared all the required data with front line reporters or used it manage performance
- All had too many overlapping and inconsistent communications tools (e.g. email and so forth) — though even in November 2015, it was clear to some that better approaches existed (e.g. Slack)
- None had yet to codify or share digital story forms as tools reporters could use to increase efficiency and effectiveness

Culture, organization and resource gaps:

- "We're stuck in an endless cycle of managing decline."
- "In a world already dominated by social and mobile, we have one — count her, one — social editor"
- "Honestly, though there are resource constraints, I do not think it's that hard for our company to find and hire talented, enthusiastic and mission-driven folks with digital skills. But it is hard to keep those folks enthusiastic in the face of the overwhelming print culture."
- "As recently as last year (2014), I was in a meeting about mobile and the very first question asked was, 'Why would we care about mobile? It's just a passing thing.' "
- "I just came from one more senior management meeting where the focus was entirely on the print numbers."
- "There's no way at all we'll ever have the 40 to 50 coders in our newsroom like the *Washington Post* has."

- "We have colleagues who actually — even proudly — are dismissive of readers, especially readers who seek content these colleagues feel is not important enough."
- "We have a legacy environment with a sense of entitlement."

Different contexts — different game plans

These shortfalls and concerns did not surprise anyone. They mirrored other metro, local and regional publishers across the industry. The picture echoed what had been described in a range of previous reports including *Digital Leads* (Stewart et al, 2014), *Innovation Report* (New York Times, 2014), and *Stickier News* (Hindman, 2015).

The pressing question was how each of the four metros would go about implementing table stakes. Their choices reflected a key lesson from the effort: *each of them — like any other metro, local or regional publisher — had to craft a pathway that made sense in light of their unique market and enterprise contexts.*

Philly: The Philadelphia Media Network includes *The Inquirer*, *The Daily News* and philly.com. Two have storied histories; all three competed fiercely with one another. In November 2015, the 250 plus folks in the three newsrooms remained physically and culturally separate and were unionized — making the challenges of getting to table stakes harder. In addition, a decade-long, revolving door of ownership had confused instead of clarified the path forward. Each new owner chose a new direction and approach; none of the directions took hold before another new owner came onto the scene and changed things yet again.

Gerry Lenfest began to restore stability after gaining full ownership in 2014. The following spring, PMN's top leadership adopted a new vision and strategy. That summer Lenfest hired Terry Egger as publisher, and Terry wisely embraced the work instead of shifting vision and direction yet again. Among other things, the new strategy spawned a 'real time news desk' aimed at better matching the timing of digital publication with audience presence. In addition, Lenfest announced his intention to create a new nonprofit Institute for Journalism in New Media that would own PMN — a transition that became official in January 2016. (For more on what is now called The Lenfest Institute, see *Could It Be Sunny In Philadelphia*, Knight Foundation/Griggs, 2016.)

Minneapolis: The StarTribune also got a new owner in 2014 — Minnesota native Glen Taylor. Like Philly but unlike Miami and Dallas, the Strib's 250-person newsroom is unionized. Unlike Philly, though, Minneapolis had pursued a clear direction and strategy ever since Mike Klingensmith became publisher in 2010 — a strategy focused on being the dominant news source in Minnesota through, among other things, careful attention to branding, advertiser market segmentation, and using events and other methods to engage with folks whether or not they were subscribers. By November 2015, Klingensmith's approach had paid off in many ways, including — when compared to Philly, Dallas and Miami — stronger print and financial performance.

Like Miami, Minneapolis had a metered paywall. (Philly did not; and, Dallas had tried twice but took it down each time). Executive Editor Rene Sanchez and Managing Editor Suki Dardarian had taken advantage of moving to a new building to redesign the newsroom in ways that were more digital-friendly while also hiring more folks with digital savvy and skills. Just prior to the initial Table Stakes gathering in November 2015, and somewhat like Philly's 'real time news desk', Minneapolis had designated a 'quick strike team' for breaking news.

Dallas: 2015 was a big year for *The Dallas Morning News* and it's parent Belo. In February, Mike Wilson became Executive Editor and invited Empirical Media to work with DMN teams to completely reimagine DMN. That summer, the teams and Empirical recommended an overhaul of the newsroom into a truly digital-first operation organized around content areas called verticals and hubs plus passion-driven arenas called obsessions. A print team would curate from digital content. In short order following the adoption of these recommendations, Robyn Tomlin joined as the new Managing Editor; DMN offered folks across the newsroom the buyout option of leaving or sticking around for serious change; the newsroom took steps to shift to a new CMS that had worked well in a 2015 inside-the-newsroom digital start up called GuideLive; and, planning started for the process by which everyone in the newsroom would reapply for jobs.

Meanwhile, Belo had shifted its enterprise direction and strategy. The company sold assets such as Providence Journal and refocused on building a multifaceted ecosystem aimed at becoming the go-to place in North Texas for content marketing, events design and management, digital optimization services, digital marketing, warehousing, distribution, direct mail and other services. The digital-first reorganization of the newsroom was essential to Belo's strategy to grow consumer and business audiences, and then monetize them with an ecosystem of business-to-business and business-to-consumer services.

Miami: Miami's participation in Table Stakes included two flagship publications: *Miami Herald* and *El Nuevo Herald*. In addition to publishing in two languages, Miami also differed from the other three by being part of the McClatchy chain. The two Miami newsrooms were also smaller. Instead of the roughly 250 in each of the others, Miami Herald had 115 and El Nuevo Herald 45. And, while all four were resource constrained like metros, regionals and locals in general, Miami was the most constrained of all.

Miami also had opportunities unlike the others. In general, geographically bound markets — e.g. Minnesota for StarTribune, North Texas for Dallas, greater Philly for PMN — impose scale limitations on metros, regionals and locals that, by contrast, are not an issue for companies like Facebook — and *New York Times* and *Washington Post* — with reach beyond any geographic limitations. Miami, however, is the "capital of Latin America" with reach well beyond Southern Florida.

The different contexts yielded different choices for implementing table stakes:

- **Miami** chose to (1) use consumer/user-centric design thinking to reimagine the audiences and purposes of Miami.com; (2) embark on out of market pilots aimed at serving Latin America and Hispanic audiences more broadly; and, (3) initiate a series of "Incs" (e.g. Food Inc) that would deploy targeted content for targeted audiences run by 'mini-publishers' in the newsroom.
- **Dallas** focused on getting the reorganized newsroom up and running with a vision to transform DMN "from a newspaper company into builders of valued and valuable audiences" — audiences that, among other things, might gain from and generate value for the ecosystem strategy of Belo. The Dallas team separated the many tasks (including, for example, finishing the process whereby folks reapplied for jobs, launching Slack across the newsroom, expanding the new CMS, choosing and implementing obsessions, establishing audience goals for verticals and hubs, re-designing and re-launching the website and more) into three phases to make

manageable an array of changes that might have been chaotic.

- **Minneapolis** used criteria — (a) evidence of user passion; (b) the newsroom was or could be best at covering the content in question; (c) we already have staffers who want to participate; and, (d) there's a reasonable path toward monetization — to pick targeted content areas with which to test, learn and expand on audience engagement approaches. A second team challenged themselves to significantly increase Strib's performance results in social and mobile vis a vis local competitors who were out front. And, by the time the Table Stakes teams gathered in May, Minneapolis had added a third effort aimed at closing table stakes gaps across the entire newsroom.
- **Philly** faced one overriding 'must do' challenge: *create one newsroom out of three*. In addition, they embarked on shifting this single newsroom toward audience-first approaches using data and analytics, skills assessment and training, and adding key people with social and audience development skills. Philly also launched an innovative effort to use data as well as third party providers of that data to build shared understanding across the whole enterprise (newsroom, marketing, sales, senior management) about what made audiences valuable.

While these pathways varied to fit the unique circumstances of each metro, the teams soon discovered that each pathway depended on a common range of tactics and approaches, including:

- Shifting the focus and timing of editorial meetings in ways to serve digital audiences first, with particular emphasis on publishing content when those audiences showed up as opposed to according to the print schedule
- Expanding, customizing and sharing data and analytics throughout the newsroom
- Assessing skill gaps and then tailoring workshops, training, editorial meetings and access to experts to close those gaps
- Beefing up social, audience development and coding efforts in the newsroom

- Using the mini-publisher concept to support audience focus and general management orientation at the desk level while using performance expectations and scorecards to reinforce accountability and build confidence
- Identifying, building, experimenting and — when the experiments worked — deploying tools that optimized instead of despaired over CMS realities
- Deploying Slack to make real time communications more effective while also weaning folks off a hodgepodge of email and other approaches

Overarching Table Stakes

As described earlier, the four metros began the Knight Temple effort by defining table stakes and identifying gaps and shortfalls — then shifted to choosing and getting going with a range of initiatives aimed at closing the gaps and putting the table stakes in place.

By the time the teams gathered in February, seven common themes had emerged to tie together the granular, more specific table stakes for work, workflow, roles, skills, technology, tools, organization and culture.

All seven put the *audience first*:

1. Serve targeted audiences with targeted content

Your enterprise must be audience driven. Identify and focus on particular, target audiences with needs, interests and problems that you can address well and derive revenue from. Use your local market knowledge, perspective and presence to serve these audiences far better than competitors. In doing this, don't trap yourself into serving individuals alone — don't overlook businesses and organizations as potential content customers you can serve.

2. Publish on the platforms used by your targeted audiences

Go to your audiences rather than expecting them to come to you. Take responsibility for distribution by publishing and promoting on the platforms used by each of your chosen target audiences. Do so in ways that serve their needs and interests in using each platform and take best advantage of the particular features and dynamics of the platform, ways that are platform optimal versus platform agnostic.

3. Produce and publish continuously to match your audiences' lives

Organize to provide an 'always on, always there' flow of digital-first content matched to the life rhythms and habits of your target audiences, their time and attention availability, and their interests, needs and problems of the moment, across the platforms they use. Get beyond either/or-ism of digital versus print. Use the audience-centric approach to go digital first, print later AND better.

4. Funnel occasional users to habitual and paying loyalists

Guide your audience through the stages of a funnel from random or occasional use, to increasing use, to habitual use, to paying for your content, products or services, to recommending your brand and content to others. Use the same step-by-step funnel approach to maximize the value of your audience to advertisers. Do this through the focused use of data and analytics, technology, content and platform tactics, multiple types and approaches of "offers" and "asks", and continuous testing.

5. Diversify and grow the ways you earn revenue from the audiences you build

Innovate, test and develop as many ways as possible to gain revenue from the audiences you build, and the relationships you develop. Avoid the search for silver bullets — for *the* answer to *the* new business. Do this by collaborating across all functions of your enterprise with a focus on innovating to growing consumer revenue and advertising and creating, testing and growing a range of new products, services and businesses of value to your target audiences and community.

6. **Partner to expand your capacity and capabilities at lower and more flexible cost**

   Use partnerships, third-party services, shared resource arrangements and flexible staffing to expand your capacity and capabilities across all areas of your enterprise: content creation, marketing and distribution to target audiences, new services and products, access to needed skills, technologies, tools and data, and more. Do this in ways that lower investment requirements, reduce and add flexibility to your cost structure, increase speed, and better share risks compared to doing it on your own.

7. **Drive audience growth and profitability from a "mini-publisher" perspective**

   Drive growth and profitability in your chosen target audience segments and key publishing platforms by developing cross-functional "mini-publisher" teams and team leaders who use a general management perspective and strong sense of ownership and accountability for performance. Expand the scope of these teams' responsibility beyond content creation, content distribution and audience development to include revenue generation, financial contribution and brand development.

2

A word on the design of this manual: We've intentionally left as much white space as possible so that you and your colleagues can make notes in the manual.

What you'll find in this report[2]

This report includes a chapter about each of the seven overarching table stakes. In each chapter, you'll find:

- What the Table Stake is
- Why it is Tables Stakes
- How to assess gaps in your newsroom
- Why these gaps exist
- What success looks like in closing the gaps and getting to table stakes
- Specific actions to close gaps
- Measures of success and tracking progress in closing gaps — scorecards to use to motivate and evaluate success

Each chapter has specific tools, frameworks, and disciplines you can use to implement table stakes in your newsroom plus illustrations and lessons learned from Miami, Minneapolis, Dallas and Philly and occasionally other enterprises as well.

You face fundamental transformation — a challenge you and your colleagues will embrace only if you build a shared understanding of the table stakes, why they are table stakes, and why gaps exist in your newsroom and enterprise. To help you and your colleagues build that understanding, each chapter provides a quiz you can use to identify and discuss gaps — as well as explanations for those gaps and the table stakes themselves.

So, we've provided you tools and approaches to discuss and agree on the need for change. Without taking such steps to build shared understanding and motivation, though, you won't make the changes required to get in the game of 21st century news and information, let alone win that game.

Take a moment now to reflect on any serious changes you've made, whether personally or professionally. If you succeeded, that achievement was grounded in the motivation to change and an understanding of why the change was needed as well as some credible path forward.

Consider this: over the past 14 years, U.S. newspaper enterprises' revenues have dropped from over $60 billion to under $15 billion.

Are you dissatisfied with that? Are you dissatisfied with the economic and financial condition of your news enterprise? Are you concerned that these vulnerable economics: (a) imperil your job; (b) your relationships at work; and/or, (c) your sense of personal purpose and aspiration? When you look around, even read through the table stakes for required roles and skills, do you feel motivated to learn what's required for you to practice journalism in the 21st century? Do you believe journalism can make a difference to democracy? Are you motivated by the opportunity to embrace the table stakes as a path toward connecting with audiences in ways that fulfill that democratic aspiration?

"Necessity", the saying goes, "is the mother of invention." Well, dissatisfaction and motivation are the 'mother of change'. Absent them, you will not make the effort. Nor will any of your colleagues who lack dissatisfaction and motivation.

In addition to motivation and dissatisfaction, you and your colleagues must increase your grasp of the changes ahead and a believable pathway to making those changes. Look again at the structure of each Table Stakes chapter — what the table stake is, why, how to assess gaps and shortfalls, why those gaps exist, what success looks like in closing those gaps, actions to take and, finally, the goals and scorecards to use to monitor progress. When combined, these elements provide the explanations, tools and illustrations you and your colleagues need to surface and discuss dissatisfaction, understand where you're headed, and map a credible path forward [3].

There is a lot of useful stuff in the report — a treasure trove of specific guidance for transforming your newsroom to get in the game of 21st century local news and information.

The core question facing you and your colleagues is: *How best to go about using this report to support your transformation efforts?*

You and your colleagues should start pondering this question by reflecting on **what not to do**, including:

- **Running away from, and even arrogantly dismissing "managing":** Transforming your newsroom — indeed your news enterprise — is *managerially intense* at every level and for every individual and team involved. Don't kid yourselves that there's some silver bullet, new business model, or magic formula the incantation of which makes all that's happened over more than a decade just disappear with a return to newsroom folks just 'doing journalism'. That's nonsense. It's true that many journalists say, "I didn't get into this to be a manager." Okay. Fine. But you're in this now. And the only way you and your colleagues can continue making

[3]

Folks who've studied and guided fundamental organization change often frame what's required with a kind of formula: Change = D×V×P. Note first, that D×V×P is multiplicative, not additive. Without even knowing what the letters represent, if you don't have D or V or P, you get no change. D stands for dissatisfaction, V for vision and P for process. V is about vision — or the broad direction and aspiration sought. P is for process, which really means the key steps needed to attain the vision. D — dissatisfaction — is the source of motivation — of energy and effort — needed to fuel the hard work of change.

the journalistic difference you do and should care about is through learning and getting good at managing yourselves and how you connect to audiences in ways that make a difference to them.

- **Failing to connect newsroom transformation with the purposes and strategy of your news enterprise:** Your enterprise now must compete with many other enterprises for the loyalty and support of audiences. That support is no longer guaranteed. You must earn it. And you must figure out with all the other folks in your enterprise how best to gain and then monetize that support. Your enterprise has scarce resources and serious economic and financial constraints. All of you — edit and business — must figure out together how to get the greatest bang for the buck of those resources. And that means whatever choices your newsroom makes for moving forward must reinforce and be informed by the choices made by your enterprise as a whole.

- **Skimming through this report for 'tips' and 'best practices':** People who confront serious change — who must learn and practice new skills, attitudes and ways of working with colleagues — only succeed when they know why and how their efforts and risk taking matter. As just mentioned, this requires you and your colleagues to connect the changes you might make to the overall direction and success of your enterprise. Absent that, you'll spin your wheels. You'll continue to read blog posts, go to conferences, and pick and choose tips from this report only to find the 'best practices' fail to make any sustainable difference.

- **Privileging — or dismissing — print:** Either/or-ism imperils serious change. For far too long, the legacy news discussion has gyrated back and forth between 'either print or digital'. Print pays the bills. Therefore, print. Digital is the future. Therefore, digital. That either/or approach wastes time and dissipates scarce resources and energy. Your enterprise's future lies in finding a sustainable path for both print and digital, both digital and print. Based on the progress in Miami, Philly,

Minneapolis and Dallas, the sturdier both/and approach is to put audiences first, then serve your chosen audiences through both digital first and print later and BETTER.

- **Failing to insist on, answer, and hold yourselves accountable to the results that define success:** Most change efforts fail. Ouch! But true. Research and reports have pointed to a pattern. Whether the focus was total quality, reengineering, acquisitions and mergers, best place to work, new strategies, or other serious changes, typically between 60 to 80 percent of the efforts fell seriously short of expectations. Many reasons explain this prevailing pattern: poor leadership, bad choices, arrogance, legacy inertia and more. Among them all, though, is a primary root cause: *pursuing change for the sake of change*. The surest way to avoid that trap is to define and hold yourselves accountable to performance results, not change. Indeed, this is so important that the next chapter provides guidance for how to use a focus on performance as the touchstone for the steps detailed in this report to implement table stakes and get into the game of 21st century news and information.

With a clear sense for what not to do, you and your colleagues can use the next, second part of the Introduction to begin embracing what you should do as you take on the significant challenges of transformation.

Focus On Performance Results in Using This Manual

Performance is the primary objective of change. Not change.

Change is a large word. It can mean any of the shifts described in this Table Stakes report. Moving from a general store providing general news to general audiences to serving targeted audiences with targeted content is change. Publishing on platforms used by your chosen audiences as well as continuously publishing to meet the needs of those audiences: both are changes. And so on for the rest of the Table Stakes (funneling, maximizing revenue from audiences, partnering to expand capacity and capabilities, and using the 'mini-publisher' perspective). All are changes.

There are numerous specific changes described in this Table Stakes report including: assessing skill gaps, then the training, work-shopping, knowledge management systems and more to close those skill gaps; deploying "Inc's" (Miami) or 'obsessions' (Dallas); shifting the timing of daily editorial meetings while making them audience-and-digital first instead of print centric; using teams; experimenting with new products, services, revenue and audience approaches; installing new technologies, tools, data and analytics and getting front line journalists and others use them; hiring and/or partnering to expand scarce skills related to data or audience development; renovating platform presences whether social, mobile or otherwise; navigating shifts among behemoths like Facebook; finding and delivering actual, demonstrable value to what is local — all of these and more involve change.

And all are changes your newsroom and news enterprise must make to get in the game.

Yet, the surest path to confusion and failure is to focus on change for the sake of change — to make change *the* objective because you've failed to clarify:

- How any of these changes fit in, and contribute to, the direction and strategy of the enterprise as a whole
- To whom the changes matter and why
- What success at the changes looks like in terms of results and outcomes as opposed to the activities described by the changes themselves

Here's what happens when change is pursued for its own sake instead of performance that matters to direction and strategy:

- People asked to change do not grasp why those changes matter to them and their jobs — nor how they would know if the changes to their work make a difference
- Change becomes just one more thing to do — a recipe for failure in the already overwhelmed news enterprise
- Managers and front line folks alike spend too little time, attention and persistence at what matters most. Episodic bursts of energy arise. But those dissipate; and, instead of demonstrable progress, failure spiced with cynicism spreads along with deep frustration
- Change remains at the margins — instead of the core — of the "way we do things around here"
- No one knows if the changes work — if they have positive impact.

Avoiding these traps demands keeping performance as the primary objective of change. And that, in turn, requires answering for any given change, "What does success look like?" in terms of SMART outcome-based goals — then holding folks (including yourselves) accountable for achieving those goals, or, failing that, learning what works, what doesn't work, and adjusting accordingly.

This chapter provides guidance — and illustrations — for:

- Articulating SMART outcome based goals that answer, "What does success look like (for any given change)?"
- Identifying where performance happens and who must be accountable for delivering it
- Managing across the different time frames in which real performance and change happen

Use SMART outcome-based goals to answer, "What does success look like for the change at hand?"

As described in the Introduction, once the teams from Miami, Minneapolis, Philadelphia and Dallas had defined table stakes for roles, skills, work, workflow, technology, tools, organization and culture, each choose a set of initiatives aimed at putting the table stakes in place.

For each initiative, the teams answered, "What does success look like in terms of SMART-outcome based goals?"

For readers not familiar with SMART-outcome based goals, they describe the results, impacts, or outcomes: that is actual differences made by actions taken[1]. They are not activity-based goals.

Here's an illustration contrasting an activity-based goal with an outcome-based goal for getting journalists to master the art of headlines in the digital space:

- *Activity-based goal:* By December 15th, we will train all reporters in how to use headlines to drive traffic.
- *Outcome-based goal:* By December 15th, all reporters will be have used headlines to increase overall traffic by a minimum of 10%.

"We will train all reporters" is an activity, not an outcome. When you articulate goals in terms of activities, you trap yourselves in a self-fulfilling prophecy. In this example, imagine the conversation after December 15th:

- Manager: "How did we do at the goal?"
- Staff: "We did great! We trained all reporters in how to use headlines."

But, no one knows if the training made any difference.

Training is a terrific idea. So are other useful activities such as workshops, the 'headline rodeo' used in Dallas, coordination with SEO and audience development experts, A/B testing and so forth. All of these, though, require two conditions to make any difference:

---

[1]

For more, see *Make Success Measurable* **by Douglas K. Smith**

the reporters take the training in such things seriously; and, they actually use what they learn on the job.

- Both conditions are far more likely to happen when performance results, not activities and not change, are the primary objective. Indeed, the teams from Philadelphia, Dallas, Miami and Minneapolis all recounted frustrations of having devoted time and attention to training only to find too many of those trained reluctantly attended and/or never tried to use what was covered on the job.
- When the goal is for reporters to achieve minimum 10% traffic gains, the odds go way up that they will take training seriously, use what's learned on the job and see and experience making a difference. In addition, managers and staff alike know what's working, what's not working and how best to adjust going forward.

This illustrative outcome-based goal related to 10% traffic gains is also SMART:

- *Specific:* Reporters get better at using headlines to drive traffic
- *Measurable:* 10% increase
- *Aggressive yet achievable:* 10% is a stretch goal — yet one that is do-able
- *Relevant:* Direct cause-and-effect relationship between headlines and traffic
- *Time-bound:* December 15

Here are SMART outcome goals from some of the initiatives of the four metros:

Philadelphia had a key initiative seeking to build a better-shared understanding of valuable audiences across marketing, sales and the newsroom. The purpose — the hypothesis — was that, through understanding more about audiences of higher value to advertisers, the newsroom could serve these audiences better and, in doing so, create more value for the audiences as well as the advertisers seeking to reach them.

Now, quickly: this was not anything even remotely about Advertiser X dictating content to the newsroom. Instead, to illustrate, it was about building a shared understanding that, say, "men between 35 to 50 seeking healthier life styles" also had higher than average eCPMs in the Philly area. By understanding the data, Philadelphia's health, sports, and life style desks could provide targeted content to this targeted audience (see Table Stakes #1) — content that men needed to be informed about, and make better health choices.

When asked to define success for this initiative over a 10- to 15-month time frame, the Philly folks chose this:

> "By the end of 2016, create data bridges to connect content and sales to reach the highest value audience. With this, we will realize a 10 percent increase in eCPM, improve customer/advertiser retention by 5 percent and grow overall digital revenue by 5 percent."

Dallas embarked on a major reorganization to make its newsroom digital first, print later and better. The vision was to "transform from our newspaper company into builders of valued and valuable audiences." Among the ways Dallas answered what success looked like included:

- Grow overall digital uniques by 15%
- Grow local digital uniques by 25%

In addition, Dallas gained commitments from each of its verticals and hubs to (1) increase average monthly uniques by 10% more than the previous year's average; and, (2) maintain or increase scores against a specially constructed engagement index that monitored 13 specific elements spread across four broad areas: (i) overall audience size and time spent; (ii) local audience; (iii) loyalty; and, (iv) social media engagement.

Miami sought to take advantage of being the 'capital of Latin America' by finding ways to servo and monetize audiences from beyond South Florida. In one of the experiments selected, a Miami team identified services and content sought by relatively well-heeled Latin Americans seeking to live, buy homes, start businesses or regularly visit Miami. Here's how success was defined:

"In 6-12 months, we will innovate at least three products or services that this higher-end audience will pay for (such a real estate database or luxury travel or a database of medical, legal and business specialists or home decorating packages). Within the first year, this effort will grow to 1-2 million page views a month, and be gaining $500,000 to $1 million for premium advertising"

Recall that **Philly** had to physically (and culturally) combine what had been three separate newsrooms: *Daily News*, *Inquirer* and philly.com. Here's how they answered, "What would success look like?"

"We will complete the job of creating a single newsroom to eliminate redundancies, maximize effectiveness and free us up to cover more of what our audience wants. By Q12017, our in-market audience will increase by 35% and our content production will increase by 20%."

Identify where performance happens and who is accountable for delivering it

SMART outcome-based goals define performance — which, if you think about it makes sense because *you cannot manage performance if you have not defined performance*.

Managing performance also demands understanding *where performance happens* and *who in the news enterprise (individually and together) delivers it*.

Twenty plus years ago, where performance happened in metro publishers, and who delivered it was crystal clear:

- The newsroom covered the news using a beat structure plus investigative/enterprise efforts. Reporters, editors, copy editors and others created and delivered news articles every day in time for the print close.

- Circulation sold and managed subscriptions, using a plethora of price, time frame (length of subscription) and other options.
- Distribution delivered papers to subscribers and managed single copy sales
- Advertising sold ads across a range of offerings including classifieds and coupons. Because most metros had dominant market positions, advertising as often as not did not sell as much as take orders from customers.

All the functions of the news enterprise had, in the words of a Dallas marketing executive, "their own performance swimming lanes." The functions only occasionally needed to coordinate (e.g. policies about when to hold the paper for late closure).

Today, where performance happens, who's responsible and the requirements for cross-functional coordination are more complex. For example, the newsroom reports, edits and otherwise shapes and publishes content in traditional and untraditional (e.g. aggregation) ways across multiple formats and distribution channels (platforms) in order to grow, retain and serve audiences. In doing all this, the newsroom must deliver performance results — sometimes themselves yet often with others across the enterprise — against a more complicated range of outcomes, including:

- Content choice, format, quality, story form and time of publishing and blended average cost of all content through use of aggregation, bots and so forth
- Platform and distribution choices and implementation (including, of course, print)
- Traffic and engagement on digital platforms, including platforms owned and operated by the news enterprise as well as platforms belonging to others (e.g. Facebook, Twitter, Snapchat and more)
- Target audience selection and service
- New product and service innovation
- Partnering with others
- Mastering technology and tools (including selection and review of whether any particular technology/tool works)
- Reinventing and revitalizing what local journalism does and for whom

The newsroom cannot do these alone. Consider, for example, what to do about ad blockers? Choices for how best to respond to ad blockers requires agreement about the nature and quality of the audience experience, technology options, and brand, and revenue alternatives that, in turn, require perspectives of the newsroom, marketing, sales, technology, finance, and senior management.

Or, take product and service innovation. It is folly to imagine your newsroom can or should pursue new products or services in the absence of coordinating with marketing, sales, technology, finance and senior management. Belo, for example, has embarked on knitting together a local ecosystem aimed at becoming *the* go-to place in North Texas for content marketing, events design and management, digital optimization services, digital marketing, warehousing, distribution, direct mail and other services. Dallas Morning News' success at building valued and valuable audiences is essential to this strategy and the odds of success rise with intentional coordination across the various companies Belo has assembled.

Ditto for Philly's experiment at building data bridges for shared understanding of the newsroom, marketing, and sales (not to mention key third parties) of what makes audiences valuable.

Or, consider Table Stake #7: "Drive audience growth and profitability from a 'mini-publisher' perspective." Will Pry, Amanda Wilkins and their team who created Dallas' award winning[2] *GuideLive* in 2015 were a prototype for the mini-publisher approach. They succeeded by using a whole business perspective to *knit together* work done by journalists, audience developers, technology, tool providers, and others in making, then acting on, targeted content for targeted audiences.

[2] **GuideLive won an International News Media Association innovation award.**

Manage performance across different time horizons

Legacy newsroom efforts revolve around the daily print cycle. Still, reporters, editors, managing editors and executive editors have lots of experience managing efforts that go beyond the daily cycle. Consider investigative and enterprise. As celebrated in the movie *Spotlight*, the *Boston Globe's* work to uncover sexual abuse scandals in the Catholic Church extended well over a year.

So, the concept of managing efforts over *different time horizons* is not some alien, never been done before idea. Think, then, about the time horizon required to implement Dallas' root-and-branch reorganization. The DMN/Empirical teams began work in summer 2015. The basics of having folks in new roles with new reporting relationships and digital-first objectives were essentially complete by spring 2016. Even then, as Robyn Tomlin and colleagues attest, there remained much to do to get fully good at the new ways of working.

As part of Knight Temple Table Stakes, Gabe Escobar and Dan Sarko of Philadelphia embarked in early 2016 on a significant innovation: using data to build shared understanding of valuable audiences across marketing, sales and the newsroom. As of this report, that effort continues to progress yet isn't complete. Some of the elapsed time could have been shortened — Dan, Gabe and others, like so many of today's metro leaders, faced significant other demands on their time and that slowed things down. Still, an innovation as fundamental as this doesn't happen in the course of the daily cycle. It takes months of effort — and months of management focus, time and attention.

The initiative to reimagine Miami.com tells the same story. Importantly, the team leading the effort got to work right away with the resources they had on hand (including free lancers) to figure out what sort of content would better serve target audiences. They immediately set goals and tried things out so that they could learn by doing instead of slipping into the trap of analysis paralysis. But the overall requirements for a reimagined approach also demanded using design thinking, McClatchy corporate resources, website and mobile redesign, rebranding and more — essential steps well beyond the daily cycle and rhythms of legacy newsrooms. It's no surprise, then, that the effort is still under way in Miami.

Well before Knight Temple Table Stakes, the Star Tribune chose the occasion of moving to a new space to launch an extensive re-branding effort. From conception through implementation, this too took over a year.

All four newsrooms worked with API to change the nature and use of data and analytics. While there was a range of time frames for the four groups, the effort to choose and put in place new data and analytic approaches took several months — again, not something that happened in a day.

Finally, every one of the four newsrooms changed the purpose, flow and timing of their editorial meetings as part of implementing table stakes. Today, each has a key meeting focused on laying out the digital-first choices that they monitor and adjust through other meetings. In Miami, this cornerstone meeting is in the late afternoon with an eye on digital for the following day. In Minneapolis and Dallas the cornerstone meetings happen early morning. In Philadelphia, largely for reasons related to the guild, the meeting happens late morning.

So, what's the time frame demanded for this change? Making the decision to shift can happen in a moment — though, the discussions and pros/cons prior to that decision likely take longer. But it's a mistake to imagine the change is simply about a decision.

Shifting the purpose, flow, approach and timing of the daily meeting schedule only succeeds fully when folks involved *get good at digital first approaches*. For example, Dallas' 'headline rodeo' changed the approach to their early morning meeting, one that encouraged, demanded and supported the use of headlines as story pitches as well as actively managing what performance results happened as a consequence. Dallas began this in late 2015. They are quite good at it today.

And they got better and better at it by doing and practicing it every day — and providing workshops and other supports along the way. In one sense, Robyn Tomlin, Amanda Wilkins and others who managed this change did so every day. But they did not stop with any single day's effort. Instead, they *managed the change* with a leader's eye on 'getting better' over the several months time.

Managing performance, then, demands managerial perspective on 'how long it will take to deliver results and get good at' any given change. Results from making a shift in the daily meeting flow can begin to happen immediately. And, as described earlier, results are more likely to begin if you and your colleagues set SMART outcome based goals that answer, "What does success look like for shifting our daily meeting flow?"

Still, consistent improvements in results — and deepening capabilities — will take two or three months or so for this change in daily meeting flow. Similarly, and assuming you set clear goals, results from training journalists in needed skills also can begin quickly — but sustained performance for individual journalists and, more critically, teams and the newsroom as a whole occur over several months. Results from the marketing, sales and newsroom data bridge effort have yet to materialize. As long as Philly sticks with this, results are likely to happen — but it will likely take over a year.

The point is that results and capabilities marking a transformed newsroom happen over various time horizons — and must be managed accordingly. Here's a guide that matches time horizons to objectives, goals and specific tables stakes as well as who is primarily responsible to lead performance and change:

TIME HORIZON	OBJECTIVES	ILLUSTRATIVE RESULTS	TABLE STAKES	PRIMARY RESPONSIBILITY
Today / This Week	Win the day throughout the day	• Traffic (especially local) • Engagement (especially local) • Timing/speed (posting time versus when audience present) • Average/blended cost of content	1, 2, 3, 7	• Audience and platform teams/ mini-publishers • Real time news desk folks • Digital experts
	Win targeted audiences	• Traffic (for target audience) • Engagement (for target audience) • Average/blended cost of content	1, 2, 3, 6, 7	• Audience and platform teams/ mini-publishers
	Win on platforms	• For owned platforms — Traffic — Engagement • For other's platform who link back: — Traffic — Engagement • For other's platforms who do not link back: — Brand awareness — Traffic — Engagement • Quality of experience: load times and so forth	1, 2, 3, 6, 7	• Platform and audience teams/ mini-publishers
	Win trust	• Impact and/or earned media or other recognition for investigative, enterprise and other efforts that serve local audiences and community • Brand value	6, 7	• Audience teams/ mini-publishers • Investigative, enterprise teams • Senior news leaders
Today through next 2 to 3-ish months	Best audiences	• Growth rates in traffic and engagement • Habitual engagement • Revenues tied to funnel • Revenues tied to mini-publisher plans	1, 2, 3, 4, 5, 6, 7	• Audience and platform teams/ mini-publishers • Biz side contributors • Partners

Focus on Performance Results in Using This Manual

TIME HORIZON	OBJECTIVES	ILLUSTRATIVE RESULTS	TABLE STAKES	PRIMARY RESPONSIBILITY
Today through next 2 to 3-ish months	*Best Talent*	• Individual and team achievement of performance goals • Closing of capability and skill gaps • Retention and advancement of high performers • Success of new hires	1, 2, 3, 6, 7, and Talent Chapter	• Individuals for their own performance and change • Teams/mini-publishers for team members • Senior newsroom leaders for teams plus key individuals
	Best Platforms	• Growth rates in traffic and engagement for owned platforms and others' platforms who link • Achievement of goals set for platforms owned by others and who do not link • Achievement of continuous improvement goals related to platform experience and performance • Achievement of learning and performance goals set for potential new platforms • Partner relationships with non-owned platforms • Speed of adoption in newsroom of new features/functions of platforms • Platform contribution to achievement of funnel and other revenue goals	1, 2, 3, 4, 6, 7	• Platform and audience teams/mini-publishers • Biz side contributors • Senior newsroom and news enterprise leaders • Partners
Today through next 4 to 8-ish months	*Best tech, tools, data and analytics*	• Install, continuously improve data and analytics needed to win • Identify, build, test and, if merited, deploy tools needed to win (and, that are consistent with whatever CMS realities/constraints you face) • CMS capabilities and ongoing improvement • New CMS	1, 2, 3, 4, 5, 6, 7	• Tech/tool experts • Senior management • Audience and platform teams/mini-publishers • Biz side contributors

TIME HORIZON	OBJECTIVES	ILLUSTRATIVE RESULTS	TABLE STAKES	PRIMARY RESPONSIBILITY
Today through next 4 to 8-ish months	*Best Partners*	• Objectives relevant to any particular partnering effort such as: — Content creation — Lower average/blended cost of content — Marketing and distribution to target audiences — Delivery of key services (e.g. events) — New services and products — Access to needed skills, technologies, tools, data or analytics	5, 6	• Senior leaders • Audience/ platform teams/ mini-publishers • Biz side contributors • Partners
	Best Innovation	• Continuous improvement as well as more fundamental innovation related to: — Identifying/meeting audiences needs (solving audience problems) — New products — Continuous improvement in exiting products, services and platforms — Reinventing and revitalizing the value in local — Partnering with others • Failing fast and failing cheap at converting serious unknowns (lack of confidence) into knowns (and confidence) • Partnering advances	1, 2, 3, 4, 5, 6, 7	• Audience and platform teams/ mini-publishers • Innovation project teams • Biz side contributors • Senior leaders • Partners
Today through 10 to 20-ish months	*Winning strategic choices about audiences, platforms, content, products, and services*	• Audience, platform and/or content performance results and whether shifts or modifications in those choices should be made and pursued • Product, service, business unit performance and any shifts/ modifications needed	1, 2, 3, 4, 5, 6, 7, Winning	• Senior leaders • Mini-publisher teams
	Winning economics and financial performance	• Enterprise financial sustainability and growth • P&L performance for audience, platform, other product, service business unit teams	4, 5, 6, 7, Winning	• Senior leaders • Mini-publisher and other product, service, business ownership teams

TIME HORIZON	OBJECTIVES	ILLUSTRATIVE RESULTS	TABLE STAKES	PRIMARY RESPONSIBILITY
Today through 10 to 20-ish months	*Winning brands*	• Brand(s) awareness, recognition and trust	1, 2, 3, 4, 5, 6, 7, Winning	
	Winning ecosystem	• Audience and financial/economic performance for elements in ecosystem — whether those elements are owned (as with Belo/Dallas) or done through partnering	4, 5, 6, 7 and Winning	

Look particularly at the first time horizon called "Today/This Week". Now look at the column "Primary Responsibility": other than paying attention to winning trust, senior newsroom leaders should NOT be spending much time on 'today/this week.' Instead, for metros, locals and regionals to be in the game, front line desks and other leaders must manage today/this week while senior leaders shift attention to the medium-to-longer time frames within which real performance and change — *and your news enterprise's best future* — happen.

This doesn't mean senior newsroom leaders must stop concerning themselves with the news and what's important. Not at all. But, it does mean senior leaders have to dramatically shift their time and attention to managing — to guiding their newsrooms and news enterprises transition to 'getting into the game.'

In doing so, and to summarize what's required, senior newsroom leaders must act to insure:

- Performance is the primary objective of change, not change
- Folks throughout the enterprise know who and where performance results happen and hold themselves accountable
- SMART outcome-based goals defining success get framed and used to drive accountability
- Regular performance reviews happen across the differing time horizons within which news enterprises will win or lose the game of 21st century news

Table Stakes
Number 1
Serve Targeted Audiences with Targeted Content

1. The Table Stake
Serve targeted audiences with targeted content

Your enterprise must be audience driven. Identify and focus on particular, target audiences with needs, interests and problems that you can address well and derive revenue from. Use your local market knowledge, perspective and presence to serve these audiences far better than competitors. In doing this, don't trap yourself into serving individuals alone — don't overlook businesses and organizations as potential content customers you can serve.

2. Why this is Table Stakes

a) The lost past of general news for general audiences

This first Table Stake goes to the heart of what has destabilized metro newsrooms with the rise of digital media over the past 20 years. In the past, metro newspaper audiences (readers) were defined in broad terms. Publishers offered a daily bundle of content that spanned a great range beyond news — everything from comics to stock quotes. The audience was anyone interested in any part of the content provided. This audience and content strategy was sometimes described as "general news for general audiences" but it was also "lots of stuff for lots of people."

In this approach, little was required in terms of really understanding any particular audience or targeting content to serve their unique needs. At most, the circulation department might develop survey-based statistics on the basic demographics of subscribers and use accepted formulas to derive the estimated total number of readers based on copies circulated.

Today, much of the audience for much of that "stuff" is gone, siphoned away by specialized websites and apps, aggregation sites offering even more stuff, search sites that handle specific queries, and social platforms that flow news and information into the friends and family stream of people's personal lives. This includes audiences for the actual news content, particularly national and international news.

The advertising base that supported all that general content is also shrinking rapidly, stripped away directly and indirectly by new players. Facebook and Google directly amass and precisely target a far larger audience in a metro newspaper's local market than the paper can or ever could. Less directly but just as effectively, programmatic advertising networks amass and target a large local market audience by aggregating traffic across a wide range of content websites, often including your metro, local or regional enterprise.

It's a completely disrupted and entirely different world. National and global players such as Facebook reach more audiences in your local market than you do yourselves. The market outsider knows more about the digital presence, behaviors, needs and habits of the local audience than you, the market insider. And these outsiders use this knowledge to precisely target audience segments in and across local markets.

b) The imperative to focus on audience segments in the face of unprecedented competition

Local enterprises faced with game-changing disruption from outside competitors must get much clearer about which customers to serve and how to serve them better than those outsiders — as with Main Street merchants contending with Walmart or any retailer facing Amazon's direct delivery. Start by thinking about audiences not as a single undifferentiated group ("the public") but rather as a series of audience segments, each with differing needs, interests and problems that your news enterprise can serve well with your local perspective.

Metro newsrooms can't compete with Facebook or Google on the scale of their virtual networks or their myriad knowledge of the transactional links within those networks. But your newsrooms can use your deeper understanding of local

HOW WELL DO YOU COMPETE AGAINST FACEBOOK IN LOCAL AUDIENCE?

If your metro area has 4,000,000 residents and Facebook is used by 65% of them on a monthly basis, they have a monthly reach of 2,600,000 local uniques. If these users access Facebook an average of five times a week, they amass over 56,000,000 monthly visits in your market. How do these Facebook in-market uniques and visits compare with yours?

HOW WELL DO YOU COMPETE WITH FACEBOOK ON KNOWING YOUR LOCAL AUDIENCE?

Facebook knows a great deal about its users in your market — their friends and family members, their personal timeline, all their "likes" and activity on other sites (through Facebook log-ins) — and uses this information to target ads and content to them. This raises the challenge of how your newsroom can know and serve its local audience better than an algorithm with a rich data feed.

audiences' needs, interests and problems to solve to build loyal, more connected networks of audiences within your market. Doing this, though, requires stepping back and reversing the usual flow of newsroom thought and practice.

c) Thinking audience first, always and in all ways

It's traditional for newsrooms to organize around subject areas as embodied in desks and beats. Journalists figure out "what's the story" within the boundaries of those subject matter areas. Only then, perhaps, do journalists give thought to audiences for the story at hand.

This pattern needs to be flipped:

1. Think audiences first — who are the segments of people and enterprises in your community that your newsroom can best serve and "own" and what are their needs, interests and problems?

2. Then think about content and experiences for those audiences — what news, information and opportunities for connections can your newsroom provide that meet and serve audience needs, interests and problems?

Audience first is not just a catchphrase. It is a fundamental shift in a newsroom's orientation and mindset that changes everything from the conversations in daily meetings to the design of workflows to the roles and skills that are most valued to the tools and technology required.

Audience first is also a required, mandatory change imposed by digital media realities. It is Table Stakes — without it, your news enterprise cannot be 'in the game.' Equally important though is this: putting audiences first not only gets you into the game but also far better positions your newsroom to provide more effective journalism whose relevance and value better serves the needs, interests and problems of target audiences. In other words, audience first is essential to fulfilling your journalistic mission.

3. Assessing the gap in your newsroom

Being audience driven shifts how you make and implement choices — not only to find sustainable paths forward but also to fulfill your historically critical mission of public service. Audience first approaches do not in any way diminish that mission, which is essential to continue. Why? Because serving 'the public' is at once broader and more general than identifying and responding to the needs, interests and problems of target audiences.

Take the following quiz for a quick read on where your efforts stand vis a vis this Table Stake. The statements in this assessment reflect observed practices in newsrooms that mostly continue to provide general news for general audiences, even if many practices have changed and more of the published content is locally focused in response to the rise of digital media.

Please note: these statements are phrased so that a 'yes' answer indicates your efforts have gaps — that is, fall short of what is required. And, the more yesses, the more gaps you face.

It is worth having many folks take these quizzes, including people in the newsroom as well as from technology, marketing, sales, HR and finance. Compare and discuss your respective responses for where you have agreement or not. Use these discussions to identify and highlight the most significant gaps you face and what steps you might take to close those gaps.

	YES	NO
1. Most people in our newsroom would say our audience is the "general public" or "citizens" of our metro area.		
2. We do not have at least five specific audiences that we absolutely "own" in our metro area (meaning we reach more of them and have more of their attention than any other local media, from local TV to niche websites).		
3. We use social media to build referral traffic, find sources and get user generated content but not to listen to audiences and track their current interests and concerns.		
4. We herald traffic on stories that become viral hits but do not routinely ask how much of that traffic is within our market.		

Table Stakes #1 Serve Targeted Audiences with Targeted Content

	YES	NO
5. Our primary digital measure in the newsroom is total page views from all sources.		
6. We usually review audience data in aggregate, e.g. total page views and unique visitors for the newsroom as a whole.		
7. We have tension in our newsroom between some folks trying to drive up traffic on a story and others who see such efforts as 'click chasing'		
8. There is concern and hesitancy about making story-level data available to individual reporters, including "real time" data (e.g. Chartbeat).		
9. Our desks/departments are described largely by the topics, institutions and entities they cover (city hall, arts orgs, major employers, etc.)		
10. Covering meetings is a mainstay of some reporter's beats.		
11. Our current beats are largely the same as they were three years ago.		
12. It would be hard to say to what degree a given desk/department has done quantifiably better over the last year in regard to audience development.		
13. Editorial meetings focus almost entirely on stories — what's developing, what to cover, who's covering it.		
14. The question "who's the audience for this story?" is rarely asked in editorial meetings.		
15. Most stories originate in response to an event or something the newsroom senses is important rather than thinking about audience needs and interests.		
16. Our stories are driven by covering the "who, what, when and where" of the story itself more than tying it to the needs, concerns and interests of the audience.		
17. Most of our stories follow a standard form; we don't often use different story forms to engage audiences in the content based on their needs and interests.		
TOTAL		

4. Why these gaps exist

"The public" and the "public interest" are undifferentiated terms. This Table Stake is about differentiation. It requires you and your colleagues to define and select target audiences, identify and understand the needs, interests and problems of those audiences, and then figure out how best to serve them.

A range of root causes explains the gaps between serving a generalized, undifferentiated 'public' versus differentiated, target audiences, including:

Traditions and habits related to 'getting the story' and 'what's the story?'

Journalists' best traditions revolve around discovering and getting the story within newsworthy occurrences ("what's the story?"). The journalistic drive and competitive impulse is to get scoops and be on top of stories as they occur. These are what the best journalists are best at. Relatively fewer traditions and habits link to understanding the daily lives and needs of specific audiences — of putting audiences first.

The daily/hourly pressures to produce content

Your newsroom produces and publishes content. The most immediate concerns are how to fill tomorrow's space in print or refresh digital content for noon hour check-ins and so forth. This means it is natural to think in terms of content and having the audience be just what you hope will follow. It takes time and a change in mindset and focus to think about audiences first amid the daily grind of the newsroom

Legacy habits make it easier to start than stop efforts

Monopolistic and oligopolistic market power produced hugely profitable metro, local and regional news enterprises that, in turn, fostered newsroom choices about what to do that were often *free of economic and resource tradeoffs*. "Should we do X?" was determined by journalistic value — not cost. Yet, when digital disruption forced metro, local and regional news enterprises to cut costs, the response focused mostly on head count and not on work. "Tighten our belts" led to fewer folks in the newsroom doing pretty much the same amount of work. The pattern became 'doing more with less' as opposed to 'doing less with less' — that is, making choices about what to stop doing. Indeed, all four metros in Table Stakes shared how difficult — yet essential — it was for them to stop doing things. And this trap compounds the adverse effects of daily and hourly content production just mentioned above.

The security and convenience of reliable story sources

Regularly covering local meetings guarantees you'll have stories as well as ready and known sources to question and quote. Established meeting schedules also provide a convenient way to plan your coverage calendar. But, this sort of coverage relates more to the *institutions that hold the meetings as opposed to audience interests and needs that might — or might not — pertain to such meetings.*

There is, of course, a small, target audience for such coverage — the officials in the meeting and being interviewed. Those officials might be important to you and your journalistic mission — for example, if your news enterprise seeks to help shape and set the local agenda and narrative of public action. Still, your newsroom must weigh the value you deliver with this coverage (and how you monetize that value) in an era of shrinking resources, intensified competition, and alternative, cheaper ways of providing readers' content (e.g. aggregating meeting minutes instead of reporting on those minutes).

Assumptions about knowing what's important to, and needed by, audiences

Understandably, the subject matter knowledge and experience that journalists develop can mean folks in newsrooms confidently believe they know best what should be covered and what is in the public interest. "We know what to cover" and "we know best," though, can also lead to one-way instead of two-way journalism — to 'telling' audiences instead of both listening and telling. These habits can be subtle ones. For example, journalists who 'know best' might trap themselves into believing they are already audience focused — or, if pushed, might contend an audience-first approach is pandering to the audience in ways that distract from what those audiences *ought* to read or see or hear (often this is characterized as making audiences "eat spinach").

Concerns that audience focus diminishes public value and public service

Some widespread audience-building tactics among digital publishers — e.g. click baiting — tarnish notions of public service and public value. Arguably, though, click-bait practices actually reflect a content-first --- not audience-first approach — because it focuses on *whatever* content is most likely to catch the eye and distract the interest of *whatever collection of individuals* pass by in the moment. When this happens, audiences remain ill defined in favor of what works in drawing clicks (cats, puppies and, as one Table Stakes participant said, 'scantily clad women'). Little to no attention is paid to understanding the needs, interests and problems of a particular audience, or building engagement or loyalty with that audience.

Thinking all digital audience traffic is the same

Too many newsrooms only distinguish print versus digital. When this happens, newsrooms are prone to thinking "a unique is a unique,", "a page view is a page view,", and that what particular kinds of audiences and traffic get built does not matter as long as traffic grows. Relentless traffic growth trumps engagement and loyalty — an approach even more likely within advertising heavy business models. In comparison, too little attention is paid to the value of engaged, loyal local audiences for subscription income, higher value advertising, sponsorship, events, and other revenue sources. (See Table Stakes #4 and #5.)

5. What success looks and feels like

This Table Stake requires a fundamental internal organizational shift in orientation — a turning of the collective eyes in your news enterprise toward external, targeted audiences. Success manifests itself both internally in skills, attitudes, behaviors and ways of working with one another and externally in how audiences and advertisers perceive and, then, put a value on your efforts.

This shift can be expressed in a series of "From-To" statements that contrast the current "as is" state with the desired "Table Stakes" state. (These From > To's depict typical metro newsrooms circa 2016 and convey the dimensions of change required. You and your colleagues can develop your own "from/to's" to more accurately describe your situation — which, by the way, is a good way to engage folks in identifying paths through transformation.)

	FROM	TO
Audience focus	Our audience is defined in general terms as "anyone who reads our content"	Our audience is defined as *multiple audiences*, each of which can be clearly described and spoken of in terms of their interests, passions, needs and problems
	Our digital sites are known as *a* place to go for general news from the metro area	We are the undisputed go-to source for a defined number of targeted audience/content areas that anchor our reputation as *the* preferred local news site
	There's no particular "content strategy" driving the work of desks, departments or verticals — it's a mix of gut, experience, reacting to events and sporadic new ideas	There's a defined strategy and documented playbook for every target audience, informed by audience data and including needs and interests, ways of listening, content sources, story forms, style and voice, and platforms of choice.

	FROM	TO
Audience growth	Overall digital traffic is growing	*In-market* digital audience is growing faster than out-of-market traffic and becoming more engaged and loyal
Advertisers	Local advertisers view your audience in general terms and run-of-site placements are common	Local advertisers are eager for placements and sponsorships around content where they know you have a highly engaged and loyal audience
Audience data	Audience data is available in the newsroom but regularly looked at only by those directly concerned with "audience"	Audience data is used daily and hourly by everyone in the newsroom to inform their work and decision making
	Audience data is available but we have to seek it out.	Audience data is visible in the newsroom on monitors and available to everyone on desktop, laptop and mobile, whether in the newsroom or working remotely
	Audience data is retrospective and delivered in fixed formats (e.g., last week's traffic report)	Both real-time and historical data is readily available and easy to cut different ways and drill-down on (e.g. all stories from a desk with certain tags over the last 30 days)
Newsroom	Our desks work traditional beats, established sources and set topics	We have teams focused on serving target audiences, listening to those audiences, and seeking sources and stories that address their interests, needs and problems
	Our reporters work individually under the direction of an editor	Our reporters/producers work as a team with a team leader to reach, engage and earn the loyalty of a target audience
	We manage available staff resources by allocating headcount across the newsroom	We manage staff resources by focusing on productivity (the audience value of content versus the time cost of producing it) and priorities (stopping one thing to free resources to do a more important other thing)

Table Stakes #1 Serve Targeted Audiences with Targeted Content

6. Actions to close the gaps

This section describes steps you must take to get good at serving targeted audiences with targeted content in competitively sustainable ways.

The first three steps help you shift the skills and attitudes of the entire newsroom toward being audience-first:

a) Set, measure, and hold the newsroom accountable for audience traffic and engagement goals while stopping non-mission critical coverage that fails to serve audiences
b) Require an audience-first perspective across your newsroom
c) "Learn by doing" what works, what doesn't, and why

The next three steps start the newsroom on its way toward serving targeted content to targeted audiences.

d) Start finding competitive advantages that combine (1) significant audience needs and opportunities and (2) what your news enterprise is or could be best at– particularly your strengths and knowledge related to what's *local*
e) Use criteria to select some target audiences and audience-focused teams to get going with
f) Hold the selected teams accountable for "content plus" strategies aimed at success

The last step requires senior newsroom leaders to manage overall newsroom transformation toward the full implementation of this Table Stake #1.

g) As rapidly as possible, organize your newsroom around audience-driven teams and the data, analytics, shared resources and management disciplines required for success

a) Set, measure, and hold the newsroom accountable for audience traffic and engagement goals while stopping non-mission critical coverage that fails to serve audiences

What gets measured gets done[1]. Or, as described in the Introduction, Part 2: performance results are the primary objective of change, not change.

If you want to shift your newsroom to an audience-first approach, then you must set and hold the newsroom accountable for audience goals. No amount of training, town hall discussions, strategy studies, brown bag lunches or other approaches to describing and encouraging audience-first changes will gain as much traction.

Miami's newsroom leaders, for example, set a goal to grow traffic by 7.5% — then provided folks access to Chartbeat to help them monitor progress against that goal.

By taking this key first step, Miami put the newsroom's focus in play — that is, while some folks (not all!) grumbled, all of them experienced a new reality — a new question: *is our audience responding to what we do*?

Not: was this a great story in our own estimation?

Not: did I/we get this story on A1?

Not: did I/we hold this important story for Sunday?

Rather: did the audience respond? And, if so, why? Or, if not, why not?

Start with setting goals for traffic and engagement. Here are some tips to guide how to set targets:

- **Benchmarks.** Benchmarks — knowing some base line starting point — can help you choose target goals. You might find benchmarks internally (metrics you already keep) or externally (for example, information you have about top performing sites in your market) or both. If you use external sources from competitors, though, make sure the competitors are going after the same audiences

[1] This rule of thumb cuts both ways. If you measure — and reward — the wrong things, those will also get done. So, for example, newsrooms that perpetuate monitoring A1 placements lock themselves into a print-centric past that doesn't work instead of embracing an audience-first present and future that can.

you are. Another approach is to ask yourselves, 'what is our 'fair share' of the audience we seek to serve?" For example, one could argue Pepsi's fair share of the cola market is, perhaps, at best half of it.

However you go about finding benchmarks, do so fast. For example, if you turn to competitor data or estimating your "fair share,' remember you may well be doing 'back of the envelope' estimates. In other words, *do not fall into the trap of wanting too much precision or analysis*. Instead, even if you cannot easily find a benchmark, then forget it. Set some traffic and engagement goals, and get going! Within a month or two, you'll have the benchmark — the baseline — you need to calibrate whether the goals you set were aggressive — or, more likely, not aggressive enough.

- **Include "stretch."** The most useful goals are stretch goals –ones that are aggressive and achievable. Try to avoid setting goals that are simply too easy (you'll not learn anything) or too hard (demoralization sets in).

- **Choose actionable time frames.** It's fine to set traffic and engagement goals over, say, 'the next 6 plus months.' However, if you do this, make sure those goals are translated into nearer term goals with shorter cycles such as, say, 2 to 5 weeks. "6 month" goals by themselves will not initiate focus or action. Instead, folks will likely forget about them. Shorter cycle times — 2 to 5 weeks — produce the kind of rapid experimentation and learning that sustain a focus on what is working and what is not working in terms of audience response. They also help you figure out when goals are either too easy or too hard — and how to adjust quickly.

- **If needed, differentiate goals among desks:** Some desks — some content areas — may well have different limits for audience appeal. It's possible, for example, that sports will more easily attract audience traffic and engagement when compared with, say, coverage of environmental policy. Audience-first approaches can surprise you and even disprove such assumptions. Still, if setting a different bar for some coverage areas versus others will help your newsroom embrace and go after traffic and engagement goals, then do so.

- **If needed, make the first phase exclusively about learning:** Ultimately, newsroom folks must be held accountable for audience goals — anything less will fail to move your newsroom and news enterprise to sustainable success. Still, many newsrooms have no history or experience in accountability for performance — for knowing that job security and advancement turns on delivering results. If this is the case for your newsroom, then clearly communicate that the first phase of goal setting and measurement is about learning what works versus what does not work as opposed to personal performance with job consequences. If you choose this route, you must also be clear that following such an initial phase, the job consequences will become reality.

Once you have set target goals, make sure your newsroom folks have at least some data tools — such as Chartbeat — to monitor their performance (see below for a more extensive discussion about data and metrics). And, require desk editors to regularly review and report on performance against the goals — as well as what is being learned.

Finally, use actual performance results to drive choices for how you allocate time and resources. As part of this, *make sure to stop coverage that fails to attract audiences*.

This does not mean: stop doing mission-based work. It does not mean failing to hold powerful people and institutions accountable in the finest traditions of journalism.

Rather, it means to force yourselves to ask, discuss and decide whether coverage that fails to attract audiences truly is core to your mission — or, as is often the case, just a reflection of cherished beliefs.

Remember: a message to be a message must be heard. The best, most insightful coverage of what you might consider mission-oriented work is unsuccessful if no one reads it. And, it consumes time, energy and resources that can better support serving audiences in ways they benefit from and respond to.

b) Require an audience-first perspective across your newsroom

Learn about the needs and interests of audiences from *their* perspective (not yours)

Audiences have choices — lots of choices. So, it is imperative that your newsroom understand the needs and interests of audiences from *their* perspective, not yours. This is not that easy for legacy newsrooms. The temptation is to jump to topics that *you* believe matter to audiences based on your journalistic background, expertise and assumptions. This leads you to continue the same coverage and content you already produce — and, in effect, imagine that your efforts have an audience focus when, in fact, they don't.

To avoid this trap, start with *questions* about audiences — then use what you learn to guide content choices that inform audience lives, interests, needs, and problems — as well as to guide desk-level reviews of what is working and what is not working regarding audience goals:

CONCERNS	NEEDS	CONNECTIONS	PASSIONS	PREFERENCES
• Who and what do they really care about? • What day-to-day concerns occupy their minds, what daily problems are they trying to solve? • What uncertainties keep them up at night? • What big life decisions do they wrestle with? • What public issues are they wrestling with?	• What do they need to navigate through the day and help with in-the-moment decisions? • What do they need to know to address their range of concerns? • What affects their lives that they need to stay current on? • What are they not even aware of that they need to know about?	• What networks do they likely have? • Who would they want to share with? • Who would they be interested in knowing about? • What organizations or institutions would they want to be "in the know" about?	• What do they want to experience? • What can they never seem to get enough of? • What prompts them to engage — to like, share, comment, sign-up?	• When would they want to see certain content? • In what form would they like to see certain content (length, text or visuals, etc.)? • What would they like pushed to them? • What would they want to save and read/view at their leisure?

1) Ask, "What job(s) are we doing for our audiences?"

Require folks in your newsrooms — particularly at the desk level — to ask themselves, "What job(s) are we doing for our audiences?"

There are five jobs you might be doing, each of which is phrased from the point of view of an individual member of your audience. That is, imagine an individual in your community who needs help from your newsroom in one or more of the following ways:

- Help me be an informed citizen in the **place** I live: Three particular sources of news and information can help you keep your audiences informed as citizens in the places they live: *breaking news* relevant to that place; *trending news* or information relevant to that place; and, *calendar-based events/information* relevant to that place.
- Help me solve the *necessities of my life*: Your audiences must find ways to navigate the complex realities of the 21st century in the **places** they live: housing, health care, jobs, commuting, finance and money matters, technology choices and more.
- Help me *improve the quality of my life beyond the necessities*: You can help your audiences seek to enrich and enjoy their lives beyond necessities: arts, entertainment, sports, vacations, learning opportunities, socializing, discovery and more.
- Help me *connect and work together with others to make the place we live together better*: You can help folks in the places you serve connect with one another — even work with one another — in several ways including (1) using your convening power to gather folks with shared interests and purposes; (2) deploying social media in ways that connect people who have common interests; (3) reporting on and enhancing/growing organizations and coalitions tackling key local challenges — and more.
- *Hold those in power accountable*: This is, of course, core to your classic journalism mission and purpose. In delivering this value to local audiences, it's key to remember that in today's market-driven society, holding the powerful accountable is not limited to government. It also includes holding the ever-more-powerful private sector accountable. For example, are banks and financial institutions serving your communities well? Health

OBSESSIONS

Quartz's idea of obsessions, circa 2012:
- "... an ever-evolving collection of phenomena — the patterns, trends and seismic shifts that are shaping the world our readers live in ... We call these phenomena our 'obsessions'"

DMN's adaptation of the idea with their definitions
- "An Obsession is ... a reporter's focus or fixation on a phenomenon that is affecting people locally, whose coverage is guided by a strong sense of audience, and whose coverage (at least at this stage) supports at least six months of regular reporting."
- "Phenomena are the patterns, trends and seismic shifts that are shaping the world our readers live in."

insurers? Major employers? Private sector polluters? And so forth.

2) Choose topics and content that matter to your audiences

Choose the topics and stories that best fit what you have learned about the needs, interests and problems of your target audiences. Redefine your beats in audience-first ways. Move away from broad generalities (government, business, the environment and so forth) in favor of audience-driven, audience-perspective beats. For example, instead of a desk or beat about education broadly, direct journalists, editors and those who support them (social editors, audience developers, product managers) to find, report and share information that helps parents navigate school choices, gain insights that matter to them and their kids about education policy choices, find opportunities for their own continuing education and so forth. (See the side bar on the concept of "obsessions" versus "beats".)

c) "Learn by doing" what works, what doesn't work, and why

Establishing and holding folks in your newsroom accountable for audience traffic and engagement goals will get their attention.

Requiring them to explore, listen, learn from and use an audience-first perspective will help them achieve the traffic and engagement goals through selecting topics, coverage and stories responsive to audience needs, interests and problems to be solved.

This third step — 'learning by doing' — is your newsroom's path toward figuring out what works best and most sustainably.

"Learn by doing" means requiring newsroom folks to embrace a continuous, short cycle 'test and learn' discipline — something also called 'design/do.' In this phrase, 'design' means 'decide' or 'choose.' It means journalists — as individuals and teams — make a clear audience-driven choice about topic, content, story, coverage — as well as platform and publication timing (see Table Stakes #2 and #3) — choices the journalists believe will both serve audiences well and drive success at traffic and engagement goals.

Once the choice is made, 'do' means just that: Do it! And see what happens. Does the choice lead to better traffic and engagement? Does it exceed expectations? Fall short? And, in either case, why? (For more on the data and analytics needed to support design/do approaches, see below.)

The design-do cycle of driving audience growth and engagement

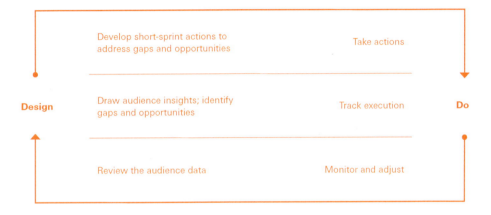

There is a key additional advantage to using this approach: through continuously using design/do, teams, desks, individuals accustom themselves to using and relying on data. As a result, folks in the newsroom learn through experience that the best choices reflect a combination of journalistic experience and intuition **and data**. In particular, newsroom folks tend to experience a path characterized by:

- Working strictly from gut and assumptions in a manner they have always done ... TO
- Seeing some data that, because it's incomplete and often only shared randomly and episodically leaves folks suspicious of the intent and uncertain of its value ... TO
- Accepting that data in the newsroom is here to stay but not being sure how to use it ... TO

- Having real-time access to more complete and relevant data in ways that help folks *see* and *use* that data as *numbers* that quickly show what does and doesn't work tactically at the individual story level (e.g. the impact of having Chartbeat everywhere in the newsroom) ... TO
- Understanding data as *feedback from audiences* and using it to better understand their needs and interests ... TO
- Using insights from data to guide what is written and produced for an audience and when ... TO
- Embracing data as a means to reach a larger local audience, reach them more often, and serve them better — and doing all this as an integral part of achieving your journalistic mission.

d) Start finding competitive advantages that combine (1) significant audience needs and opportunities and (2) what your news enterprise is or could be best at — particularly your strengths and knowledge related to what's *local*

This step begins your transition from instilling an audience-first perspective across your newsroom toward getting good at identifying and serving *targeted* audience segments.

Remember: metro, local and regional news organizations no longer enjoy monopoly or oligopoly market positions that assure financial success. Instead, you compete with many, many others. That means you must find competitive advantages on which to build journalistic and financial sustainability.

Moreover, because metro, local and regional news enterprises are so often geographically constrained, competitive advantages and sustainability will most likely arise from audience needs and interests that are *local* (whether entirely or just significantly). Yes, scalable strategies *might* emerge from serving audiences beyond your geography. For example, the Boston Globe has launched a medical/health related effort called STAT that is growing audiences far beyond Boston.

STAT, though, is an exception. It is more likely that your news enterprise's competitive advantages and sustainability will come from creating and monetizing value locally — within and not beyond your geographic footprint.

Your challenge, then, is finding competitive advantage sweet spots where sizeable and attractive audiences' *local* needs overlap with your enterprise's existing and/or new strengths, brands and assets.

Put differently: *Where is the overlap between what local audiences want and what you are or could be best at?*

1) What local audiences want/need

Three audience characteristics — separately and in combination — mark attractive opportunities:

- **Shared/common interests:** When the Minneapolis Star Tribune sought to learn more about an audience-first approach, they decided to experiment with local audiences they believed were passionate. And, because it was late winter/early spring, one of the audiences selected were Twins fans. Similarly, when Miami experimented with the "Inc" approach, they began with "Food Inc." Each of these — sports, food — is an example of defining and serving audiences based on the shared/common interests of those audiences. Others might include entertainment, music, movies, hiking, biking, automobiles, education, commuting, retirement — frankly, zillions of things.

    The key is defining and delivering content from the perspective of the audience's shared interest, not from yours. For example, you and your colleagues ought to discuss the different implications for coverage between, say, Twins versus Twins fans, food versus foodies, commuting versus commuters, education versus parents, students and teachers — and so forth.

    Also remember that organizations of all types — businesses, nonprofit, religious, governmental — can have shared interests. Dallas Fort Worth, for example, has a concentration of aviation, airline and aerospace enterprises while Philadelphia has a high concentration of colleges and universities. These enterprises, in turn, have audiences of leaders, employees, employee families, suppliers, customers and supporters who also share common interests for professional and economic reasons.

- **Shared purposes:** There's a powerful distinction between folks who share a common interest versus people and/or organizations that actively pursue that interest *together for shared purposes*. In this situation, *communities* emerge that are built around these shared purposes. And stronger, more loyal audience connections become possible because, on top of the shared/common interests involved, shared purpose communities also might look to your content, coverage, convening power and other approaches to (1) help them as communities *stay connected to one another* and their purposes; and, (2) help them a*chieve their shared purposes*.

    Consider people and organizations that work together to make folks in your markets healthier — or better housed, better banked, better educated and so forth. Or, think about clubs of various sorts — exploration, athletic competition, arts, etc. Or, think about religious or ethnic groups who band together for various shared purposes.

    You can discover such communities of shared purpose in real life as well as online. Shared purpose audiences may be smaller than audiences built on shared/common interests. But, because of these audiences' strong connections to one another and their purposes, their value as audiences (especially those that also include organizations) rises because of a stronger propensity to become loyal paying customers, greater likelihood of appealing to advertisers, higher odds of providing additional revenue sources (e.g. events) and greater likelihood of sharing your content and value with others.

- **Place:** Place — where people and enterprises live, work, operate and exist — also might give rise to a strong sense of shared identity, especially when history, language, weather, and other elements of local culture reinforce that identity. Yes, technology, markets, and networks have disrupted the way folks live and experience place. But these forces have not eliminated place — have not eliminated local realities.

Your local audiences still must navigate much of their lives locally. As described earlier, they need to be informed citizens in the places they live — and solve the necessities and enhance the quality of their lives locally. And, plenty of folks (and organizations) band together to make the places they live better.

Discovering, covering and informing uniquely local aspects can differentiate what you do from other and especially national or global news and social media competitors. Consider, for example, health care. Yes, your newsroom might cover the national political aspects related to health care. It's not clear, though, what or how such national coverage differentiates you or provides a source of competitive advantage. On the other hand, pretty much everyone who lives in your metro area must figure out how to deal with health *locally*: how to live healthier, find affordable health insurance, navigate choices of local health care providers and so forth.

These local needs and interests cannot be served well by national or global news organizations. Nor is it likely that social platforms will have full-time employees dedicated to understanding and responding to such uniquely local phenomena. But you can.

2) What you are or could be best at

Three potential sources of strengths — separately and in combination — mark attractive opportunities:

- **Drawing on the best parts your newsrooms' past:** Your legacy news enterprise has a range of capabilities, track record, brands and other assets on which to build competitive advantages in providing value to audiences, including your:

    — Authenticity of perspective and voice based on physical presence in the community
    — Trusted brand
    — Credibility based on decades of reporting on the same place

- News judgment of what matters based on wide knowledge of the community across time
- Insights developed through knowledge of, and access to, better sources
- Authority based on years of service to the community
- Convening power

- **Tapping into your strengths that link to place and what is local:** Your newsroom knows — or should know — your communities socially, politically, economically, religiously, culturally and otherwise. You have decades of unique local knowledge, sensibilities and perspectives that are difficult for others, including scale-based digital media efforts, to replicate:

  - Placing and translating national and global issues and phenomena into the local context — "Why and how does this matter to where I live, work, and play?"
  - Making connections across the metro area for audiences with shared/common interests — "Are there others nearby who share my interest and concerns?" "I'm part of how this community is changing but what do I need to know about its past and understand about its workings in order to fit in and be accepted as who I am and be part of its future?"
  - Identifying and serving existing and emerging shared purpose communities– "When and how do we come together as a community to solve X?"
  - Identifying and informing as well as convening and encouraging people and organizations wishing to make the place you serve better

- **Shaping a narrative that expresses the uniqueness of your place:** Your newsroom is uniquely positioned to serve your community of place more generally by developing, playing-up, and branding yourselves and your efforts around a strong curated and understood "sense of place" that is unique.

  For example, in revitalizing Miami.com, the Miami Herald worked with the adage that "in Miami even the locals sometimes feel like tourists" to define a target audience of those interested in discovering and experiencing the city, whether arriving tourists looking "to do what the locals do," or long-time residents just trying to keep up with what's happening in the ever-changing city. And in defining its audience focused "obsessions," the Dallas Morning News included "Texana," which informed and celebrated what being a Texan is really about and really means in today's Texas — all toward developing an inclusive Texan identify that went well beyond the traditional clichés of cowboys with or without ten gallon hats.

e) Use criteria to select some target audiences and audience-focused teams to get going with

Get going! The best way to learn how to serve *targeted* audiences with targeted content is to 'just do it.' You should, of course, be smart about choosing the target audience focus with which to start — and this section provides guidance for that. But don't fall into the trap of using the criteria and process described here as a crutch or excuse to delay. Get going now!

Using defined criteria for making key decisions is an enormously important discipline to build in your news enterprise and newsroom. In the case of selecting target audiences, criteria ensure better decision making by:

- **Making thinking explicit.** Too often, the factors guiding individual judgments go unspoken. In contrast, when folks discuss each factor for consideration and write down what's learned and used, they are far better positioned to implement, review and adjust choices

- **Calibrating against biases and assumptions while surfacing insights.** Discussing and defining criteria helps reveal unique perspectives — whether blind spots and prejudices that hurt or insights that help.

- **Allowing for weighting.** Once criteria are explicitly defined, you have the option to weight them differently if some factors are more important than others. This, too, works better than having each individual alone implicitly weight each factor.

- **Providing consistency in evaluations.** Too often — and not just in the news industry — discussions of one option focus on one set of factors while the discussion of the next option shifts to a different mix of factors. Assessing each option against the same agreed upon list of factors ensures each option gets the same treatment.

As mentioned earlier, Minneapolis initiated the journey toward audience-first approaches with, among others, an effort aimed at Twins fans. Miami began with some "Incs": Food and Cuba for example. And Dallas invited folks in the newsroom to propose and get going with what they called 'obsessions.' All used explicit criteria to make choices. Minneapolis, for example, weighed the following:

- This audience has enough potential users with strong passion to move us closer to our digital subscription goals
- We can be best or tied for best at producing key elements of the content needed
- We are already devoting resources to this
- We have staff who want to do this
- We can see a path to generating decent early stage revenue

Your criteria should fit your context and aspirations. And, while you may identify quite specific and unique factors, the core criteria you use should draw from the following:

Target audience prioritization and selection criteria

TRAFFIC/ENGAGEMENT POTENTIAL	CAPABILITY AND WILL TO SERVE AND ENGAGE	REVENUE POTENTIAL
• In-market size of segment (based on basic demographic analysis and assumptions) • Likelihood to share content (multiplier effect) • Availability of influencers and opinion leaders to promote content • Orientation to social and mobile usage • Shared interests/passions • Shared purposes • Potential for place-based/local differentiation • Other?	• Long-standing assets such as brands, convening power, credibility and authority that link to the target audience in question • Newsroom knowledge and experience relevant to the target audience in question, including insights into what is/are uniquely local • Skill at shaping a narrative that can build a strong sense of shared identify for the target audience in question • Whether there are any competitors who can serve the targeted audience better than you • Existing reporting staff enthusiasm about audience-first approaches • Availability of freelancers and/or relevant potential partners with expertise and networks • Other?	• Likelihood to pay for content • Value to advertisers and sponsors • Potential interest in events, services, products, or other revenue generating approaches • Other? (see TS #5 for more on potential revenue sources)

Senior newsroom leaders along with the publisher or publisher's designee should put together a small team to choose the criteria and make the assessments. Make sure to select folks who already think audience-first while also tapping into a broad range of knowledge, expertise and perspective. This group might include:

- Reporters and editors who know your metro area well, naturally focus on audience, and think in terms of communities of interest (versus beats and institutions);
- Audience development staff who think in terms of how each audience can be reached and grown;
- Business and sales staff who can provide advertiser and sponsor interest as well as any other revenue potential
- Technology and tool building staff who understand and can articulate audience preferences and implications related to platforms, your CMS, and tech tools

In addition, this team should structure a clear process for applying the criteria and making decisions. Your team should design the process to fit your unique circumstances. Make sure you consider the following steps:

- Decide whether your team will nominate and choose target audiences and audience-based teams to serve them — or, in the alternative, whether your team will invite newsroom folks to submit proposals based on the criteria.
- Either way, identify/nominate target audiences through some combination of (1) data, analytics and experience with target audiences you already serve; (2) target audiences that competitors currently serve yet you believe you could serve better; and, (3) target audiences not yet being served in your market.
- Require specific and nuanced profiles of target audiences and the opportunities to serve them well. You might even ask folks to use personas — made up descriptions of individuals whose interests, needs, problems, media using behaviors and so forth characterize the target audience in question.
- Ask each team member to *independently* rate each of potential target audiences against the criteria using the shared spreadsheet.
- Meet to assess the collective ratings. Make sure to discuss the audiences with the greatest variation in ratings so that your team builds a shared understanding about the reasons for the differences and gains a common perspective on the ratings.
- Choose how to move quickly to gather any additional information needed to clarify and decide among the audiences.
- Make your selections and then challenge the teams selected to get going.

The selected teams should include reporters/producers and a leader. The team's primary focus is serving the target audience. These teams will vary in size depending on the nature of the opportunity and the size of your newsroom. Teams might just include two or three folks. More than seven or eight becomes difficult and may indicate too broad of a target audience for most metro newsrooms.

The team needs to use the classic team discipline[2] to be effective, meaning that across the team members there must be:

- A common understanding of the target audience, the team's objectives and goals for that audience, and the "content plus" strategy the team will use to achieve those goals (for more on this, see the next section);
- Mutual accountability for meeting the team's goals and objectives as well as individual accountability for one's own work;
- A commonly understood and agreed upon way of working together regarding such things as coverage planning, digital skills development, and collaboration on everything from headline writing to partner development;
- Use of common tools for communications and coordination (e.g. Slack channels) and content production (e.g., story templates).

In staffing these teams, do your best to assemble folks with the range of complementary skills and perspectives most relevant to serve the target audience. *In addition, don't automatically assume the current desk editor is the best choice for team leader.* She/he might be of course! But other candidates could include reporters more adept at an audience orientation and/or digital skills as well as audience developers and/or social media editors.

Finally, your senior leaders should charter the team to:

- **Develop an ever increasingly clear understanding of the target audience while sharpening the content-plus strategy to serve them**

    - Think "audience first" and always ask what audience needs and interests are served by every piece of content
    - Use audience data continuously to better understand what content actually attracts and engages readers and viewers
    - Develop over time a clear profile of the audience being served and a deeper understanding of its needs and interests
    - Articulate and document this profile so it can be communicated to others (e.g. advertising)

[2] See *The Discipline Of Teams* and/or *The Wisdom Of Teams* by Jon R. Katzenbach and Douglas K. Smith

- **Drive audience growth and engagement through intentional, ongoing, rapid *design/do* experiments and improvements**

    — Set short sprints (2–4 weeks) with just one or two focused experiments or improvement areas at a time
    — Make sure these experiments test actions aimed at distribution (social platforms, promotion, distribution partnerships, etc.) as well as content
    — Use a simple work plan to write down planned actions and track their status during meetings (a very simple listing of actions, timeframe, responsibility)
    — Check in weekly as a team to assess what is working or not and why. Use those insights to identify and take appropriate follow steps
    — Keep a growing list of "what works" and what works best in what situations so these best practices can be shared and used across the team; add them to the team's playbook.

- **Develop and use an audience scorecard**

    — Develop, use and refine the audience scorecard itself (see below under Section 7).
    — Use the scorecard to conduct regular reviews of audience development, content performance, and individual reporter/producer performance.

- **Develop the team's skills and capabilities**

    — Assess skill levels and identify gaps for team members
    — Require team members to commit to specific skill development plans that link to performance goals — then tap into specialists, experts, training and coaching resources to help team members learn 'just in time to perform' (just in time to deliver results)
    — Develop points of expertise among team members and share skills as needed

- **Work across the organization to earn revenue from the target audience**

    — Understand what drives ad revenue

— Work collaboratively with marketing, sales, technology and others to use Table Stakes #4 (funneling occasional users into paying loyalists) and #5 (diversify and grow the ways you earn revenues from audiences) to identify, test and expand revenues from the target audience

f) Hold the selected teams accountable — to themselves as teams as well as to senior leaders — for "content plus" strategies aimed at success

The audience teams you select should start by defining success — that is setting specific traffic, engagement, revenue and/or other goals — then craft 'content plus' approaches to succeeding.

The content that best serves a target audience differs from traditional newsroom thinking about beats and news coverage in several ways:

- It is first, foremost and always driven from the perspective of the audience — again, contrast content relevant to commuting versus *commuters*.
- It makes choices about and describes the target audience and the interests, needs and problems to be solved of that target audience.
- It is proactive rather than reactive in the news 'we break' for — as well as information and content we provide to — the target audience.
- It looks forward and specifically calendars information and stories the target audience will need in the coming weeks and months.
- It seeks out stories, data, information and coverage that surprises the target audience in unexpected ways.
- It is framed from a *local* perspective.
- It is defined both by what you choose to cover and *what you choose to stop covering*

A content strategy becomes "content plus" when audience teams specify:

1. **The methods the team will use to *listen* to the audience — not just once as part of the initial work but in ongoing ways that continually inform and update the team's efforts:** Social media provides an extraordinary opportunity to find, listen to, and even see your audience in order to learn how those audiences identify and define themselves, what are their needs, interests and problems, and how they connect with one another. Still, don't limit yourselves to social networks. In addition to Facebook groups and pages, Twitter sources and hashtags, Snapchat and so forth, audience teams should learn from what competitors are doing — including informal efforts by bloggers and so forth. And, use readily available tools to sort through and track what is being learned about the target audience — for example, Storyful, Facebook Signal, Geofeedia, Dataminr, Groundsource, Public Insight Network, Hearken and others. However you choose to listen and discover, it is essential to write down, share and discuss what you are learning about target audiences, then act on the insights to see what happens in terms of audience response.

2. **A robust range of content sources (including aggregation) they'll use to serve the target audience.** Content sources might include:

   - Individuals and organizations who are part of the target audience and have signed-on to be sources (through a tool like the Public Insight Network);
   - Subject matter experts who understand the needs, interests, and problems of the audience and can frame and translate their knowledge in accessible, meaningful ways;
   - Data sources of recurring interest to the audience (surveys, public records and reports, statistical databases maintained by others, etc.);
   - Sources the audience regard as influential (recognized leaders and personalities, individuals in positions of power, informal opinion leaders and influencers);

- Potential content partners who know the audience and subject matter (individual bloggers, niche sites, organizations, etc.)

3. **The mix of content and story forms required to meet target audience needs.** Serving a target audience well requires a rich suite of story forms — far more than the standard 300, 600, or 1200 word text-based story with an accompanying photo. The range of story forms should reflect:

- **The audience's time requirements.** Audience-first means serving content to audiences when the audience — not the newsroom — is available and seeking content, and doing so in ways that fit how much time the audience has available. This means understanding and responding to the audience's daily and weekly routines. And, it requires story forms/treatments that target audiences can absorb within the time frames they have available — from a 30 second check while waiting in line to an end-of-day 10 minute read before the lights go out. And, it involves not just different story forms but how to treat the same story across each of the time-based forms.

Time-sized Content

> **Bites** (*not ready yet)
Photos, quotes, tweets, updates

> **Snacks**
Featured information with image and short description, videos, summaries, lead-ins

> **Meals**
Complete stories, documentary videos, galleries

> **Feasts**
Enterprise, investigations, narratives, interactives

Time is the new Inches

CASE ILLUSTRATION

The Dallas Morning News used food metaphors to convey the idea of audience's needing story forms that fit the time they have available — whether it's just a quick bite on the fly or plenty of time for a sit-down feast. To drive this point home to legacy print-oriented folks, Dallas also declared, *"Time is the new inches"*

- **Audience format preferences.** Learn and respond to the ways your audiences prefer to absorb and use content. Choose among the potential elements of a story and how best to combine them to meet these target audience preferences:

- Visual treatments (graphics, slide shows, gifs, videos, etc.)
- Text forms (text blocks, bullets, pull quotes, etc.)
- Audio (podcasts, etc.)
- Embeds and links to others' content (Tweets, Instagram, etc.)

Do not reinvent this every time for every story. Rather, develop, catalogue and share a repertoire of story forms that select and combine elements in ways that match different kinds of content and audience preferences. This ensures a better match of story form to your audience's needs and makes treatment decisions faster, easier to communicate, and quicker to execute.

4. **The styles and voices that convey the authenticity, credibility and authority needed to earn and keep the targeted audience's trust, reliance and loyalty.** General news for general audiences meant writing in one "general" style or voice. Focusing on a target audience is different. You and your colleagues must get good at adapting and varying style and voice in ways the audience prefers and responds to. Doing this fosters opportunities for adding personal voice and identity in appropriate ways. For example, you might post/publish the collective profiles of the team serving the target audience, personal profiles of individual contributors, and commentaries and personal narratives — all aimed at letting the target audience get to know the newsroom team just as the team gets to know them.

5. **The platforms and publishing schedule that will best reach and serve the target audience.** See Table Stake #2 (platforms) and Table Stake #3 (continuous publishing) for more.

6. **What the teams will stop doing.** Audience teams will fail if they attempt to craft and implement a content plus strategy while perpetuating all other traditional desk-related content.

7. **Clear objectives about how the audience team will blend the value they will create for audiences with the costs of doing so.** Different story forms and approaches have different costs. For example, the cost of an originally reported and edited piece is higher than the cost of content that is aggregated. "High cost" might but does not necessarily equate to "high value" to the audience. Nor does "low cost" necessarily equate to "low value." And, value-to-the-audience might arise from more than the content itself — for example, when target audiences find what they want, when they want it, and in forms they prefer, value rises. In this sense, a quickly done, highly relevant aggregation post might have as much or more value as a traditional enterprise piece. Audience teams need to set and manage goals for the average blended value/cost of content, paying particular attention to how best to use your scarcest resource: the skills, time and attention of your journalists.

g) As rapidly as possible, organize your newsroom around audience-driven teams and the data, analytics, shared resources and management disciplines required for success

As described above, you must get going *now*, first, to foster an audience first approach across your newsroom — then to select some teams to begin learning-by-doing how to shape and deliver targeted content to targeted audiences.

Eventually, you should organize the whole newsroom around audience-driven teams and, as Table Stake #7 describes, have mini-publishers drive those efforts. The following picture from Table Stake #7 describes stages through which newsroom leaders can guide the transition from current approaches to mini-publishers — in effect, a picture or vision for where you're headed.

Spectrum of development of audience-based mini-publisher teams

	CURRENT NEWSROOM	STARTING AUDIENCE TEAM	WELL-DEVELOPED AUDIENCE TEAM	AUDIENCE-BASED MINI-PUBLISHER TEAM
Organization unit/staff	• Conventional beat, desk or vertical structure	• Core newsroom team with audience-first focus supported by platform and other newsroom specialists	• Core team as described with working relationships with business-side	• Cross-functional core team with full P&L responsibility for target audience
Charter, Work, Accountability	• Story focused • Cover institutions, organizations related to beats • Deliver on assignments	• Audience-first focus • Serve targeted content to targeted audience • Accountable for audience growth and engagement across platforms	• Convert/funnel occasional users into habitual, monetized loyalists • Wide distribution in concert with platform specialists • Content partnership development • Audience revenue experiments	• Audience growth (all dimensions) • Revenue growth • Cost management, including average content cost through blending hi and lower cost approaches (e.g. aggregation) • Net financial contribution (attributable revenue minus expenses)
Success metrics	• Meeting deadlines • Some overall traffic numbers	• Traffic, local vs non-local uniques by platform • Reporter- and story-level traffic performance	• Local audience engagement and loyalty measures • Attributable revenues from funneling	• P&L performance • Performance of partnerships
Knowledge, skills and tools	• Beat reporting editing	• Understanding audience needs and interest • Audience focused story telling • Audience engagement skills • Access to basic data and analytics	• Understanding of specific problems being solved for audiences • Story form and platform experimentation and learning • Content partnership development • Customized data and analytics	• Partnership development and management • ROI thinking; contribution management • Project management

Table Stakes A Manual For Getting In The Game Of News

	CURRENT NEWSROOM	STARTING AUDIENCE TEAM	WELL-DEVELOPED AUDIENCE TEAM	AUDIENCE-BASED MINI-PUBLISHER TEAM
Key relationships	• Other folks on the desk and/or in the vertical • Sources within institutions, organizations being covered	• Platform, audience, social and other specialists • Tech/tool providers	• Platform teams • Business side colleagues • External partners	• Senior enterprise leaders

Note: all dimensions are cumulative; each level builds on the foundation of the prior level

Table Stake #7 also lays out the progression toward having mini-publishers drive your platform efforts too. And, of course, all seven Table Stakes — and the step-by-step guidance contained in this manual — will help you make the full transition.

For now, though, your senior newsroom leaders need to move as quickly as possible toward the second and third stages described in the above table. As you do, keep your eye on driving toward more and more teams serving targeted "content plus" approaches to target audiences. In particular, senior leaders must hold themselves accountable to:

- **Assign staff and provide resources**

    — Assign staff for the target audience teams
    — Assign additional staff as shared resources to the audience teams (e.g. specialists in social media, audience engagement, coders/developers, video/photo and so forth)
    — Make sure to set explicit expectations for how much effort is required from these shared resource folks
    — Assist in developing any external partnerships that will help audience teams succeed

- **Set objectives and review performance**

    — Set and pace audience development goals and objectives, including weekly, biweekly, monthly, quarterly targets (whatever combination makes most sense)
    — Conduct regular review sessions to assess performance, raise and resolve issues, and identify next steps

- **Providing ongoing support and coordination with the rest of the newsroom**

    — Advise, coach and support audience team leaders regarding audience growth strategies/tactics, continued development of the team's content strategy, and team member skills development
    — Make sure teams have support for the audience data, analytics and reports they need
    — Ensure needed social media and other audience development support
    — Resolve any issues among audience teams as well as among audience and platform efforts that they cannot resolve themselves

There are multiple pathways[3] for moving your newsroom through the stages described earlier. In a sense, though, all these choices sit between two basic approaches:

[3] See Introduction for similarities and differences in the pathways taken by the four Table Stakes news groups.

TRANSFORM THE EXISTING NEWSROOM ORGANICALLY AND IN TEAM BASED INCREMENTS	< — >	TRANSFORM THE EXISTING NEWSROOM WITH A COMPLETE AND THOROUGH REORGANIZATION
Identify and launch a small number of audience teams. Then expand on their efforts organically and incrementally across the entire newsroom.		Switch to a new audience-driven, digital-first newsroom organization structure in one big move — then develop audience-focused teams within the new structure.
Case example: Within its existing structure, the Miami Herald experimented with one audience team and then moved to four more. These teams helped foster audience focused thinking and analysis in ways that led to reallocating staffing across desks, shifting more staff to The Herald's Central News Desk, and making additional staff cuts from an audience perspective. None of this was done according to a predefined master plan. Yet, the results after a year was still a major transformation of the newsroom organization.		**Case example:** Based on a through newsroom-wide organizational review, deep analysis of audience data, and sweeping recommendations, the Dallas Morning News restructured its entire newsroom around new digital content verticals and more audience-focused "hubs" within the verticals, along with an entirely separate print publication team. This redesign included many newly defined positions and extensive revisions of others. Over an intense three-month period everyone in the newsroom had to reapply for jobs as part of putting the new structure in place. Once that was done, Dallas then focused on implementing the new structure — making it work as intended — through such steps as skills training, implementing of a new CSM, instituting redesigned workflows (e.g. their morning 'headline rodeo'), and asking reporters to develop and pitch "obsessions" to instill an audience focus (see the earlier sidebar on obsessions in Section 6b(2).

7. Measures of success and tracking progress in closing the gaps

This section describes ways to track progress and measure success at mastering how to use targeted content to serve targeted audiences. The first five steps (a through e) guide how folks in your newsroom (e.g. audience teams, audience developers and others) can work with analytics and technology folks to design, build, test and continuously improve data-driven metrics and related scorecards to support excelling at this Table Stake #1.

Part f below can help managers distinguish the data, analytics, scorecards and managerial reviews to drive improved performance and skill results across the three time horizons in which real performance and change happens: (1) weekly/biweekly sprints by which teams progress; (2) monthly/bimonthly progress reviews of team performance by senior leaders; and, (3) one-to-three month periods within which individuals set and achieve personal performance and skill goals.

Finally, part g can help senior news leaders see and manage targeted audience efforts as a portfolio within which to set and achieve overall news enterprise goals.

a) You cannot become audience-driven in the absence of data and audience teams using that data

Being data-driven goes hand-in-hand with audience first approaches. Data provide audience teams a direct view into the size, behaviors and preferences of the target audiences served.

Digital audience data has been available to newsrooms for years and its use and reach continues to spread. Yet, the sheer volume of data plus the variety of available metrics can sow confusion and a lack of confidence about what data to look at and how to figure out what to do with that data. Too often, a focus on one metric in one conversation bears no relation to the focus on a different metric in another. Or, conversations happen at either the very micro or very macro level.

Target audience teams have an opportunity to give more effective focus and purpose to using audience data to drive audience growth. Such teams are small enough to use and learn from data in more practical, actionable ways than, say, top newsroom leaders trying to make sense of all of the audience data from the newsroom en masse. Audience teams also provide a practical, actionable context for individual reporters to translate audience results into *team* strategies and approaches as opposed to merely looking at individual data and celebrating or despairing over whether its good or bad news.

Teams are better positioned to make choices, act on them and learn from data about what works, what doesn't and how to adjust moving forward.

b) Marry clear audience purposes to the audience data you choose, share and use

In the absence of clear and shared audience purposes, objectives and goals, you're at risk of drowning in the wide array of digital audience metrics, using data that reveals too little insight, or both. Your audience purposes emerge from exploring *questions* about what data can best help. These questions start at a high level and drill-down to specifics:

- Very broad questions about the *basic dimensions* of the audience – its size, location, behaviors, sources, and screen use;
- More specific questions that dig further about **types** of *audience measures* — e.g., "consumption," "attention," and "loyalty" when looking further into the audience's behaviors;
- Still more specific questions within these types of measurement to select specifics — for example, choosing "time spent per unique" to measure how much total attention do you get from an audience member over a given span of time.

Together these provide audience teams a typology to customize based on team purposes, objectives and goals. (See the table below).

Typology of audience-focused digital metrics

DIMENSION	TYPE/SUBTYPE OF MEASURE		SPECIFIC MEASURE*
Audience location: where are they physically?	• How many are coming from locations from outside our local market?		• Out-of-market traffic (filter for other measures)
	• How many are coming from locations in our local market?		• In-market traffic (filter for other measures)
FOR IN MARKET TRAFFIC			
Audience size and composition: how many are there and of what sort?	• **Reach** — how many people are we reaching?	• How many people are "coming in the door" • How many separate individuals are coming? • How well are we doing at attracting individuals from within our market?	• Visitors • Unique visitors (uniques) • In-market share (%) of total uniques
	• **Demographics** — what's the profile of our audience?	• What's their age? • What's their gender? • What's their income?	• Age distribution of uniques • Gender % of uniques • Income distribution of uniques

DIMENSION	TYPE/SUBTYPE OF MEASURE		SPECIFIC MEASURE*
Audience behaviors: how engaged are they in our content?	• **Consumption** - how much of our content do they view?	• How much in total? • During a single visit? • Per person over a given period of time?	• Total page views • Page views per visit • Page views per unique
	• **Attention** — how much of our audience's time are we capturing?	• How much in total? • During a single visit? • Per person over a given period of time? • Do they stick around?	• Time spent total • Time spent per visit • Time spent per unique • Bounce rate
	• **Loyalty** — how often does our audience come back to us?	• How often do people come back on average? • How much of a habit are we for our audience?	• Visits per local unique • Percentage of uniques at defined habituation levels (e.g., >20 visits/month)
Audience source: how do they get to our content on our sites?	• **Direct** — how well do we do as a destination site for our audience?	• How well overall? • How well relative to other sources?	• Total direct referral visits • Direct visits as % of total
	• **Search** — how well does our content do via search?	• How well overall? • How well relative to other sources? • How well by each search site?	• Total search referral visits • Search visits as % of total • Breakdown of each search source as % of total
	• **Social referral** — how well do we do in getting click-throughs from our presence on social sites?	• How well overall? • How well relative to other sources? • How well by each social site?	• Total social referral visits • Social visits as % of total • Breakdown of each social site as % of total
	• **Other referral** — how well do we do in getting click-throughs from other sources of referral?	• How well overall? • How well relative to other sources? • How well by each other referral source?	• Total other referral visits • Other referral visits as % of total • Breakdown of each other referral source as % of total

DIMENSION	TYPE/SUBTYPE OF MEASURE		SPECIFIC MEASURE*
Audience by device: what sort of screen are they viewing our content on?	• for **Reach** — what share of their traffic (visits) is on which screen?	• How much on desktop? • How much on mobile? • How much on tablet?	• Desktop share % of total visits • Mobile share % of total visits • Tablet share % of total visits
	• for **Consumption** - what share of their content consumption (page views) is on which screen?	• How much on desktop? • How much on mobile? • How much on tablet?	• Desktop share % of total page views • Mobile share % of total page views • Tablet share % of total page views
	• for **Attention** - how much of their attention (time) is spent on which screen?	• How much on desktop? • How much on mobile? • How much on tablet?	• Desktop share % of total page views • Mobile share % of total page views • Tablet share % of total page views

* All measures within a given time frame (e.g., week, month)

This typology is useful in two ways. First, it provides a mental model for thinking about audience metrics overall and how individual metrics fit the larger picture. Second, it keeps clear why teams track any given metric — that is, the questions teams seek to answer. *If there's no clear and important question, there's no value in tracking the metric.*

In this typology, take special note of the first dimension, audience location. It is key to distinguish your *in-market* audience since the primary purpose of audience teams is to grow engaged and loyal *local* audience rather than attracting a churning, fly-by, high bounce rate audience from anywhere.

Yes, out-of-market traffic and page views have inventory value for programmatic advertising. That is a piece of the revenue puzzle to solve. Still, audience teams must go beyond programmatic to build local audiences from whom revenue can be earned in multiple ways: higher value advertising and sponsorship opportunities, local sponsored content, subscriptions, events, and more. (See Table Stakes #4 and #5 for more on revenue possibilities and practices for realizing them.)

Moreover, in-market and out-of-market audiences likely have different behaviors. Blending the data will distort the profile of the in-market audience and make it difficult to accurately understand local audience behaviors, needs and interests.

c) Ask audience teams and analytics plus technology folks to work together to develop and use audience team scorecards

Having a good understanding of audience data and being able to view it in an analytics system is a start but won't do much to drive the performance of your audience teams. To be really useful, the data needs to be fashioned into a scorecard as a tool that serves multiple purposes. A well-developed scorecard:

- Tells the story of the audience and the audience behaviors you want to grow and tracks your progress in reaching set objectives.
- Focuses on the questions and measures that matter most and provides a logical path for drilling deeper on questions as needed with additional measures.
- Serves as the focal point for regular team meetings to review audience results, to see and discuss what is and isn't working, and to identify the next round of improvements to make.

Scorecards don't have to be elaborate. In the beginning, for example, scorecards might comprise a handful of key measures manually pulled and tracked each week on a spreadsheet. That can be enough to get started with weekly review meetings. The important thing is to have and use some sort of scorecard from the start with the team and build from there.

With this in mind, here's guidance for developing scorecards audience teams should use to continually improve performance.

> **NOTE TO READERS**
> This view of digital metrics and analytics is from an audience perspective. Table Stake #2 provides another view of digital measures from a platform perspective for managing platform performance, though many of the same measures and metrics are involved. And Table Stake #4 focuses on metrics for "funneling" fly-by readers and viewers to become loyal audiences with a "willingness to pay" in one form or another.

d) Determine the scorecard specs

While you might start with a manually kept scorecard, you will soon want to shift to one that is automatically generated by whatever analytics system your newsroom uses. In making that shift, develop the specifications for your scorecard through:

- **Selecting the audience measures to track.** Use the typology of measures to pick wisely among the range of possible things to track. In the beginning, focus on fewer rather than more. Recognize that your choices may change over time as the audience teams evolve. For example, audience teams might initially choose to build traffic and engagement and later move to increasing reach, loyalty and monetization.

- **Adding content measures.** Content helps drive audience. So, make sure the team's scorecard includes some basic measures to track how the volume and effectiveness of the content published by the team is affecting audience numbers. These can include:

    — The count of stories published by all the team's contributors
    — Percentage of stories with unique visitors *above* a threshold number (e.g. % of stories with >= 3,000 uniques with the threshold set as a target that's well above the current average)
    — Percentage of stories with unique visitors below a threshold number (e.g. % of stories with <= 100 uniques with the threshold set at a level deemed not to have been worth the time and effort)

- **Setting the reporting frequency for each measure.** As the list of measures gets longer, you can and should distinguish between *tracking* measures and *diagnostic* measures. Tracking measures are those your team reviews to monitor progress while diagnostic measures are those the team uses to understand what is happening and why.

    — *Tracking* measures include a smaller set of measures that teams likely should review once a week — long

enough to smooth out day-to-day variations yet not so long as to preclude action (for example, monthly intervals might cause the team to forget what to do and why).
— *Diagnostic* measures are reviewed to drill-down on more specific questions and analysis of particular issues and opportunities. They are a longer list of measures that facilitate and support teams taking deeper dives. Consequently, monthly time intervals are quite likely more useful than weekly ones.

- **Including goals for the measures.** Scorecards must include the current goals set for the team. Otherwise, they are no more than a table with numbers. Goals should cover all of the team's tracking measures and perhaps some of the diagnostics measures. Time frames for goals will include but also extend beyond weekly intervals.

e) Work with your data/analytics colleagues to ensure the scorecard meets your chosen specs

It is key to include your data, analytics and technology colleagues from the beginning of your scorecard discussions. In particular, engage them about:

- **Capturing all the data.** Make sure to capture data from all the platforms where the audience team's content is published. This includes your own websites, mobile sites and apps. To the degree possible, it should also include available data from other's platforms where the team's content is read and viewed directly on their platform (for more, see Table Stake #2).

- **Providing multiple data views in the same format.** Three different cuts of the data going into the scorecard are needed for three different purposes. All three versions should look the same. This is important for ease and speed of viewing and to reinforce the audience story reflected in the main scorecard.

— **Team performance:** how the entire team has done on key measures. This version is the main scorecard and used for the weekly team meetings and deeper-dive monthly sessions.
— **Individual performance:** how each individual contributor to the team has done on key measures. Among other things, this view is key to use in a one-on-one review and coaching sessions and in evaluating relative performance across the team's content contributors.
— **Content performance:** This version helps the team better understand what kinds of content and story forms work best or not.

- **Displaying trending.** Teams use the scorecard to drive growth and improvement, which mean scorecards must include *rates of change from period to period*. This can be done numerically with percentage changes from the last report or against a rolling average for the measure (e.g. the rolling average of unique users for the last 4 weeks). Showing a graph for how things trend over an extended period is the best way to see what's happening.

- **Ensuring usefulness to the team.** Just as with a website or app, the user experience is important. Is everything clearly and meaningfully labeled? Is there a good flow to the order and layout? For example, it's worth first doing a wire frame mock-up, just as you would a website. Similarly, for viewing the scorecard on-line, layout the navigation and places where you'd most want to drill-down for detail.

- **Providing access.** To be as useful as possible, make sure folks have access to the scorecard by desktop, mobile device and printout. Managing who has access is also important to think through. Open and more access is a better rule than closed, narrow access.

- **Making trade-offs.** You will probably confront challenges around data availability, data quality, and the reporting limitations of your analytics systems. Tradeoffs, next-best alternatives and workarounds will be required. So, the better your analytics folks understand your scorecard needs, the better, most pragmatic will be the choices and approaches.

f) Use three time horizons to guide and manage audience team performance

Senior leaders along with audience teams and team leaders must use the goals and scorecards to drive performance, skill building and change. Three time horizons or cycles are key to guiding and managing overall progress:

1) Weekly (or biweekly) team meetings to stay focused on design-do experimentation and improvement

Weekly audience team meetings establish a performance rhythm that keeps the design-do cycle moving. Daily meetings don't allow enough time to make choices, act on them and see results. Yet, if these meetings happen less than biweekly, too much time lapses between check-ins, disrupting the rhythm of progress. Following a set agenda keeps these meetings brief and effective.

- **Review scorecard results and trends for the prior 7-day (or 14 day) period.** Identify and discuss what did and didn't work based on the audience data, what did and didn't happen as intended, and what insights can be gleaned and acted upon.

- **Identify and check in on the progress of "sprints" to improve performance in focused ways.** "Sprints" come from the world of agile software development where work is broken down into short, iterative cycles with each cycle sharply focused in terms of activity and objectives. These short cycles typically last one to two weeks, sometime as long as four. For example:

- Focusing on a particular skill and practice across the team (e.g. writing better social heads);
- Trying quick experiments to test specific ideas (e.g. a new type of aggregation).
- Asking team members to adopt practices that have shown progress, whether those practices arose within or beyond the team (e.g. story forms that have proven successful in other audience teams)

- **Calendar ahead for content and coverage**, including the content flow for the next one-to-two weeks, further out content items that are emerging possibilities or date-pegged opportunities, and planning lead times for stories requiring early coordination with specialists (e.g. visually rich story projects).

2) Monthly (bi-monthly or every 6 week) reviews with the senior newsroom leaders

The senior leaders to whom the audience teams are accountable should gather the teams every 4 to 8 weeks to (1) evaluate progress, (2) discuss and identify insights from design/do sprints, (3) raise and resolve issues and challenges needing senior management input or decisions, and (4) do deeper dives into particular issues or opportunities that benefit from more senior perspectives or cross-team sharing about what's working versus not working.

In addition, senior leaders need to set aside time to review skill-building efforts, including candid discussions about gaps between the skills, attitudes, behaviors and working relationships teams need for success versus the current reality — and what steps have been or ought to be taken to close those gaps (see chapter entitled "Shaping The Right Staff Roles And Skills For Your Newsroom").

And, at least 2 to 4 times each year, senior newsroom leaders should invite the enterprise's top management team to join for a more thorough, strategic review of how well each audience team's content plus strategy is serving the target audience as well as generating revenues and otherwise supporting enterprise results.

For these reviews, pull a report of every article published over a recent period of time (e.g. the last 90 days) but also published for a minimum amount of time (e.g. 7 days). With each story include the traffic data for two or three key audience measures from the audience team's scorecard (e.g. total uniques and average time spent). Then sort the stories by each of the measures to create ranked lists by each measure (e.g. one for total uniques and another for average times spent). In reviewing these lists look for:

- Consistently low performing types of stories to drop (or find more effective ways of covering the content);
- New types of content and story forms that are performing well and worth doing more of;
- "Middling" performance stories that could be boosted to "top 20%" with some reframing and better production;
- Content with good evergreen or long-tail performance that can be produced during slower periods or assigned to freelancers.

In addition, make sure to review how the team is doing on its goals for the blended cost and value of content. And, make sure top management of your enterprise understand and weigh in on how each team's "content plus" strategy might get adjusted to better link to revenues.

3) One-on-one sessions to drive performance of individual team members

These are coaching sessions, not formal performance reviews. The frequency can vary from, say, every 30 to 90 days depending on the individual being reviewed. The agenda and objectives include:

- Reviewing progress against agreed upon improvement actions identified in the last one-on-one session — what did and didn't get done, what seems to be working and what's still a struggle.
- Looking at the most recent audience scorecard for the individual and discussing improvements in recent results, shortfalls and areas for improvement moving forward, including how the individual can repeat and amplify successes.
- Discussing some recent stories — some that performed well and some that did not — and identifying specific things that did and did not work in the stories ranging from the story idea itself to specific aspects (e.g. the cropping of a photo) to publishing time and platform.
- Linking all of these discussions to the individual's skill,

attitude, behavior and/or working relationship gaps/shortfalls to be closed.
- Agreeing on specific improvement opportunities over the coming period; and, make sure to ask/discuss steps for where, how and from whom the individual can get help. Remember to keep notes so you can come back to items at the start of the next review session.

Use this same approach with freelancers who are essential to the team's success. Freelancers will appreciate the feedback and discussion since they are less likely to get it elsewhere. (And, if they don't appreciate the feedback, it's a sign you should seriously consider cutting ties.) It also can help motivate freelancers to make your newsroom their top client priority. Finally, if the team has any critical content partnerships with other organizations, it's key to find ways to review those as well.

g) Manage across the portfolio of target audience teams

From the perspective of the entire newsroom — indeed the entire news enterprise — target audience teams comprise a portfolio that senior leaders must manage and migrate toward audience and enterprise success. Each audience team is best viewed as a mini-enterprise that, when fully formed, has a business strategy and plan for success — not just a content and audience plan. (See Table Stake #7: Drive Audience Growth and Profitability From A "Mini-Publisher" Perspective)

Managing this portfolio of mini-enterprises involves:

- Setting performance expectations for the portfolio as a whole that, in turn, get allocated to the audience teams as well as the entire newsroom. (Newsroom-wide audience development can be tracked with a newsroom scorecard using the same design as the audience teams' but inclusive of all traffic.)
- Regularly reviewing the performance of the audience teams collectively using the common scorecards that have been developed for them. Such reviews should include the participation of groups beyond the news-

room — sales, marketing, events, technology, etc. — that need to be actively working with and across the audience teams.
- Assessing where to add or shift reporting and other resources across the target audience teams based on their performance and opportunities.
- Identifying where target audience teams need to be added, redefined or reconfigured.
- Working with the publisher, marketing, ad sales and others to convert the growth in local audiences into revenue opportunities and results.

Table Stakes Number 2
Publish on the Platforms Used by Your Target Audiences

1. The Table Stake
Publish on the platforms used by your target audiences.

Go to your audiences rather than expecting them to come to you. Take responsibility for distribution by publishing and promoting on the platforms used by each of your chosen target audiences. Do so in ways that serve their needs and interests in using each platform and take best advantage of the particular features and dynamics of the platform, ways that are platform optimal versus platform agnostic.

2. Why this is Table Stakes

a) The audience has gone elsewhere: attention, habit and reliance

Serving your target audiences demands having their *attention*, becoming a *habit* in their lives, and earning their reliance on you as their go-to source in important moments.

Up through the 1990s, legacy metro newsrooms could still claim all three — attention, habit and reliance — despite the coming of radio newscasts in the 1920s, the development of television news through the 1950s and 1960s and the emergence of the public internet in the mid-1990s. That is not the case anymore because of the rise and dominance of digital media, social networks, and mobile digital devices.

1) Attention has fractured and shifted to Facebook and others

Initially the web and digital media fractured audience attention by offering many instantly accessible places to go for news content and diversions covering every angle of audience interests — a nearly endless source of diversion of time and attention.

More recently, the rise of social media, principally Facebook, has concentrated audience attention in the distribution channel Facebook controls. By combining personal news of family, friends, acquaintances and affiliations with a stream of public news from a variety of favored sources, Facebook now commands a dominant share of attention and is a source of news for more than 60% of the public. This dominance translates locally: for example, toward the end of 2016, Facebook had more than five times the number of local unique visitors as Philly.

Audience attention to legacy newspapers is cut by both of these developments. The fracturing of attention reduces the time once spent on print content while social and mobile developments pulls attention away from metro's digital content. The concentration of audience attention elsewhere (e.g. Facebook) leaves metros competing for even a few seconds of attention with everyone from mothers to global news sites to single topic sites. Indeed, because of these two forces metros can now claim only five minutes of digital attention per month per local resident.

2) Habits are set by the audience and not by you

Legacy newspapers once set the habits of readers through direct control of distribution, which determined when and where audiences received their news. Now audiences determine their own choices of when and where to consume news. *They — not you —* form their own habits, whether its reflexively reaching for their phone to check notifications any time there's a few seconds of waiting in line or regularly checking in on Facebook late in the evening before bed.

Your newsroom now must earn its way into these new audience formed habits in three ways:

- Be present where audiences are choosing to go.
- Make audience's experience with your content compelling, satisfying and "sticky" so that positive associations carry forward the next time they see your content (e.g., fast load times and well chosen "related content" selections).
- Move your target audiences, on the strength and appeal of your content, to seek you out directly (e.g., using apps and bookmarking websites) or glad to receive content when pushed to them (e.g., reading newsletters and opening links).

(See TS #4 for more on "funneling" audiences to habituation)

Legacy metro news organizations still have local market advantages because of their established brands and remaining print audiences. This makes all three of the actions above easier to achieve than a local start-up. But these advantages will continue to erode for metros that have yet to have the Table Stakes required to be in the game of digital. For such lagging metros, the brand image drifts toward "they aren't what they used to be." Even loyal print subscribers can and do lose the reading habit and let the papers pile up. Or, drop subscriptions altogether when, for example, cost cutting measures leave content 'thin.' Meanwhile, too little brand awareness, content presence and engagement among millennial and younger generations allow rivals to compete on near equal ground.

3) Reliance on your content must be earned anew

"Check the paper" used to be a byword for people looking for breaking news, wanting to get the full story, and search for the right facts. Now "check the paper' is mostly an anachronism heard in dated movies.

Yet an updated phrase of "check the [metro] news site" still happens — and can grow — when audiences have moments of immediate information need if and only if metros serve audiences in those moments the audience has these needs. Doing so necessitates metros that embrace digital's speed of publishing and continuous updating.

Succeeding here builds on many of the best parts of what metros have done well in the past: quick mobilization, reporting skills, editorial judgment, deep knowledge of local sources and rich archives of material. These advantages are difficult for non-local news sources to replicate and new local rivals to develop.

These advantages get wasted, though, if metros fail to publish content where the audiences are. Your newsroom must take full advantage of search, news aggregators, social sites and alert services. Only by establishing your presence in the routine, day-to-day cycle of audiences' news and information seeking do you get the chance — the opportunity — to redevelop and grow the audience's reliance on what you do so well.

b) Other players increasingly control distribution

In the early years of web-based publishing, your newsroom mostly owned and controlled the digital platforms you used. This has changed. Other companies and players (with roots in technology rather than content) created new and different platforms that they — not you — own. This has shifted control of distribution in critical ways:

- **Search engines** provide users easy access to their desired content from any source — diminishing audiences need to scan your home page

- **Social platforms** built massive audiences grounded in interpersonal relationships and networks and enabling personal sharing of content as opposed to those social platforms providing content themselves

- **Aggregation algorithms** generate personalized offerings of news as a direct service (Google News) and within feeds of social platforms (Facebook's Trending and News Feed).

- **Mobile technology** gives users nearly ubiquitous access to digital content and new user experiences.

- **Publishing templates** provide faster page loading times and better integrate publishers' content into non-publisher sites

These technology developments are user-centric — conceived, developed and constantly refined to meet user needs and create good user experiences. Through this user-centered, audience focus, major players have taken audience attention, habituation and reliance away from legacy media.

They have also taken control of much of the digital distribution playing field and *now set the conditions and rules for publishers to play on those fields*. And, they have redefined the minimum quality of experience users expect — even on the platforms that publishers still directly control. In his excellent "Stickier News," for example,

[1]

Stickier News by Matthew Hindman, Shorenstein Center, 2014

Matthew Hindman emphasizes the need for news sites to load much faster in order to meet user expectations[1].

c) Today's metro *newsroom* must manage distribution

Distribution is now an essential function and responsibility of metro newsrooms because of the loss of audience attention, habituation and reliance and the shift in control of publishing platforms to technology companies. Circulation in the print world still matters for newspapers of course. But your newsroom and not the circulation folks must now master the strategic, dynamic and externally focused demands of audiences in the digital world.

Why? Well, one explanation ought to be obvious: in a digital world, content creation and publishing is inextricably intertwined with distribution itself. Yes, you can and should tap into the expertise of audience development and social media folks. But those experts cannot entirely 'do it for' others in the newsroom in the manner circulation does for print.

Squarely taking on this larger responsibility requires your newsroom to blend strategic choices (e.g. Table Stake #1's requirement to choose targeted audiences) with operational excellence related to where and when to publish content. For example, publishing where the audience is cannot happen simply through "publishing everywhere" on every new platform that comes along. Instead, it demands you make managerial choices about which platforms to use — the ones you control as well as the ones controlled by others. And those choices must be **grounded in criteria** related to audience selection, brand aspirations, platform qualities, revenue possibilities, and considerations of costs and other scarce resources. In the case of others' platforms, it also means assessing the terms, conditions, opportunities and trade-offs of publishing in their space and on their terms.

Nor does publishing strategically mean being "platform agnostic." That's an unfortunate phrase that, while okay in terms of opening up minds to many possibilities, closes those same minds to a key question: *What does each different platform do well versus not well?* Instead of platform agnostic, your newsroom must be **platform optimal** where content is shaped to best fit the unique characteristics of each chosen platform — where each platform is seen as unique instead of the same as another. Operationally, this requires continual experimentation to learn and then codify effective platform practices. In the case of platforms and technology controlled by others, this also means staying current on their evolving practices, requirements, features and opportunities and building them into your work routines (SEO, SMO, etc.).

Unlike the print era, there is not now nor likely will there be any final, fixed solution. Such simple and fixed distribution solutions are a thing of the past that existed for print metros but not for metro news organizations competing in an era of multi-platform publishing. Instead, distribution is a portfolio challenge. Your metro enterprise is now moving from one platform (that is, the newspaper as platform) to many platforms — to a portfolio of platforms. And, just as you might personally manage a portfolio of investments to achieve various risk and return objectives so to must your newsroom manage and optimize the mix of platforms according to your enterprise's objectives regarding audience engagement, growth and yields from that engagement and growth compared to the costs and investment of staff time, skills and other resources. You have to *manage* the hard choices about whether and when to walk away from an underperforming platform, reinvest in platforms that show promise or do well and experiment with new ones.

This Table Stake #2 closely links to other Table Stakes. It grows out of Table Stake #1's requirement to choose which audiences to serve and with what to meet their interests and needs. It also blends in with Table Stake #3's requirement to produce and publish continuously to meet audience needs. It further supports your efforts to use Tables Stake #4 to funnel occasional users into habitual loyalists. All these Table Stakes advance when you publish on the platforms used by your targeted audiences.

3. Assessing the gaps in your newsroom

The gaps with this Table Stake concern how far you've come in (1) thinking strategically about your overall distribution plan, (2) using the target audience perspective to deliberately choose the platforms you use, (3) organizing yourselves to manage each platform effectively; and, (4) rigorously assessing platform performance and value against objectives you establish.

Take the following quiz for a quick read on where your efforts stand vis a vis this Table Stake. *Please note: these statements are phrased so that a 'yes' answer indicates your efforts have gaps — that is, fall short of the requirements of this Table Stake. And, the more yesses, the more gaps you face.*

It is worth having many folks take these quizzes, including people in the newsroom as well as from technology, marketing, sales, HR and finance. Compare and discuss your respective responses and where you have agreement or not. Use these discussions to identify and highlight the most significant distribution gaps you face with regard to publishing on the platforms used by your target audiences.

	YES	NO
1. We publish on multiple digital platforms, but we are not entirely clear why we are publishing on each of them, who we are trying to reach, and what we are gaining from the effort involved.		
2. We often describe the audience for a platform as anyone who uses the platform ("our audience for Facebook is Facebook users").		
3. We still have some-to-many reporters and editors in our newsroom who see getting a story published on the main website as the extent of their digital publishing concerns.		
4. We too often make decisions about publishing or promoting a story somewhere other than our main web and mobile site until after that story has been published on the main site instead of including such considerations from the beginning.		
5. Our decisions on what, how much and when to publish on a given platform are more often than not ad hoc and based on an individual's notions at the time.		
6. We do not have one individual or team directly responsible for growing our Facebook audience, engagement and referrals.		
7. Too many of our reporters and editors are confused about whom to ask for help with questions about what works best for audiences on different platforms.		
8. The people in our newsroom lack a common and ever growing view of the specific practices that have actually proven to be effective on platforms.		

	YES	NO
9. We too often fail to meet the minimum user experience expectations for platforms (e.g. speedy load times).		
10. We cannot point to enough platforms where we believe we've figured out what it takes to consistently succeed — and have the audience results to prove it.		
11. I am worried that our newsroom's lack of platform skills and expertise will preclude us getting really good at enough platforms.		
12. We too often begin publishing on a platform without setting any audience targets in advance, or setting a checkpoint in time to decide whether to continue using that platform.		
13. We have at times launched on a new platform only to have it hardly mentioned six months later.		
14. Our main website and mobile site or app are the only platforms for which we regularly track and report audience traffic.		
15. Total page views and uniques are the primary metrics we track on our main website.		
16. We do not regularly track and set goals against how we rank in our market versus local digital competitors (e.g. local TV stations but also the local Facebook presence).		
17. We pay attention to one-off stories that go viral and blow through the numbers but do not regularly track whether the average performance of all stories — or stories of certain types — are rising or falling.		
TOTAL		

4. Why these gaps exist

Gaps in your newsroom's effectiveness at publishing on the platforms used by your target audiences arise from: 1) the legacy mindsets, operations and organization of print-based distribution; and 2) the inherent complexities of navigating a world of multi-platform distribution, especially one where dominant platforms are owned and controlled by others.

a) Gaps exist because of print legacy impediments

Not surprisingly, the legacy of having once controlled distribution and publishing fosters a range of practices and conditions that slow down and clutter up how fast and well you adapt distribution and publishing on multiple platforms. Some of these have softened in recent years yet can remain significant factors in metro newsrooms.

1) The comfort of controlling print distribution created an organization culture that is slow.

Owning the means of distribution in print from beginning-to-end always had operational challenges (e.g., when to stop the presses for late closing and how best to optimize distribution routes). But those rarely caused news enterprises significant discomfort about controlling the interaction with print readers. This culture of comfort — of being in control — ill serves the radically different dynamics and unsolved challenges of distribution platforms that are unfamiliar and not totally or even partially controlled.

Even your own websites where you retain control demand audience-first approaches characterized by dynamic, fast moving uncertainties that are a far cry from distributing newspapers. And, mobile web and apps move even further away from the comfort zone because the technology requirements of different mobile operating systems come into play. Finally, publishing on platforms controlled entirely by others strips all comfort away.

Digital-only publishers have no choice but to embrace the challenges of digital platforms. Legacy metros, in contrast, can and too often have retreated into organizational habits of comfort and/ or denial — especially, the sense that your metro can dictate the terms of distribution. You don't and you can't.

2) Unchanged legacy organization structures and processes are out of sync with new demands.

Legacy metro news enterprises were functionally structured organizations whose clear division of labor spelled out the well defined, function-by-function — silo by silo — effort that linked every step from words typed on a page to a newspaper delivered on a doorstep. In this world, when one function finished work it could and did successfully hand it off to the next function. It could with good results 'throw it over the wall.'

Not today. Not in a world where content can be created and published on the same keyboard. This shift raises organizational questions about how best to publish on your own platforms and those of others, including:

- How to make decisions to start publishing on a platform?
- What are the roles and responsibilities related to each platform you use?
- Who "owns" a given platform?
- What bridges must connect editorial, technology and the user experience for each platform?
- Who develops a working knowledge of platforms owned by others — and relationships with those owners?
- Who's looking out for what's coming next and thinking about experiments to try?
- How is the overall portfolio of platforms assessed and adjusted and who's involved?

These questions cannot get resolved by newsrooms stuck in the fixed roles and functions tied to print. Yet, for too long now, too many newsrooms have put off addressing these questions in favor of improvising at the edges.

Nor does managing digital as a separate unit work any more. Small web teams in another building that few in the newsroom even knew about made arguable sense in the early days of the web. Today, those arrangements are too slow and too cumbersome.

Nor do separate teams focused on social sites and platforms controlled by others work either — for example, through staffing distinct "audience development" positions who serve as appendages to the newsroom. When this happens, the expertise too often gets stuck doing routine tasks (e.g. updating Facebook pages) for others who, with time and learning, could do it better themselves. Even worse, opportunities to 'wow' audiences through digital experiences suffer when, as one of the Knight Temple folks with digital and social expertise said, "The whole story is written before they even talk to us." While such skilled experts can and do make a difference even after the fact of content creation, their impact is severely limited in the absence of the entire newsroom's embracing and integrating audience engagement and development into how everyone — not just the experts — do work.

3) The continued financial realities of print trigger unhelpful either/or choices.

For most metros, print still generates the lion's share of revenue. It also carries the lion's share of costs. It's understandable, then, that metros perpetuate or revert to 'print first.' Understandable? Yes. Acceptable? No. It is now Table Stakes to be audience-first to be in the game of 21st century news and information. And, audience-first means shifting from print-first to both digital-first and print later and BETTER as part of a commitment to publish on the platforms used by your target audiences.

The either/or trap of print versus digital is a subtle and powerful legacy impediment. Only when your metro newsroom sees and experiences how the print product — the print reader's experience — gains from embracing the rich possibilities of digital content across multiple, relevant platforms will you find a way out of the either/or trap of sacrificing audience growth and engagement to print revenue needs.

b) Gaps exist because of inherent complexities of multiplatform distribution

Adding to these legacy-driven impediments are the complexities of navigating and managing distribution in a world of multiple and emerging platforms, some of which you own and some that others own. These complexities manifest themselves organizationally in ways that further impede effectively publishing on the platforms used by targeted audiences.

1) Ambivalence saps and wastes energy

Current publishing ecosystems mandate choices across a spectrum of possibilities: serving audiences who already come to you versus finding audiences elsewhere and trying to pull them to you versus finding them elsewhere and serving them elsewhere.

The choice to distribute on platforms owned by others provides your newsroom much wider reach. It also raises concerns about (1) loss of control, (2) undermining direct reach, (3) losing direct relationships and brand identity with audiences; and, (4) becoming dependent on and vulnerable to the actions of others. It's natural for any content producer to feel conflicted and ambivalent — especially in newsrooms with legacies of being in control of publishing.

These conflicted feelings, though, can and too often do generate ambivalence, inaction and risk avoidance. They generate either/or framing of choices ('print versus digital') rather than both/and approaches (both print and digital — both reaching audiences where they are and figuring out how to bring them to us).

They also can too easily sap energy and precious resources by triggering seemingly endless debate and discussion over platforms. Talk trumps action — unresolved debates persist instead of 'learning by doing' and 'just getting on with it.'

2) Reactiveness displaces management discipline

News organizations can be overly reactive. Ambivalence and delay turn suddenly into urgency. Platform choices leap to the top of the agenda. "We have to be on Snapchat!" "We need a special app for the bar scene!" Such efforts get launched impulsively in the absence of any managerial discipline and choice grounded in attention to target audiences, platform optimal content, publishing workflows, maintenance costs, revenue possibilities and more. While such sudden reactive efforts might produce good results, they also regularly fail to match optimistic expectations that, in turn, can leave the platforms languishing in unmanaged ways — neither killed nor developed further. When that happens, skepticism grows in ways that undermine instead of building confidence.

5. What success looks and feels like

Publishing on the platforms that your target audiences use requires your newsroom to get good at (1) how best to use each separate platform; and, (2) how best to manage your portfolio of platforms. The net effect is a publishing platform plan, action and performance that are strategically crafted, effectively managed, resilient to external changes and robust in growing your share of audience, especially in your local metro market.

Success looks and feels like the "to" side of the following:

FROM > TO shift for publishing on the platforms used by your target audiences

	FROM	TO
Strategic selection and conscious management	An assortment of publishing platforms accumulated over time	A consciously and strategically chosen portfolio of publishing platforms chosen to serve targeted audiences and continually optimized based on platform performance
	Some orphaned platforms with little audience and little attention paid (e.g. newsletters or apps started in earnest but left to drift)	Every publishing platform has an owner; every platform is tended to; every platform's audience performance is tracked
	Random, unmanaged and unshared platform approaches used or unused by reporters and editors as they wish	Performance-based and platform optimal practices actively managed by platform owners and experts and mandatory for reporters and editors to use
	Reporters and editors do not see or accept platform distribution as essential to their jobs	Reporters and editors, with rare exception, understand and incorporate platform distribution into their daily work
	Stories are created and published without consideration of a platform distribution plan	With rare exceptions, stories routinely include platform optimal considerations in the planning stages

	FROM	TO
Strategic selection and conscious management	Failure to meet key user experience (UX) expectations on each platform that matters	Meet or exceed basic user experience (UX) expectations on all platforms that matter
	Lack of platform specific metrics	Have and use metrics relevant to each platform
	Lack of engagement metrics along with page views and uniques	Have and use engagement, page view and uniques
Other's platforms	Fear of algorithm changes	Reasonable confidence in not being adversely affected by algorithm changes based on your audience targeting, content relevance and overall platform publishing strategy
	Vulnerability to traffic drops by over reliance on particular traffic sources and susceptibility to changes by those sources	A robust distribution strategy that's resilient to changes in any given traffic source based on conscious targeting of platforms to target audiences and providing content of value to those audiences
	Near dread of the "next new thing" as one more thing to deal with (or not)	Interest in the potential of the "next new thing" to better reach and serve your target audiences combined with clear approaches and criteria for evaluating and possibly experimenting with the "new thing"
Local market penetration	Traffic growth driven primarily by out-of-market traffic; out of market-traffic an increasing share of total traffic	In-market traffic growing at a greater rate than out-of-market and increasing its share of total traffic
	Lagging local market reach on key platforms vs. local news competitors (e.g. TV stations)	Consistent #1 (or at least high) local market ranking on key platforms (e.g., desktop, mobile, Facebook and Twitter)
	Monthly in-market uniques that represent only a small share of your metro market	Monthly in-market uniques that represent a larger share of the metro market than in the peak days of print

Table Stakes #2 Publish on the Platforms Used by Your Target Audiences

You and your colleagues ought to create your own version of this "From > To" statement. Doing so will help you define the changes you need to make — and explain those changes to others in ways that engage them. A from/to is also a good way to identify gaps.

Try drafting a version of from/to yourself or, better yet, with colleagues. Describe the "from" and the "to" as sharply as you can to capture your newsroom's current state versus the better state of your aspirations. Share it with others as widely as possible, and ask them to build on the needed shifts using language that makes sense to your newsroom. There should be nods of recognition when reading the 'from' side — and an energetic "yesses" when reading the 'to' side.

6. Actions to close the gaps

This section describes the key steps required to publish on the platforms used by your target audiences, including:

a) Use a strategic view of the distribution landscape
b) Pick platforms intentionally based on agreed purposes and criteria
c) Develop, use and continually update publishing plans for each platform you use
d) Designate platform owners and hold them accountable for delivering results
e) Experiment with platforms where your audience may be going or want to be

a) Use a strategic view of the distribution landscape

1) Staying grounded

Publishing and distribution platforms shift and change. New platforms emerge regularly, different audiences gravitate to them, much is written about them, cases for the pros and cons are made, urgency and anxiety about "being on" ensue, actions are or aren't taken, and then this cycle repeats with announcements of another new platform or changes to established ones. All this is driven by players outside your newsroom's control — players whose range of interests may or may not coincide with yours. It's little wonder then that developing and effectively managing the portfolio of platforms used by your audiences is new and difficult, particularly for legacy print news enterprises habituated to owning and controlling the means of publishing and distribution for print.

It's important to stay grounded in two ways:

- **Start with your audience, not the platform.** The better you have chosen which audiences you seek to serve and the more clearly you understand their needs, interests and behaviors, the easier and clearer it is for you to know which platforms to use to reach, engage and habituate those audiences.

- **Assess any given platform against how it's strengths and weaknesses serve your chosen audiences compared to other platforms in your portfolio.** Start with a simple typology of publishing and distribution platforms that provides a general framework for considering which platform to use for which audience and why — a lay of the land you use to navigate how best to match platforms to audiences.

2) Get the lay of the land through using a typology of platforms

We use "platform" broadly as any means of getting your content to audiences, directly or indirectly. The focus is on digital platforms but print and even public forums are included as well. Within the digital realm, scores of existing and emerging sites, apps and technologies fall under this definition.

To avoid the chaos of just 'one long, darn list,' you should put publishing platforms into three groups based on ownership, content control and audiences' access to content:

- Platforms you own
- Platforms others own *that redirect to your content on your platforms*
- Platforms others own *where your content remains on their platform*

This table outlines the core dynamics of these three platform types.

Three basic types of publishing and distribution platforms

PLATFORM TYPE	CONTENT CONTROL	AUDIENCE ACCESS	KEY TO SUCCESS
1. Your platforms	• You publish on your own platform, directly controlling the flow of your content	• The audience reaches you directly; you serve them directly • You must attract the audience	• Providing a great user experience on all dimensions • Keeping users returning to your platforms • Keeping users on your platforms • Migrating users from random to habitual users on your platforms (See TS#4)
2. Others' platforms redirecting to you	• Your content is aggregated, prioritized, curated and/or referenced by someone else who provides links back to your content on your platform	• You reach the audience indirectly at the discretion of others • Others attract the audience • You compete with other publishers for attention	• Maximizing user click through to your content on your platforms • Playing well by someone else's rules and criteria • Competing effectively with the other publishers on the platform under the owner's terms
3. Others' platforms where your content stays on their platforms	• You publish directly on a closed platform owned and controlled by someone else	• The audience views your content in someone else's space	• Showing up with superior content amid the rest of the crowd • Emphasizing your brand and value as worth visiting directly

3) Use criteria to evaluate and monitor the value of different platforms

Here are the criteria you should use to evaluate, monitor and update the value any particular platform has in serving your target audiences:

- **Reach:** ability to reach large audiences, especially new ones, and increase content consumption and awareness

- **Targeting:** ability to focus the reach on the audiences you choose to serve

- **Content context:** compatibility of the other content appearing on the site with your brand

- **Consumption:** ability to increase items read/viewed and time spent per session (stickiness)

- **Engagement:** ability to prompt audience-initiated actions that add reach, data and/or affinity (e.g., sharing, sign-ups)

- **Habituation:** ability to induce frequent, regular return and develop a preference over other sources to increase likelihood to return (stickiness)

- **Share-ability:** utility provided to users who want to share with others — and do so in ways that promote the value of your content and brand

- **Brand building:** ability to identify your brand with the content being viewed and distinguish your brand from others

- **Data:** availability and extent of data about audiences and their activities when reading and viewing your content

- **Monetization:** ability to monetize the audience reading and viewing your content, including driving subscriptions or other consumer based revenue as well as ad type and placement control, inventory availability, revenue sharing arrangements and ad-blocking circumvention

- **User experience:** quality and consistency of the user experience (including ease of access, load times, navigation). You need to consider this factor in two ways, depending on the basic type of platform:

  — For your own platforms, your capacity and capability to create a good user experience
  — For other's platforms, the quality of the user experience they have created and your ability to enhance it further in your use of their platform

- **Costs:** the complexity, difficulty, staff time and other cost involved in using the platform to publish

You should use these criteria to:

- **Assess platforms that you are currently using** as to whether they have sufficient value to continue using

- **Assess the value of existing platforms that you are not now using** for reaching your targeted audiences

- **Assess new platforms that come along**

b) Pick your platforms intentionally based on agreed purposes and criteria

1) Consider three different possible purposes for platforms

You might include platforms in your platform portfolio for three quite different purposes:

- **Brand-wide mainstays:** core platforms where audiences expect to find your content and where most of your newsroom's collective content is published.

- **Target-audience specific:** platforms picked to reach and engage specific target audiences (for example, newsletters of targeted content for targeted audiences, or platforms heavily preferred by certain demographics).

- **Experiments:** platforms to test, whether as potential mainstays or target-audience specific platforms. Commitment to these experiments is time and resource bound (See more on these under 6e below).

2) Use criteria tailored to the different purposes

Tailor the criteria described in the previous section to choose among the three platform purposes as follows:

- **Brand-wide mainstay platform criteria**

    Select the platforms on which local audiences expect to find your content when they seek information (e.g. for breaking news and local crises). Such platforms are your main entry doors for the metro population.

    Given the current stage of digital media, this means publishing on mobile (app, mobile web and/or responsive web), desktop web, Facebook and Twitter.

    For platforms beyond these, give particular attention to these criteria:

    — Widening your *local market* reach to create awareness, catch first-time readers/viewers and re-hook occasional readers/users.
    — Ease of sharing and recommending through multiple means
    — Ability to gain more favorable positioning on existing mainstay platforms (e.g. Facebook Instant Articles)
    — Ability to promote to boost trending opportunities
    — Ability to monetize their bulk traffic through advertising

- **Target audience-specific platform criteria**

    Choose additional target audience-specific platforms when they provide an attractive blend of niche reach, opportunities for engagement, loyalty building and habituation.

Pay special attention to these criteria:

— Ability to reach users in a particular local target audience who may not be heavy users of your mainstay platforms
— Ability to gain more data on the audience, track usage and know individual identities
— Ability to monetize specialty traffic through multiple means (see Table Stake #6)
— Ability to use effective story forms and gain greater engagement, loyalty and habituation within the platform

- **Criteria for platform experiments**

   Distinguish experiments aimed at brand-wide platform possibilities versus those aimed at adding audience-specific platforms. Use the criteria listed above for brand-wide experiments. Essentially, ask yourselves if you can quickly learn about brand-wide possibilities through rapid and inexpensive experimentation.
   Experiment with new audience-specific platforms when you can quickly and cheaply learn about the factors listed above plus:

— Indications of interest and emerging usage within your local market, not just buzz in the national media and tech press. Look to your local trendsetters and tech community instead.
— The availability of willing and cheap "experimenters" who know how to use a potential platform (e.g. interns).
— The opportunity to learn about a range of similar platforms (e.g., experimenting with one messaging app to get a feel for others or to reconceive how you approach notifications)

3) Design and use a management process for selecting platforms

Establish and use a management process for (1) selecting platforms; (2) establishing goals for platforms; and, (3) regularly reviewing if and how platform results meet the goals you've set
This requires you to:

- **Make decisions at the right organizational level.** Brand-wide mainstay platform decisions, including any experiments with possible new mainstays, belong to enterprise-wide leaders. In contrast, audience and/or mini-publisher teams might make decisions about target audience specific platforms and experiments. When target audience experiments affect two or more audience teams, it's best to have all involved participate in setting the objectives and approach of the experiment.

- **Involve the right mix of people.** This includes editors and reporters from the newsroom as well as folks with experience and expertise in audience development and audience metrics. There may be others with perspectives and knowledge to share and vested interest in the success of the platform, including business development, sales, marketing and technology.

- **Use a tool to spell out your criteria, make your ratings and capture important notes.** This can be as simple as a Google doc spreadsheet constructed and shared among participants to capture their ratings and notes.

- **Experiment before fully committing.** In the spirit of learn fast, learn cheap, it's best to start publishing on a new platform as an experiment with defined expectations and criteria that determine whether or not the experiment moves forward after the trial period. (See section 6e for more on experimenting)

Start this management process with your existing platforms, particularly any platforms about which there's confusion over purpose, doubt about value, or concern over the resources being committed. Most newsrooms have launched platforms that may have seemed promising or necessary at the time but yield little audience. Even The New York Times with the capacity to support a multitude of platforms has learned there comes a time to drop some and redeploy resources elsewhere. It is even more important for newsrooms with far smaller multi-platform publishing capacity to periodically reassess and make changes to the portfolio of platforms.

You should put together and continually update a 'platform map' that depicts your existing platforms as well as current experiments. The platforms on the map ought to reference the target audiences served as well as the core objectives you hope to achieve. Moreover, share this map broadly so that folks throughout the newsroom and beyond have a current sense for platform strategy, objectives and results.

c) Put together a publishing plan by platform

You should be as intentional about your plan for how best to publish across your chosen platforms as you are about the selection, experimentation and management of any given platform. Publishing plans for each platform begin with the audience in mind, not the platform per se. The difference is subtle but important. Avoid defining your audience by the platform you use ("Our audience is Twitter users."). Instead, define how you use a platform to better serve an audience ("We use Twitter to reach an audience that's hungry for breaking news and the doings of prominent local personalities.").

A plan for publishing across platforms includes the following elements:

- Target audiences
- Content types
- Story forms
- Voice
- Frequency of posting: weekdays, weekends, special events, seasons of the year
- Timing of posting
- Forms of promotion and "boosting"
- Relative priority and resource commitment

- Responsibilities for producing and publishing
- Traffic/engagement/brand/economic/financial/other objectives

Audience teams should take the lead on these plans in collaboration with the "continuous news desk" (or equivalent) and the platform owner (see the next section).

d) Designate platform owners

1) Your newsroom must have platform owners

You must have platform owners. You must name the folks who are accountable for *platform management and performance across target audiences*. Platform owners must coordinate with audience and mini-publisher teams. But, without platform owners, no one in the newsroom will manage platform performance. Worse, the platform runs the risk of being organizationally orphaned.

"Owning" a platform is a role, not necessarily a *position or full time job* in the newsroom. It is distinct from producing and publishing content on the platform. It's also distinct from the role of a platform editor (e.g. a mobile editor) focused on content. The focus of the platform owner is on the platform itself — understanding the nature of the platform and the user experience with the platform, setting platform performance objectives and goals, assessing platform results, developing better uses of the platform, and identifying and pursuing needed platform improvements.

In larger newsrooms, this role might be a full-time job and not just a role. And, whether a role or a job, you might call it 'product manager' instead of 'platform owner.'

2) Role of platform owners

The platform owner is the person anyone in the newsroom or enterprise can turn to with questions about the platform. Consider newsletters as platforms. When other folks have questions about the objectives and/or performance of newsletters, they can turn to the newsletter platform owner — if, of course, that role has been designated. Similarly, there should be roles as platform owners for whatever is in the portfolio of platforms selected.

Platform owners are responsible for:

- **Understanding what it takes to win on the platform** based on a solid understanding of the platform's features and uses by users, effective publishing practices and basic underlying technology.

- **Monitoring publishing on the platform** from an overall, platform user perspective across all content published on the platform.

- **Providing platform specific support to users**, whether it's answering one-off questions, offering brown-bag sessions on effective practices and new developments or providing side-by-side coaching.

- **Assessing performance of the platform**, including keeping a platform scorecard, benchmarking performance against peers and reporting on platform performance.

- **Determining and driving what's needed to grow the platform's audience**, ranging from wider use to better user training to technology investments.

3) Picking platform owners

How many platform owners you have, whether or not those owners are full-time jobs or roles, and whom you pick to be owners will vary based on the size of your news enterprise. Here are the most important considerations:

- **Time commitments of platform owners vary by importance of platform.** The platform owner of your primary website may be a full-time role or close to it whereas owning, say, LinkedIn as a platform may require a lot less of someone's time (e.g. perhaps 10-15%) — or, indeed, more depending on how critical LinkedIn is to your objectives.

- **Distinguish platform operations from platform ownership.** Your target audience teams, "continuous news desk" and audience development team have many hour-by-hour, day–by-day roles and operational tasks to perform across platforms. These differ, though, from platform ownership responsibilities related to overall platform objectives and performance.

- **You may have natural owners of some platforms.** A social media editor, for example, might be the right person to own some or all of your mobile platforms. Niche mobile apps may call for someone from the audience team responsible for the content of the app. If an audience team member is the only user of Snapchat, she or he could be the natural owner.

    (*Please note:* In cases where someone combines platform operational and production roles with the ownership role, it's especially important to make the platform ownership responsibilities a distinct and explicit part of their position description and make allowances for them in the allocation of time.)

- **Look broadly for potential platform owners.** Platform ownership is a learning opportunity. The platform owner role will help folks experience and learn general management skills as well as deepen expertise at distributing content in a multi-platform world. Depending on your size, you may also need to spread the workload of platform ownership. Consider, for example, tech folks who are super users of a particular messaging app, or have an intuitive sense of the user experience on mobile — or, yet again, for apps that have heavy tech requirements or need special expertise (e.g. Facebook Instant Articles or Google AMP). You might look to photographers or multimedia designers for a platform such as Instagram. Finally, don't limit your choices to the newsroom. Mixing in non-newsroom folks as platform owners can enrich and speed up whole enterprise thinking and action.

- **Platform owner teams may help make the management of related platforms more effective and efficient.** Such teams might still have individual team members take responsibility for individual platforms but work together to share learning about cross-platform issues and opportunities. For example, given the tight interrelationship of mobile and social, there could be a team that owns your mobile platforms and main social platforms. Another combination might be your own notifications along with messaging apps that you use.

- **Include print.** Even as newsrooms move to multi-platform digital publishing, print remains a primary distribution platform — it too needs platform ownership. In effect, for example, Dallas did this when it reorganized the newsroom to include a print team.

4) Platform owners must manage platforms as *owners*

Being a platform owner truly means owning. It means being a *general manager* — a publisher if you will — who takes responsibility *for all aspects of platform performance — strategy, operations, customers, costs and revenues*. It means setting and monitoring performance objectives for the audiences on the platform, the platform's uses across the newsroom, the time and effort invested, the users' experience, the traffic and engagement performance, and the revenues generated by the platform.

However, unlike the traditional, hierarchical general manager position, a platform owner may hold a front-line position in the organization and manage more through example, expertise, insight, relationships, influence and the development of the skills of others than authority per se. In this sense, the role is similar to the 'mini-publisher' described in Table Stake 7.

The table below details the list of platform owner responsibilities. This list is extensive — it describes the full scope for truly owning a platform. Someone just beginning in the role of a platform owner shouldn't necessarily be expected to perform all the roles from the start. But any platform owner should aspire and be held accountable to grow into the full role.

Checklist of platform management responsibilities

Knowing the platform	• Understands the platform's features and functionalities as well as any underlying technology necessary for effective use of the platform • Understands key aspects of the user experience and what matters most to users • Knows what it takes to win on the platform • Develops benchmarks for performance on the platform (what success should look like in a market of your size) • Keeps current on how the platform evolves as well as how others (even beyond news publishers) are using the platform
Assessing the user experience	• Engages with users about their experience on the platform and the newsroom's content on the platform for insights and opportunities to improve their experience • Objectively assesses critical aspects of the user experience on the platform for gaps and opportunities (e.g., load times, navigation ease, and ad experience)
Overseeing effective platform practices	• Periodically scans content on the platform from across the newsroom to assess what is happening on the platform (anything from SEO optimal headlines and tagging, to social ledes, to use of visuals, to content fit — depending on the success factors of the particular platform) • Monitors execution against the publishing plans by audience teams • Develops a sense for which individuals and teams across the newsroom are working well with the platform versus those who need support
Growing platform competence across the newsroom	• Identifies basic training and support needs and arranges/provides that training and support • Provides coaching • Holds informal skill building and practice-sharing sessions and workshops • Identifies, promotes and explains particular examples of effective content and publishing practices on the platform
Fixing problems	• Identifies problems impeding platform use or effectiveness (technical or otherwise) and takes the lead in getting them resolved by whoever needs to be involved • Is the point person for others to go to when they see or encounter problems

Tracking platform performance	• Understands, and crafts strategies, for how the platform can best contribute to financial performance (and includes those in the platform scorecard) • Understands the intricacies of the available metrics, including data quality • Identifies the best metrics for the platform in line with the newsroom's overall strategy and objectives for the platform • Creates and maintains a platform scorecard (see section 7 below) • Regularly identifies findings and "so whats" from scorecard performance results • Communicates scorecard results and findings across the newsroom (in conjunction with other platform reporting)
Aiming for "next level" audience growth for the platform	• Sets, and regularly raises, the bar defining "good" performance of posts on the platform (e.g., how many uniques a top quintile post attracts) • Conducts ongoing experiments on the platform to increase audience reach and engagement. • If and as appropriate for target audiences, makes the case for wider use of the platform across the newsroom • Identifies and makes the case for any needed enhancements and technology improvements and investments
Managing the brand across uses of the platform	• Understands newsroom-wide branding objectives and standards — and translates them into effective brand practices for the platform • Ensures consistency in branding and adherence to brand standards across multiple uses of the same platform (e.g. multiple Facebook pages, multiple Twitter accounts, or multiple newsletters) • Finds ways to strengthen the awareness and presence of the brand when published on platforms owned by others

e) Experiment with platforms where your audience may be going or want to be

Experimentation and learning are essential to growing your target audiences through building the best possible portfolio of digital distribution. Why? Because existing digital platforms continue to evolve; new ones emerge; and, how to use digital platforms to publish content and build loyal audiences demands continuous improvement and innovation.

For example, consider a messaging app that may have value today to zillions of users in general but not yet for users who consume local news. That might change. For example, you might observe or hear about local news consumers going to the messaging app. Or you hear about a use on that app that could induce local users to use it.

Here are the basics for any experiment applied to digital publishing:

- A clear idea (hypothesis) of what's being tested, including your specific performance and learning objectives.
- An outlined "lab" procedure: what will be done, what and who is needed to do it — and a commitment to deploying those resources.
- A set timeframe and defined criteria for deciding whether the experiment succeeds, fails, or must be continued a while longer.
- A plan for what happens when an experiment succeeds.

Beyond these basics, you should customize your efforts based on whether the experiment involves existing platforms or new platforms.

1) On existing platforms

Conducting ongoing experiments to improve the performance of an existing platform is an integral part of managing a platform. And it's a natural part of the platform owner's role to identify, shape and conduct the experiments in collaboration with audience teams and others in the newsroom (and beyond, e.g. an outside content partner).

Most experiments on existing platforms are likely to be aimed at continuous and incremental improvements in platform performance. These experiments might occur as a regular part of the content production, publishing, monitoring, and promotion process (e.g. headline A/B testing). Or, they might involve innovation with greater uncertainties and risks (e.g. experimenting with Facebook Live to grow younger, more visually oriented audiences).

2) On new platforms

When you are experimenting on new platforms, it's important to distinguish those that could be brand-wide mainstays versus those for narrower, target audience possibilities. Here are suggested approaches to keep in mind:

- **Make sure either an individual or group is responsible for scanning for trends and opportunities.** This could be a platform owner, another individual with the right experience and inclinations, or the collective responsibility of the platform owners as a group. Whoever has the charge must focus on emerging usage within your local market in addition to the buzz in the media and tech trade press. It's paramount to look beyond direct news competitors: many businesses, nonprofit organizations and units of government use digitally distributed content to reach customers, patrons and citizens. They have talented staff — folks with knowledge and experience to share. Hence, you should reach out regularly to these individuals as part of your informal "platform network" and find ways to follow and befriend them (e.g. look for local chapters and members of ONA).

- **Consider where your newsroom wants to be on the adoption curve.** Every innovation follows an adoption curve with different stages of adopters, from innovators (experimenters) to laggards. While there are advantages to entering in the early stages in terms of establishing market presence and share, there are costs of being too early (e.g., bigger expenses in being the first to figure

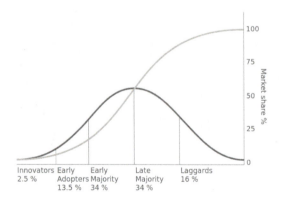

out how to make it work, time to wait for the rest of the market to develop, and greater risks of failure). Your choice for when/where to enter on this curve can vary by different platforms. Still, it's a choice you must make —

and do so with particular attention to where the platform is on the curve in your local market vis a vis your target audiences.

- **Have a process and use criteria to select platforms for experimenting.** Start with the same criteria you use to assess any platform, as discussed above in 6b but apply them more lightly since there's more uncertainty with new platforms and you don't want to over-screen at an early stage. There may also be some additional criteria to include based on unique characteristics of the platform or the nature of its potential appeal to target audiences.

- **Apply the concept of a Minimum Viable Product (MVP).** This well established, proven product development stresses getting to trials as fast as possible with product versions having just enough features to gain some valid learning about the product itself and gather enough customer feedback to know whether or not to proceed with further development.

- **Don't be afraid to put something in front of audiences.** One of the advantages of the web and digital media is low expectations by customers of permanence — something there today isn't necessarily expected to be there tomorrow. There's also an acceptance of early trials and beta versions. So, short of doing something that is blatantly brand damaging, there's little risk involved in experimenting in front of real audiences.

- **Engage audiences and experts in the experiments.** Another advantage of experimenting in digital media is the openness you can have with audiences and the informal tech and user community devoted to a platform. They can be directly engaged from the start in the fact that you are experimenting and why, and asked directly for feedback by survey or direct contact.

7. Measures of success and tracking progress in closing the gaps

You can choose among a rich array of available data and analytics to monitor platform performance. In doing this, though, avoid complexity — and the confusion, loss of focus, and lack of action arising from ill-defined, ill-chosen data and analytic approaches.

In addition, choose and monitor metrics/indicators for aspects of a platform business plan that are not addressable by data — things related to the quality of user experience, revenues, costs and so forth.

a) Platform measures

At the broadest level, there are two key categories for platform metrics:

- **Analytics-based metrics.** The familiar digital metrics of uniques, shares, time spent and the like focus on audience traffic and the audience's interactions with the platform. They help you get continuously better at using a platform to grow and engage audiences every day. They are operationally oriented.

- **Managerially focused metrics.** Managerial measures guide platform owners in managing platforms *as businesses*. They help you plan, implement and monitor performance — audience growth and retention, profitability, market performance vis a vis competitors, etc. — in ways you can compare platform versus platform as well as the portfolio of platforms as a whole. They are less operational and more strategic.

1) Analytics-based measures

Four types of analytic metrics help you focus on the audience's use of the platform:

- **Reach:** how many individuals a platform *might* help you reach. For example, Facebook might help you reach, say, 2 million users in your metro. That doesn't mean your efforts actually reach that number. But they might.

- **Consumption, time and attention:** How many users you actually reach and, for them, how much of their time you garner and the "stickiness" of their visits in keeping them with you in a session.

- **Engagement action:** what actions are taken by those you reach beyond just reading and viewing your content — for example, do they click on ads or provide you data or sign up for subscriptions

- **Loyalty and habituation:** how often do those you reach come back in a given period of time; how much of a habit you are in their lives; how often do they share your content with others.

The following typology provides a simple, illustrative overview of analytic-based measures. You and your colleagues should use it to gain a basic orientation about the nature of choices at hand. Your objective here is to become conversant with the basic choices so that you can better do the more complicated work of actually choosing the specific metrics that work with different platforms. For that work, see TS#4.

Typology of Platform Metrics

TYPE OF MEASURE	METRIC*	SUB-METRICS*
Reach	unique users	in-market
		out-of-market
	sources of users	by referral source
	devices used by users	by device

TYPE OF MEASURE	METRIC*	SUB-METRICS*
Consumption, time and attention	Click throughs	total click throughs (referrals)
		click through rate
	content views	total page views
		views per user session
	time spent	by content item
		per user session
	bounce rate	
	completion rates	
Engagement	likes/recommends	total for site/brand
		rate per content piece
	ratings	
	shares	total count
		rate per content piece
	comments	total count
		rate per content piece
	survey responses	
	self-identification	Registrations
		Signups

TYPE OF MEASURE	METRIC*	SUB-METRICS*
Loyalty and habituation	visits per unique users	
	% of unique users visiting = > threshold number of times (e.g. = > 9 visits per month)	

*All measures within a defined time period

2) Managerially focused measures

Platform owners use managerial measures to manage platforms **as businesses**. They help measure whether overall platform performance is delivering what the business needs for success: audience, market share/standing, revenue, productivity/costs and profitability:

- **Audience hurdle measures**. By 'hurdle,' we mean a threshold level above which you deem performance good and below which not good. For example, you might use a hurdle of X thousand unique visitors to distinguish platforms that perform well versus those that do not.

    Platform owners *must* set hurdles because, without them, you fail to take a position on what is good versus not good performance. This is true for the platforms you own and truer still for platforms owned by others where less information is available.

    Hurdles help you drive improved performance through comparing and contrasting different efforts on the same platform. Imagine, for example, that Facebook posts published over the past 30 days have ranged from zero uniques to 5,000 uniques and zero time to 3 minutes of engagement. You might divide up this full range into quartiles or quintiles of performance — in the case of quintiles, you figure out the average number of uniques and engagement time for the top fifth, second from top fifth and so on down to bottom fifth.

    With this information, you as platform owner might set a hurdle (threshold). For example, you let folks know you're seeking 'desired performance' equal to the averages for the top fifth — say, 3,500 uniques and 2 minutes of engagement.

    You and your colleagues can then monitor against this goal over whatever time horizon you think best: the next 30 days… the next 60 days… the next 90 days … and so on.

As platform owner, you monitor how often content reaches into the top fifth — and work with folks to understand why versus why not so that it happens more often.

(*Please note:* If this sort of internal hurdle is happening for the first time in your newsroom, you'll probably want to make clear the objectives are about learning — and not immediately about individual performance. Yes, with time, individual performance will come under scrutiny. But not until you and others learn more about how to improve results. Failure to manage this distinction can lead to anxieties that preclude instead of advance learning.)

It's worth noting that audience teams — and the mini-publishers managing them — might also set internal platform hurdles for their teams in ways that help platform owners succeed as well. For example, food related content might consistently outperform town hall meeting content on Instagram. This could mean setting a lower yet still 'good' hurdle for town hall content, yet a higher hurdle for food.

And, the hurdle you use might arise externally as well. The above Facebook example linked to internal numbers. It might, though, have come from the performance of competitors (for example, perhaps you know a local TV station routinely exceeds 3,500 uniques and 2 minutes engagement time — and that is the source of your designated hurdle/threshold).

Using this approach helps you build teams and individuals whose work consistently exceeds the hurdle level. It helps you avoid getting caught in the trap of focusing on big hit, viral stories. It provides you performance data with which to address and make choices about low performing content — and whether, why and how much of that content to create.

- **Local market standing and share.** These measure how well you do on particular platforms relative to other publishers in your market:

— **Local market standing:** an estimation of where you rank among competitors in your local market on the platform

— **Local market share:** a rough estimation of how much of the local market (or the target market within the local market) you are reaching through the platform based on demographic data for the local market.

- **Revenue attributable to platforms.** Platform owners running platform businesses need to understand how much revenue their platforms generate — or help generate. Hence the word 'attributable,' which can be direct, indirect or intangible yet still important:

    — **Direct:** on-site advertising and sponsorships; revenue shares from others' sites

    — **Indirect:** ad revenue derived from traffic sent to a directly monetized site

    — **Intangible:** reach, brand discovery and brand reinforcement

    Please note: How platform owners set and monitor revenue and revenue-related (e.g., brand discovery) goals is essential to running the platform as a business. Such revenue goals and approaches define the core objectives of the 'business' — and how those objectives relate to serving audiences and at what cost.
    For example, say you choose an overall revenue target of $10,000 from ad revenue generated by Facebook referrals. Well, what reach, click rate, share rate and share click rate would be needed to generate the needed number of main website page views at a given CPM required to reach $10,000? Once you've figured that out, set those as targets.

- **Platform productivity.** Productivity is a business term meaning: how much output do we get from a

---

ILLUSTRATION

Dallas made good use of internal hurdles in all these ways. They developed a careful index of factors. Then set hurdle goals that differed for different content types. When they rolled this out the first time, they made clear it was about learning and not individual performance — while also alerting folks that the individual performance aspects would emerge after they'd learned much more about what works and what doesn't.

given input? For example, productivity might estimate the "audience yield" you get from the content your newsroom publishes on the platform. It is best expressed as a ratio: Audience yield versus staff time involved or cost to produce content or whatever other input you choose.

Imagine, for example, that you have 50 folks in your newsroom and they average 2 hours per week on Facebook posting. That's 100 hundred hours per week — or, if we use 50 weeks per year, 5,000 hours per year. Either way, you now can construct a productivity ratio by choosing the relevant metric for audience as the output measure: "We get X number of uniques for our 5,000 hours, we get Y engagement time for our 5,000 hours … and so forth".

Platform owners can also translate the 5,000 hours into costs using wages, salaries, benefits and other direct costs (that is, not pure overhead). Perhaps the 5,000 hours equates to, say, $150,000. With either of these in hand — hours or costs — platform owners can set and monitor productivity goals.

- **Platform contribution.** By attributing revenue and costs to platforms, platform owners can gauge how much the platform is contributing to the total enterprise's economic performance. And, when this is done for all platforms, your enterprise will have a good indicator of overall platform portfolio performance as well as platform versus platform performance.

b) Platform scorecards and sharing best practices

As described in TS#7, platform owners are encouraged to be 'mini-publishers' who manage key platforms **as businesses**. *For the most important platforms*, platform owners should use a blend of analytics metrics plus managerial metrics to create and use a scorecard. It is not as important — and could be too much work — for platform owners to have scorecards for the less critical platforms — including those being experimented with. In this case, though, it's essential to have regularly scheduled group meetings to share best practices: what's working, what's not, why and agreed upon next steps.

Meanwhile, platform owners as a group along with top news enterprise leaders must manage the overall portfolio of platforms — including both key ones for which there are scorecards as well as less critical ones for which only best practice sharing gets done.

1) Scorecards

The steps and guidance for developing and using platform scorecards parallel those described for target audiences in TS#1:

- Choosing the scorecard measures: use the previous sections on analytics measures plus managerial measures to identify what to include in your platform scorecard.
- Setting the measurement interval: the measurement intervals will vary. For example, analytic measures could be monitored daily while some managerial measures are best reviewed weekly, monthly or even quarterly. Essentially, as a platform owner, you want to allow enough time between measurement/review to make progress against goals you set.
- Constructing the scorecard itself: See Table Stake 7 for guidance on this.
- Setting objectives for the platform: It's key to set SMART outcome based goals that describe what success looks like on an ongoing basis.

2) Qualitative best practice sharing

Platform owners and their colleagues must proactively seek out and share examples of what's working well — and instructive examples of what is not working well. There are a range of ways to do this such as (1) weekly emails; (2) incorporation into daily meetings; (3) posting on an internal wiki or knowledge sharing platform; and, (4) use of Slack or Slack-like channels. In addition, platform owners and colleagues should encourage informal sharing of what works and what doesn't — essentially, seek out folks and ask them to find ways of sharing on their own. Make sure to share a combination of the approaches/techniques used as well as the results along with highlighting the specific lessons to be learned and any ongoing questions worthy of focus. And, don't forget to celebrate the names of those who have acted — even in those cases where failure can be celebrated as a source of learning.

c) Managing platform performance with the scorecards

Use scorecards to track performance, identify issues needing corrective action, and spot potential opportunities for improved performance. In the case of platform scorecards this should be done on four levels.

- **The platform level.** The owner for each given platform should spend a half hour each week tracking recent performance and spotting immediate issues of concern or opportunities. Every two to four weeks, it's worth spending more time to dig deeper into the data and identify clear next steps to improve performance. Both levels of review should be scheduled on a calendar.

- **The target-audience team level.** Platform owners and audience teams should regularly hold joint reviews in which to reflect on — and identify key next steps for — how audience team efforts perform on the platforms. While the timing of these reviews will vary, it's key to make sure every audience team using the platform is met with at least every two to three months or so.

- **The *newsroom level* across the portfolio platforms.** Newsroom leaders should gather all platform owners about every four weeks or so to focus on cross-platform issues and opportunities as well as to coordinate joint efforts to improve platform use (e.g. rotating responsibilities for best practice sharing). Also, use these meetings to discuss, review and evolve the role of platform owner, and to share experiences and ideas for being more effective in the role.

- **The *enterprise level* across the portfolio of platforms.** Every three to six months, the top management of the enterprise should gather platform owners along with appropriate folks from editorial, technology, business development, sales, marketing and others to focus on current platform-by-platform performance, investments (or disinvestments) needed among current platforms, experiments with new platforms and launches of new platforms with tested audience growth potential.

This last level of review (and resulting action) is the essence of platform portfolio management. Given the limited capacity of any metro newsroom to publish on multiple platforms, this level of management is essential for making sure that capacity is deployed to publishing in the most effective ways for building a larger, more engaged and more loyal local audience to be served and from which revenue can be earned.

Table Stakes
Number 3
Produce and Publish Continuously to Meet Audience Needs

1. The Table Stake
Produce and publish continuously to meet audience needs

Organize to provide an 'always on, always there' flow of digital-first content matched to the life rhythms and habits of your target audiences, their time and attention availability, their interests, needs and problems of the moment, and the platforms they use.

Treat print as *a* unique platform that benefits by curating from the rich content of continuous digital first publishing rather than *the* platform that drives the schedule, workflows and resources of the newsroom. Put differently, get beyond either/or-ism of digital versus print. Use an audience-centric approach to digital first, print later AND better.

2. Why this is Table Stakes

a) Audiences expect fresh digital news on their own schedule

Audiences have always had their own particular habits and patterns for consuming news. Even in pre-digital days not everyone did all their reading of the paper the moment it was delivered. It might happen through the day and into the evening. Or the next day. Or days later when the paper was picked up and given another look just before throwing it out.

But none of that mattered. Legacy newsrooms captured all of that readership so long as the paper was delivered on time every day. There weren't competing sources of news to turn to at any given moment and there weren't expectations that the news would be fresh every time they picked up the paper.

Today, audiences' habits and patterns matter far more. Audiences can catch up on the news at any moment they choose, from any number of sources, on any number of digital devices, anywhere they are. They expect the news to be fresh in the moment they choose. If it's not, they can move on to another source in an instant.

The chart below illustrates how these audience patterns look through the day, by platform, for one digital publisher[1].

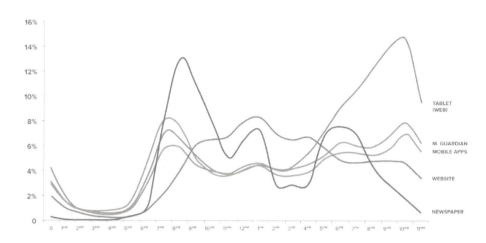

Source: Reuters Institute Digital News Report 2014; Guardian audience research

1

Not shown in these patterns is the constant potential for usage to spike on various platforms instantaneously at any moment with breaking news and viral stories.

Stated simply, your target audiences look for news throughout the day with varying patterns of peak usage on different devices. To meet their needs and expectations for fresh content, you need to be publishing in sync with their patterns and habits.

b) Yet, too many newsrooms provide news on their own print-driven schedules

The audience patterns of news seeking may already be familiar to you because your own habits likely reflect them. *But do you know how well your newsroom's digital publishing patterns actually align with them?*

It's an obvious question — and answering it can be surprising. It was for Minneapolis and Philadelphia who looked at the data and drew charts comparing their daily digital audience traffic rhythms to their digital publishing times.

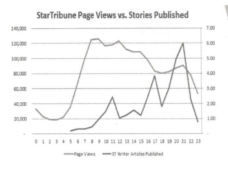

Minneapolis Star Tribune   **Philadelphia Media Network — Philly.com**

The mismatch was immediately obvious and attention grabbing. Less obvious but critically important was that this analysis was for their *existing* audience, an audience already shaped in part by the newsroom's existing publishing timing and practices. It did not account for further mismatches arising from contrasting usage patterns of the *entire* local market's digital audience across all local news publishers — including underserved audiences (e.g. millennials) Minneapolis and Philadelphia sought to grow.

Someone from one of the Knight Temple newsrooms used an analogy to an out-of-step restaurant to drive the point home:

> *In pre-digital times a legacy newsroom operated like a restaurant geared to preparing and cooking a very large meal overnight that it then served to all its customers at breakfast time in the morning. Customers ate some of it then and used that same meal to nourish themselves throughout the day and even into the evening (unless an evening meal was ordered from the "evening" restaurant).*
>
> *Now, with mobile digital media, customers can get something fresh to eat all day long, from early morning to late into the night. And they can choose anything from snacks to full entrees, with expectations for a selection of cuisines and a choice of formal and informal atmospheres. Yet many legacy newsrooms, despite years of attention to digital content, are still operating largely in their traditional print-driven "one big meal a day" mode.*

c) Everyone loses out

This mismatch results in everyone in the metro area losing out:

- **Local digital audiences** miss seeing stories as soon as there is something to tell from a trusted news source they can always turn to for the latest local news they need to know.

- **Local print audiences** miss the benefit of stories that have been re-versioned, enriched and sharpened through digital publication throughout the day as well as story selection informed by digital metrics of audience interest and engagement

- **Journalists and the newsroom** lose by having fewer people see their work, missing opportunities to get the story in front of readers earlier to flesh out more sources and story angles, and being scooped by faster-to-publish sources. Journalists also lose by not developing and honing the skills they need to be personally competitive as an audience-focused digital reporter, producer and publisher.

- **The news enterprise** loses by not attaining its full digital traffic and engagement potential — and the related revenue, missing opportunities for more frequent visits per day that build habit and loyalty, not developing audience habits that lead to subscribing or paying in other ways, and weakening its brand value as the local market's leading news source.

d) Continuous digital publishing as a Table Stake capability

Digital news consumption rhythms and habits are trackable thanks to the ongoing flow of digital usage data. The costs of not matching your digital publishing to these rhythms are clear and substantial. This makes it a Table Stake to intentionally publish when the audience is there — and doing so on the platforms where your target audiences are. Put in the reverse, your newsroom *cannot* successfully serve and grow digital audiences if you fail to publish content when and where the audience seeks content.

But this Table Stake involves more than a single adjustment of posting more content earlier in the morning (though that's a good place to start). The broader capability required is to publish *continuously* and *responsively* to match the news consumption rhythms and habits of your targeted audiences in terms of both general patterns and specific opportunities.

And, while perhaps an obvious Table Stake, it's not one that's easily achieved. It requires resetting deeply ingrained rhythms and practices that go back some 170 years to an earlier technology driven transformation brought on by the invention of high-speed rotary presses. These print-driven rhythms and practices are embedded in every aspect of the newsroom — roles, skills, workflows, technology, work schedules and meetings. Fundamental changes are needed across all these areas to move to truly digital first continuous publishing. But the changes should not be seen as a win-lose matter of digital *versus* print or digital *over* print. They are about seeing yourself as a truly audience-focused, multi-platform publisher seeking to optimize the use of every publishing platform — including print as a platform *that benefits from digital publishing first and continuously*.

3. Assessing the gaps in your newsroom

a) Gaps: Shortfalls in continuous, responsive digital publishing

Consider each of the statements below. Answer "yes" if the statement is either entirely or mostly true for your newsroom. Answer "no" if it is not true at all or only to minor degree.

	YES	NO
1. Our editorial meetings are scheduled at the same times they were two to three years ago.		
2. We spend most of our time in editorial meetings on story selection and placement for print.		
3. Our newsroom starts to fill-up around 11 a.m. and really comes to life in the afternoon.		
4. Our reporters think in terms of what their daily and weekly output should be for print but don't have the same sense of how much and how often they should be publishing digitally.		
5. Stories have print deadlines but not separate digital deadlines.		
6. A majority of our digital posts for the day are published after 5p.m.		
7. Our daily budget covers only print.		
8. Our budget includes some digital publishing but the budget tool is print-based.		
9. Our workflows tie to print publishing deadlines and/or our print CMS.		
10. Less than half of our reporters and editors can build and publish a complete digital story (e.g. with headline, SEO head, text, tags, photo, hyperlinks, embeds).		
11. Most of our digital production and publishing work is done by dedicated digital producers and audience "specialists" rather than our newsroom's reporters and editors.		
12. Little special attention is given to headlines for digital posts; the print headline usually suffices.		
13. Stories are "held for print" (e.g. the Sunday paper) for good print reasons but without corresponding arguments for digital publishing first.		
14. Our reporters know how many stories they've had on A1 last month but couldn't say for sure how many of their stories were in the top 10% of page views, unique visitors or time spent.		
15. Management may not be aware that the website was down for a time but would certainly know if a press run finished an hour late.		

	YES	NO
16. More of our staff time is spent specifically on print production than on digital production and publishing.		
17. Key staff (e.g. visual specialists) are pulled for days at a time to work on big projects that appear only in the print edition.		
18. Major enterprise, investigative or other editorial projects are conceived and planned with print foremost in mind; the form, timing and promotion of digital publication happens late in the game.		
TOTAL		

Note: The statements in this assessment are based on observed practices at newsrooms that have not yet reached the Table Stakes for continuous and responsive digital publishing.

Add up the number of "yes" marking to get your assessment score. The higher your score the bigger your gaps.

To calibrate your own score, ask others in the newsroom to take it as well and then meet together to compare answers on individual items and overall scores. Use the ensuing discussions to calibrate your gap assessment and develop a shared understanding of the nature of your gaps.

b) Gap: Identify the misalignment between your target audiences' news consumption patterns and your publishing schedule

Identifying this misalignment — and monitoring it — is a key discipline for:

- Using the audience data you have available to get a clear view of the usage patterns and habits of your audience;
- Tracking your posting timing to see how well it matches your audience's patterns; and,
- Constantly looking for gaps and opportunities to better match your publishing timing to the usage patterns.

In doing this over time your newsroom will develop a keen sensibility for staying in sync with your audience.

Start by:

- Picking a long enough period of time to smooth out weekly variations (e.g. the last 4-6 weeks)
- Determining and graphing the number of posts (URLs) published to your primary platforms (website and mobile sites or apps) by hour for weekdays, Saturdays and Sundays separately.
- Pulling and graphing your traffic data for unique visitors to these same platforms by hour for the same time period, again separating weekdays, Saturday and Sundays.
- Overlaying these two sets of graphs to see how well your current posting times align with your unique visitor traffic patterns on weekdays, Saturdays and Sundays. (See the earlier examples from Philadelphia and Minneapolis in Section 2).

If you wish to go deeper, you can also analyze and depict such gaps by:

- Device by weekdays, Saturdays and Sundays
- Finer time periods — e.g. weekdays between 6 a.m. to 9 a.m. in quarter hours
- Facebook posting to your main Facebook account versus when unique visitors arrive via Facebook
- Major traffic sources beyond Facebook — e.g. search, other social referrals, etc.

Finally, an important nuance to consider: Try to find data for overall audience traffic patterns in your market — that is, not just your own audience traffic. Why? Because your current traffic may not reflect the full picture. For example, your mismatch gaps along with other factors could provide a distorted picture if the traffic coming to your sites differs significantly from the news seeking behavior of the target audiences you wish to serve. Anything you can do to get a fuller picture of overall audience traffic patterns in your local market will give you a more accurate picture of your total market potential and current publishing gaps (e.g. data on leading local digital competitors).

c) Gap: Identify workflow performance gaps

Workflow performance gaps arise from unproductive step-by-step approaches to getting work done. For example, performance shortfalls arise from a workflow in which reporters complete stories for print first and only then either they or others (e.g. digital producers) make any changes or additions relevant to digital audiences. This print-first, digital-as-afterthought workflow can cause performance gaps related to extra time, misuse of resources, errors that require rework, lower quality audience experiences, and failure to capture traffic and engagement.

Identifying workflow performance gaps is tricky, though, because *workflows, roles and skills, and technology and tools are highly interrelated*. Look at the chart below:

Triangle of Interdependence

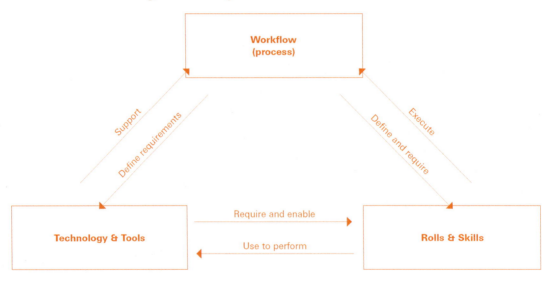

Notice that workflows require people in the right roles having the right skills and using the best technology and tools. If any part of this interconnected triangle is ineffective, the associated workflow suffers. For example, if technology and tools are weak (illustration: no universal budget), workflows become longer and more elaborate with workarounds and added steps, which in turn require more skills, experience and cleverness. Skills and workflow end up propping up the technology rather than being supported by it. And when skills are narrow (illustration: too few reporters can create a fully digital story), workflows are fragmented into more steps and handoffs that require extra coordination and supervision.

The opposite also holds: When more folks have deeper, more practiced skills, they can contribute to more roles — and the more roles folks can do, the fewer the workflow steps and handoffs required. Similarly, the better the tools and technology, the fewer the manual tasks required and the shorter and faster the workflow.

Getting all three elements aligned and in balance is essential to three dimensions of digital publishing performance:

- **Speed and placement of audience-focused publishing** to ensure your target audiences see your content when and where they are;
- **Effectiveness of publishing** to ensure every story has all the needed elements to attract and engage an audience, and that your newsroom quickly seizes on traffic trends and opportunities;

- **Efficiency of publishing** to insure your already constrained staff maximizes overall digital output at the best possible cost.

Failures in any of the three elements — workflows, roles-skills or technology-tools — lead to specific performance gaps in these three key elements — gaps that add time and delays to digital publishing, take more resources, time and talent that could be put to better use, create errors requiring rework, generate extra work in finding, checking or fixing content, lower the quality of the output, deliver unengaging user experiences, or lead to the wrong output such publishing stories of little interest to an audience or unsuited to a platform.

To identify such workflow performance gaps, start by considering a "one person" workflow as a baseline. Today — as long as he or she has the right skills and technology — an individual can perform all the tasks of a digital publishing workflow. Indeed, this is the workflow used by digital natives — folks who grew up with today's technology — to publish in your local market — whether as a lone blogger with a loyal following, a digital-only startup largely replicating the one-person workflow across a digital native staff, or a savvy local TV newsroom that's broken from its own broadcast-centric legacy.

With this one person workflow in mind as a comparison, use the following steps to fully map out your current workflow and identify shortfalls and gaps:

10 steps for workflow mapping

1. Pick three or four people who collectively know the day-to-day workings of the newsroom. Get together in a room with lots of whiteboards or wall space for placing sticky notes and give yourselves a couple of hours of uninterrupted time.

2. Start with the workflow to publish a typical "daily" story. Make sure to include all the basic elements for the story, including those that are part of digital as well as others (e.g. text, photos, simple embeds, etc.).

3. Draw a box or use a sticky-note to identify the person who starts the story chain. If more than one person initiates the action, draw or use whatever number of boxes or notes are needed. Mark the title or position of the person in the box/note and list all the discrete tasks that person does before handing the story off to another person.

4. Add a box or sticky note for that next person and list all the specific tasks that person does before handing the story off to the next person. Draw the connecting arrow between the two boxes to show the direction of flow. Keep adding boxes/stickies for each person in the

chain. If the process ever goes back to a person already included, still add a new box for them and list the tasks they do at that point in the process.

Note: If you run into questions along the way about how things really work, check quickly with someone who knows. But don't let that delay your work. Make notes of the questions and who to check with later and keep going to get a full first draft laid out. Similarly, keep track of any "ah ha" insights you have or problems you spot along the way but don't stop to devise fixes yet. Keep focused on mapping the entire process to be sure you have whole picture first.

5. Any time information or story assets are put into an information system of any sort (even a WORD doc on a desktop computer) create a box or note for that system. List the information or assets that are created or put into systems and draw an arrow from the person inputting. Likewise, draw an arrow from the system to the person who accesses and draws the information out of the system.

Note: It's visually helpful to make the information system block a different shape (e.g. boxes for people and circles for systems) or the stickies a different color to distinguish systems from those for people.

6. When the process flow diverges for different platforms, show the branching with arrows and layout the sequence for each platform. If one platform loops back into or feeds another platform, show the connections.

Note: Again, you can use different color stickies or a different shape to indicate a platform.

7. Don't stop your process mapping with the publication of a story. As with the one person workflow, continue to map the steps involved in how traffic is monitored on the story as well as steps to promote, update or re-version story.

8. Once you have a first pass at the entire workflow, step back to review it to be sure it "flows" (even if poorly) and no steps are missing. If you logged questions along the way or think it needs another set of eyes, bring in others

as needed to review it with them and make corrections as needed.

9. With the whole workflow before you, review it to identify significant delays between one step being completed and the next one being started and note the reasons (e.g., lack of capacity and "stacking up" at that stage, lack of information that something's now ready for the next person to work on, slow systems processing or cycle times). Also identify causes for where the workflow breaks down (e.g. errors made in prior steps, missing information or story assets, lack of clear communications).

10. Make sure to fully capture your work. The easiest way is taking pictures that can then be used to recreate it in document form such as PowerPoint. (Be sure the shots are taken close enough to be able to read all the detail.). And, if possible, keep your whiteboard drawings or sticky notes up for a time to facilitate further conversation and problem solving. But, again, make sure to take the pictures in case someone unwittingly clears the board.

Once you've laid out the workflow for a basic daily story, you can build on and differentiate it for other key efforts such as:

- An enterprise story incorporating more complex visual elements (heavily edited video, multiple graphics, interactives, etc.);
- A multi-part enterprise or investigative series that involves more extensive planning, editing and development of many multi-media elements.

In the course of mapping your basic workflow, you will come across some head-slapping moments of saying, "why do we do that?" — the sorts of questions that are often answered, "because we've always done it that way" without thought as to why or to what end. Mark those down — but keep going with the workflow mapping.

Once you've finished, collect all such questions and insights, then add to them by identifying additional gaps in adding value from an audience perspective as well as optimizing the efficiency and effectiveness of scarce staff and other resources.

To help, here's a guide to common workflow issues:

AREA	POTENTIAL WORKFLOW GAPS
Poor digital workflow design	• **Digital holds** where content is first reviewed for print placement, published digitally only after print production is finished (published from print), and/or held for print-first publication without due consideration of the digital audience • **Missing steps** that limit the potential reach and engagement of digital stories (e.g. proper tagging and SEO headlines) or result in added work in later steps (e.g. steps for digital asset tagging and filing) • **Unnecessary steps** that add little if any clear audience value and are habits carried forward from a different era • **Redundant steps** where work is duplicated or redone without adding any clear audience value (e.g. added layers of editing) • **Missing information flows** that should accompany process steps and hand-offs but don't, resulting in errors or added work to loop back to get the needed information • **Lack of early planning involvement and adequate lead times** with shared specialists' resources that result in crash assignments and crunch workloads for individuals and delays in publishing other stories • **Missing feedback loops** that could improve the audience focus, reach and engagement of future stories (e.g. audience traffic data, periodic reviews of story content and production)
Unclear or unperformed roles and responsibilities	• **Sloppy hand-offs** due to a lack of definition of "clean handoff" requirements or poor execution by individuals, resulting in problems, added effort and publishing delays down the line (e.g. digital assets filing) • **Lax enforcement** of specified workflow steps and/or views that some steps are merely optional instead of required, resulting in suboptimal digital posts (e.g. lack of photos, missing tags) • **Passive or reactive communications** rather than clear responsibility for proactive communications across the workflow, resulting in unnecessary points of confusion, frustration and conflict. • **Double work** because two people think they're responsible for the same thing (or don't trust the other person to do it right or do it their way)
Skills limitations	• **Extra hand-offs** because a person doesn't have the skills to do the next needed steps (e.g. adding steps to involve producers and specialists because the reporter has few if any digital production skills) • **Added inspection and rework steps** to cover for the weak skills of individuals who can't be counted on to do work at an acceptable level of quality (e.g. some editing steps). (Note that such work-around steps allow the weak skills to persist as part of the workflow rather than being addressed directly.)

AREA	POTENTIAL WORKFLOW GAPS
Tools and technology limitations or absences	• **Extra steps** required by working between multiple systems (e.g. cutting and pasting from a word processor to a CMS or from one CMS to another CMS) • **Duplicative tasks** from having to work in multiple unintegrated systems (having to enter the very same information in two different places) • **Fix-it steps** to cleanup or add back items lost in the transfer of content between systems (e.g. having to redo hyperlinks) • **Workaround steps** that overcome technology limitations and problems but would not be necessary with better technology • **Missing information** due to a lack of universally used tools such as calendars and budgets that would provide one place to find all the information needed by any user at any step in the workflow. • **Processing delays** and the resulting hang time caused by lack of CPU power, data transfers across systems and platforms, too infrequent of updating cycles, etc.

4. Why these gaps exist

a) Root causes of newsroom's slowness to publish continuously

In working across metro news organizations to define this Table Stake a number of root causes were uncovered that underlie the resistance and slowness to make the changes needed to serve audiences across the times of day when they are seeking news. Many or all of them may be quite familiar to you.

- **Prevailing operating assumptions about print.** Given print's long legacy and continued revenue generation, there can be many prevailing assumptions about how it must be treated in the transition to digital:

    — Print is still driving the revenue so it should still drive the publishing cycle.
    — The print product will suffer by publishing everything on digital first.

— The print product will suffer if any fewer resources are dedicated to it or if too much attention is given to "digital first."

So long as these assumptions, spoken or unspoken, remain unquestioned and untested they discourage experimentation and constrict actions that can *both* transform digital publication *and* improve the print product.

- **Known versus unknown consequences.** Print deadlines are very clear and real. And the consequences of not meeting them are obvious and material — press overtime, delivery delays, subscriber complaints, etc. Digital has no mandated deadlines. And the consequences of missing a digital publishing "deadline" may be understood conceptually but is not felt directly — e.g., when did a reader ever call to complain that a story arrived too late to their smartphone? It's human nature to give more attention to consequences that are known and felt over those that are conceptual.

- **Tangible vs. intangible success and rewards.** A front page is still something you can see on the street; a front-page article is still a success you can clip and save. Topping the website homepage is ephemeral unless you screen grab and print it in the moment, the traffic count on a story is just numbers, and a URL isn't something you can clip and tack-up. Feeling the personal value of reaching a digital audience happens only once you're begun to realize the potential of reaching a far larger audience and become attuned to different forms of positive feedback.

- **Existing skills and identities.** There's pride in the mastery and confidence in the work product that comes from well-honed print skills — pyramid-style story writing, space budgeting, page layout, section design, supplement production, etc. It's harder to have confidence or claim mastery when the digital publishing environment keeps changing, when there's no one proven and enduring model of success to follow, and the skills needed keep morphing and expanding.

- **Lack of sunk cost and opportunity cost thinking on technology.** The newsroom's print-based CMS may be widely recognized as *the* biggest factor impeding earlier and more continuous digital publishing but it's accepted as a given for the present. Besides the high costs of investing in new technology, there's also uncertainty about actually getting a better system — "There's no perfect CMS" — and reluctance to take on the huge task of converting to and learning about a new system.

  Day-by-day it's easier to stay with "the devil you know" and live with the cumbersome steps to do simple digital tasks, use the skills and tricks you've learned to make it work better, and keep developing work arounds to make incremental improvements for digital publishing. And while you manage through each day, the true costs of the current CMS in terms lost productivity, accumulated frustrations, and missed digital audience opportunities remain unexamined and unconsidered.

- **Personal factors.** Newsroom staff are comfortable with established workflow routines that give a known pace to the day. Work schedules are arranged around these workflows and their timing (i.e. print deadlines) and, in turn, personal and family schedules are organized accordingly (school drop-offs and pick-ups, spouse's work schedule, daily and weekly living routines). The prospect of disrupting such intertwined schedules can in itself be a source of reluctance to change.

b) Addressing the root causes requires focusing on performance management and accountability

Many of these root causes concern personal mindsets and behaviors that both shape and are reinforced by existing roles, skills, workflows, shared habits and cultural norms across the newsroom. You can't just exhort or order "be digital first" and expect anything much to happen. It's not a matter of just giving new instructions to someone who already knows how to follow them and is most willing to do so. Because it involves deep-seated behavioral changes in terms of mindsets, skills, roles and ways of working, continuous digital first publishing is inherently much harder to achieve.

These mindsets and behaviors will shift and change only when individuals actually do things differently as opposed to talking about doing things differently. And getting the staff of your newsroom to do things differently will only happen when they have clear performance objectives that are only achievable by doing things differently. As emphasized in the Introduction part 2: Focus on Performance, performance objectives and results are the primary objective of change, not change per se. And these performance objectives must be clearly tied to compelling personal and enterprise needs and interests, that is, the consequences of not reaching the objectives and the aspirations and sense of purpose fulfilled in achieving them.

So, for example, if you set audience traffic goals that can only be reached when content is published at the times the audience is seeking content, the changes in workflow, skills, habits and culture will have reason to follow as essential actions. Through the experience, learning and realization of success in actually growing audiences by making these needed changes, mindsets will shift and the needed behaviors will change.

Through all of this, it is useful to keep these root causes in mind in managing the process of performance improvement and organizational change. It will help in understanding and navigating through points of resistance and reluctance and in guiding how best to recognize and communicate early signs of success.

5. What success looks and feels like

This Table Stake is about changing the basic rhythms of publishing and a successful transformation results in a newsroom with a fundamentally different feel and even look. One way of envisioning success is to contrast the 'as is' current state with the desired future state in a "From/To" depiction.

Here is an illustrative set of From > To statements for a newsroom transforming to continuous digital publishing:

	FROM	TO
The newsroom	Our newsroom doesn't really come to life until about 11 am or later	Our *physical* newsroom is alive (at least in pockets) from early in the morning until evening Our virtual newsroom is alive nearly 24/7 using Slack channels (or equivalent) and Twitter, checking traffic, and watching trending.
	Our newsroom becomes increasingly animated as print deadlines approach	Our newsroom is most animated when … … seeing an important story doing exceptionally well in-market … developing a trending story in real-time … collaborating in small groups on how to shape a story or write a headline that really engages an audience.
Meetings	Our editorial meetings consist mainly of list recitations and discussion of when stories will be ready	Our editorial meetings are energized by discussions and idea generation of how to deliver a selection of stories with effective digital headlines that will engage audiences at the times throughout the day those audiences show up — along with real time debriefing of what's working and what's not.
Print publication	Shifting attention and resources to digital is seen as necessarily diminishing the print product	A mindset of "digital first and print later and *better*" drives how we work to better serve audiences across all platforms.
	The print product is produced according to well established print practices	Print production is informed and invigorated by the audience insights and the flow of story versioning from digital-first publishing
	Print is *the* platform that drives workflows and publication timing for digital platforms	Print is *another* very important platform with its own production workflows, roles and skills, apart from and not affecting digital publication.

	FROM	TO
Publication timing	The timing of the digital posting of many stories is driven by traditional print considerations, priorities and assumptions.	Digital publication for all stories is based on data about audience usage patterns and understanding of their daily life rhythms and needs of the moment.
Roles and skills	Most of our reporters hand off their stories for digital publication and consider their work done.	All of our reporters think about when to publish and how to promote their stories, actively watch their story traffic, and look for ways to build on and boost audience engagement.
	Audience development is something of a separate function whose staff get involved after reporters finish stories.	Audience development staff are at the very center of our newsroom, working side by side with reporters and editors in a "digital hub," and contribute to and/or lead editorial discussions
	Our reporters work largely by themselves and with their editor in developing and writing stories.	Our reporters/producers collaborate actively with others across the newsroom on developing story angles, shaping digital and social headlines, watching traffic, and enhancing, re-versioning and promoting the stories as they develop.

	FROM	TO
Workflows & technology	Stories move first through a print workflow and then on to a digital workflow	Workflows are digital first with print workflows curating from digital content in ways that make the print stories better.
	Extra steps, hand-offs and staff time are required to produce and publish a digital story because we lack basic digital skills across the newsroom.	Everyone in our newsroom can produce and publish a complete digital post (i.e. text, photo, headline, tags, basic video and embeds) without help from specialists
	Our workflows are shaped largely by the limitations, peculiarities and work arounds of our CMS.	Our workflows are shaped by the steps needed to create engaging stories and publish them at the right time for audiences.
	We spend too much unproductive time doing routine digital production tasks because of technology limitations and lack of tools	Our workflows are simplified and accelerated by technology and tools, allowing us time to focus on better content and audience engagement.
	We do not have a clear technology architecture or strategy, leaving our newsroom frustrated by CMS limitations	Our technology architecture and strategy balances addressing needed fundamental changes with pragmatic workarounds and other solutions that get the most out the existing limited CMS while avoiding the illusion of a 'perfect' CMS.

Crafting your own set of From > To statements is valuable to both crystalize your thinking and communicate needed changes to others across the newsroom. It's a *qualitative* way of confirming where you are now versus what success looks like once everything is in place and working right. (Developing the *quantitative* definition of success is addressed in Section 7 of this chapter.)

Start by tailoring and adding to the statements in the version above — or, even do your own from/to's from scratch. Develop a first draft by yourself, with a colleague or small group. Once you have a draft, share, test and refine it with expanding circles of people across the newsroom. The value of the From > To's arise from discussing, debating, shaping and internalizing each statement. It's a first step in engaging others in the work to be done.

To develop your own From > To statements for this Table Stake, consider these questions:

- What do you observe now in your newsroom ("From") that is most indicative of the gaps you have in the flow of your digital publishing — the ones that irk you every time you see or think of them? Then what do you imagine observing in your newsroom ("To") that would be tangible evidence — real proof to a colleague at another newsroom — that you've transformed your digital publishing practices?
- For the "To" side of the statements, what new inputs are needed in terms of skills, roles, workflows and technology? What new *outputs* arise in terms of what's published? What new *outcomes* happen in terms of audience traffic and engagement as well as newsroom confidence and spirit?

6. Actions to close the gaps

This section describes the following steps you and your colleagues can take to produce and publish continuously to meet audience needs:

a. Reset the rhythms of your newsroom to match the rhythms of your audiences
b. Redesign workflows to ease and speed continuous digital publishing
c. Broaden skills and combine roles to enable more efficient workflows
d. Provide the tools to support better workflows and broader roles
e. Re-organize to be digital-first, print later and better
f. Address the technology drags on digital publishing

a) Reset the rhythms of your newsroom to match the rhythms of your audiences

Start by setting a clear goal to close the gaps you identified in Section 3 related to misalignments between when you publish content versus when and where your target audiences look for content. In effect, this goal seeks to have the line of when you post track exactly with the line of when/where the audience shows up (see graphs of misalignment at Star Tribune and Philly in Section 2). Then take the following steps to achieve that goal:

- Match deadlines to audience windows while setting expectations that journalists monitor and update stories as merited by audience response and opportunity
- Change shifts so that folks show up to work earlier and provide continuous coverage
- Modify key editorial meetings in terms of timing, purposes and participation.

1) Match deadlines to audience windows

Deadlines powerfully shape journaltic workflows and practices — especially deadlines that carry the traditional force of print deadlines. Unlike with print, though, newsrooms can't be in the game with 'once a day' deadlines. Instead, to close misalignment gaps, you must match deadlines to the realities of conitinuous digital news consumption throughout the day.

One way to do this is to set deadlines to match two types of audience-driven windows:

- **Persistent, repeated windows of audience usage** based on target audience seeking and reading habits. For example, the Miami Herald frames its weekday daytime publishing in these four windows:

Early Eyes	Cubicle Crowd	Lunch Bunch	Weary Workers
6–8 a.m.	8 a.m.–noon	Noon–2 p.m.	2–5 p.m.

- **Windows of high audience interest** driven by breaking news and trending stories. While these are unscheduled and of uncertain length — maybe a few hours within a day, maybe over several days — they still have rhythms against which deadlines can be set. e.g.:

BREAKING NEWS	TRENDING STORIES
• First alert — being first (and right) in notifying your audience • Continuing coverage — giving reasons to keep checking • Follow-on coverage — engaging through other angles and underlying issues	• Spotting early • Promoting and positioning • Building-on and extending

Review your analysis of your audience's usage patterns (and/or, as suggested in Section 3, the usage patterns of desired audiences in your market that you fail to serve or underserve). Define your own digital publishing windows for both regular audience usage patterns and opportunistic moments of audience interest linked to breaking news and trending stories. Coin meaningful and memorable descriptions for these windows (e.g. Miami's "lunch bunch"). *Finally, set and hold folks in your newsroom accountable for meeting deadlines linked to these windows.*

In addition, you must reset journalistic expectations away from the "once and done" approach of print and toward creating short versions as previews of the fuller story to come, producing multiple posts from one story, updating and versioning stories that continue to develop, and later aggregating the story with related pieces. One essential aspect here is shifting journalists' mindset from a focus on A1 placement and how many inches a story has to a passion and focus on serving audiences well wherever and whenever those audiences seek out content. In this regard, Dallas Morning News leaders proclaimed, "Time is the new inches." Administratively, it's also key for folks in the newsroom to enter stories underway and update their status in the budget, work with the central news desk on scheduling against the best audience window, and collaborate with platform and audience specialists on enhancements and promotion of stories with particular audience promise.

2) **Change shifts so that folks show up to work earlier to provide continuous coverage**

Having one deadline a day kept staffing schedules relatively simple for print workflows. Staffing for digital publishing across persistent as well as episodic (that is, breaking news and/or trending story-related) audience windows is more involved. In general, three areas of change are likely involved:

- More staffing earlier in the day — e.g., shifts starting at 6 a.m. or even before for some folks; an 8 or 9 a.m. start for many more; and, moving staff (e.g. copy editors) from evening/night shifts
- Longer hours of continuous coverage — e.g., 18+ hours a day, 7 days a week
- More varied shift structures to cover all the publishing needs

    — Split role shifts — part of a continuous shift in one role and part in another role
    — Split time shifts — a day's work split into two shifts with time in-between

Making these changes can trigger concerns if the new work schedules disrupt personal patterns related to child care, schools, spouse's work, etc. In addition, such changes may demand changes to union/guild work rules. If so, then the shifts might need to be considered in the context of other negotiations. All of these factors underscore the importance of advance planning, communications and discussion of rationales and necessities, and sufficient lead times for making personal adjustments.

3) Modify key editorial meetings in terms of timing, purposes and participation

Daily editorial meetings are a telling artifact of a print-driven legacy. You can tell a good deal about a newsroom's progress on this Table Stake by noting when these meetings are held and what's discussed. Correspondingly, making fundamental changes in their timing, purposes and participation instigates and signals fundamental change. In particular, you must make these changes with the objective to be *driven by* digital publishing — not just to accommodate it.

To give a sense of this, here's a profile of changes made by three of the Table Stakes newsrooms to their morning editorial meetings:

NEWSROOM	FROM	TO
Philadelphia	**10:30 a.m. meeting** — print focused — begins with foreign and national news — cursory review of online traffic at the end	**8:30 a.m. teleconference** — key editors — run by website's RealTime news desk — focuses on identifying and directing online content for morning and afternoon **11:30 a.m. meeting** — all desks — begins with discussion of website analytics — focuses on identifying and directing online content for afternoon and evening — includes digital story pitches and headline tryouts
Minneapolis	**10 a.m. meeting** — paper budgets — discuss print newspaper section targets	**Starting at 5 a.m. on Slack "am plan" channel** — Quick strike teams and department digital reps identifying and discussing upcoming stories and reporting digital plans **8:15 a.m. digital huddle/brainstorm** **10 a.m. meeting** — digital metrics — digital plans for the day
Dallas	**10:30 a.m. meeting** — department heads — share budget lines to slot stories into next day's paper	**9 a.m. headline rodeo** — editors (and anyone else) — write headlines conveying essence of the stories — discuss/question/improve headlines — vote for headlines to lead digital — analytics debrief on what is and isn't working digitally

Note that these changes go beyond resetting the start time of morning meetings to also include:

- **Shifting the purposes and focus of meetings away from story status toward audience reach and engagement.** Traditional, print-centric editorial meetings too often focus on who's working on what stories, when those stories will be ready, and when and where the stories will appear in the paper. Even worse, such meetings can be no more than recitations of information that should be but isn't available in easy to use budget tools. Instead, the purposes and focus needs to shift from stories per se to audiences and how the stories can better serve audiences:

— What stories do we have and/or need to meet audience interests and needs in the coming audience window(s)?
— How can audience appeal and engagement be sharpened? What is or are the best headline(s) for digital platform(s)?
— What story forms should be used and how do those fit audience needs such as how much time they have to read, view, absorb?
— What is the story's visual appeal? Is there video to include?
— How should stories be socialed and possibly promoted?
— How might stories be versioned for earlier initial publication and extended play?

- **Changing the dynamics of the meetings.** Meetings that are largely round-the-table recitations of story lists feel perfunctory and lifeless. Meetings characterized by sharing, learning, problem solving and collaborating — with the audience in mind –are animated and energizing. Consider, for example, Dallas' "headline rodeo." It combines a focus on better digital publishing (better headlines) with real-time skills training and workshopping headlines as a group. Indeed, the focus on the best possible headline doubles as a powerful crucible for developing strong points of view about what is this story, which audiences does it serve, and what are the needs, issues and problems of those audiences to which it

  responds.

  - **Modifying the participation and leadership of the meetings.** The participants in print-focused editorial meetings typically mirror the structure and hierarchy of traditional newsrooms (i.e. desk or department heads with the managing or executive editor leading). In contrast, digitally focused editorial meetings should include folks leading digital publishing and audience teams (Table Stake #1), key platform owners (Table Stake #2), and digitally skilled audience developers, social leads and others. Moreover, inviting — even at times requiring — others from across is a great way to spread digital skills, reinforce workflow changes and spot new talent.

Moreover, consider changing who leads some of these meetings. For example, the Miami Herald's 4 p.m. meeting is led by a young staffer who is their social media lead and who has demonstrated great ability on their Central News Desk. You can also rotate leadership.

- **Continually reworking the overall schedule of meetings and check-ins to keep planning ahead of publishing windows that can vary by platform.** Given multiple digital publishing "windows" across the day, editorial meetings need to be scheduled for planning *ahead* of each of these defined windows so that your effort stays proactive instead of reactive or retrospective. For example, the Miami Herald's 4 p.m. meeting is now focused on three objectives: late afternoon publishing that is in process, plans for evening publishing and lining up the following morning's "early eyes" window.

b) Redesign workflows to ease and speed continuous digital publishing

If you have not done so already, use the workflow mapping steps described in Section 3 to identify workflow performance gaps. This mapping will identify a whole range of performance gaps, issues and challenges that should fall into three categories of fixes based on their difficulty and the time frame required to address them. Use the following to create — then execute — a road map by which to arrive at a true digital first workflow within a reasonable time frame, say 10-12 months:

1. **Relatively quick and easy fixes through clarifying and changing workflow steps or roles without significant skill or technology considerations.** These "do now" fixes can include:

   - Eliminating low value tasks within the workflow;
   - Consolidating tasks to reduce handoffs where significant new skills are not involved and the task instructions can be readily learned;
   - Establishing standards for "clean handoffs", including clarifying the roles and responsibilities on both sides of the handoff (e.g. with simple checklists);
   - Codifying, documenting and recommunicating workflow steps where there is confusion or conflicting practices (again, with simple checklists);
   - Strictly enforcing adherence to workflow tasks as "non-optional."

   There may also be simple tools that can be adopted to make discrete tasks within the workflow faster, easier and simpler to train on (e.g., a better suited software for photo cropping, sizing and format conversion) or relatively inexpensive hardware upgrades that can ease process bottlenecks.

2. **Multi-month drives (e.g waves of 2 to 4 months each) to close workflow performance gaps through broadening digital skills and digital-first practices across the newsroom.** Broadening digital skills and digital-first practices will get your newsroom significantly closer to the "one person" digital workflow. Yet, because they require folks in the newsroom to learn new skills, adopt new mindsets and break old habits, you ought to expect the full transition to happen through a series of successive waves of action.

   Broadening digital skills involves identifying the specific skills needed, assessing current individual and team skill levels against those requirements, setting expectations for digital self-sufficiency, and providing needed support. For more, read 6(c) below as well as the chapter entitled Shaping The Right Staff Roles and Skills For Your Newsrom.
   Shifting to digital practices involves getting reporters and editors:

- focused first and foremost on digital publication with an understanding (and belief) that print will emerge from their good digital work;
- writing, producing and publishing throughout the day rather than working to a single print deadline
- thinking always in terms of audience, starting with audience listening for story insights and carrying through to audience traffic monitoring for story feedback.

Hands-on newsroom leadership direction, demonstration and reinforcement is needed — sometimes starting with clear "permission" that it's now okay (and expected) to *really* focus first on digital.

Take time to think through the planning and preparation for these efforts. But avoid one, huge, all consuming "change program." Like other changes described throughout this report, you can move forward on a small scale with certain individuals and groups based on readiness and then expand and accelerate later across the newsroom. In addition, remember to ask folks who have — or build — digital skills to help others in peer to peer ways. Moreover, your effort can be a self-feeding movement. Those who already have the digital skills and are most critical for providing the needed skills instruction and coaching to others (i.e. producers), will have more of their time freed from routine production tasks as more reporters and editors become more self-sufficient, freeing more of their time to do more skill development.

Along with building digital skills, multi-month waves might also address workflow gaps that arise from ineffective technology and tools. Prime among these are getting a "universal" budgeting system and choosing/using a common platform for real-time communications and coordination (e.g. Slack). See section 6f for more. These are tools that are readily available, don't require large investments, can be implemented with relative ease, and are likely to be seen as being necessary to implementing many of the most basic changes required.

3. **Major technology changes and investments required to fully simplify workflows and convert to digital-first, print later and better publishing.** These are changes aimed at eliminating any added workflow steps, workarounds and other complications and impediments arising from operating in a mixed print and digital CMS environment.

Start with using your workflow mapping assessment to make the case for, and define the requirements of, a CMS environment that supports rather than hinders digital first publishing. While the cost of such investments are often viewed as prohibitive, the workflow inefficiencies and staff time costs of *not making* the investments too often go unquantified and just accepted as part of ongoing operating costs. And, yet, they *are* costly.

As part of this clear-eyed assessment of existing technology costs, you may have a situation where the print CMS is the primary, "originating" system that either feeds the digital CMS very poorly or requires manual reentry of content into the digital CMS. If so, decide to flip that by making the digital CMS the primary authoring and production CMS that feeds the print CMS. If necessary, consider "cutting-and-pasting" digital content into the print CMS. Though far from ideal and likely to shift the burden of added workflow steps and workarounds from the digital side to the print side, the net effect may be positive for spurring the newsroom's full conversion to audience-driven continuous digital first publishing and print from digital curation while waiting to fund and implement better overall technology solutions. (For more, see 6f below.)

c) Broaden skills and combine roles to enable more efficient workflows

Use three steps to broaden skills in support of more effective workflows:

- Define and build the skills required for digital publishing 'self-sufficiency' across the newsroom
- Reposition producers and digitally skilled specialists to help others practice new skills while also being masters of enhanced storytelling and innovators
- Think in terms of roles instead of positions while shifting many traditional positions into combinations of roles

1) Define and build the skills required for greater digital publishing "self-sufficiency" across the newsroom

Newsroom folks always name digital skill building as crucial. Yet, far too often skill building efforts are poorly designed, ad hoc, and disconnected from performance goals and requirements. Instead of falling in these traps, start with a clear objective: *every reporter and editor should have all the skills needed for the "one person workflow" for creating, producing, publishing and monitoring a basic digital story on the major publishing platforms used by your newsroom.*

With this objective, define at a granular level the specific skills required, assess individuals' current skill levels against these requirements, and set expectations that folks will do whatever's needed to learn and use required skills. Finally, set — and demand individuals to achieve — specific traffic, engagement and other goals whose success depends on digital skills.

As a first step, define the skills needed for digital "self-sufficiency." Start by specifying the elements of a "good digital post." Include both the tangible elements of the post itself (text, visuals, links, embeds, etc.) as well as the practices needed for audience-focused digital storytelling (e.g. social listening). Use these specifications to lay out the necessary skills along the workflow stages of the "one person workflow." For example, for your main web and mobile web site this could include:

Audience needs and interests identification	Text	Text	Publishing	Audience monitoring
— social accounts setup and use (FB, Twitter) — social listening points and practices **Audience news behavior understanding** — drawing insights from audience data across all your stories **Multi-post planning** — developing and feeding a story through multiple posts	— writing for digital **Visuals** — photo shooting basics — video shooting basics — uploading photos/video from the field — creating simple data charts **User Generated Conent** — sourcing UGC — verifying and gaining rights to UGC	— composing in the CMS — pull quote use and placement — self-editing **Headlines** — story headline writing for digital — SEO head construction **Visuals** — photo cropping and sizing — video simple editing — metadata tagging — loading/searching in asset mgmt system — placement in body text in CMS — caption/narrative writing — source crediting **Links/embeds** — hyperlinking in text — tweet and YouTube embedding **Related content** — content selection — reference placement	— publishing posts — scheduling posts for later publication	— data access (desktop and mobile) — metrics interpretation — key metrics to watch **Follow-on publishing** — updating and enhancing — reversioning — self-aggregating

Note: basic journalism skills and ethics are not included here and assumed for this skills need analysis

You can then expand your requirements for self-sufficiency by adding other primary platforms where audiences expect your staff to be able to post, e.g. Facebook or Twitter. Add any elements and skills not already covered that are specific to these platforms. For example, in the case of Facebook, this could include effective story selection and writing an engaging headline and social lead.

What you choose to include in your "self-sufficiency" specifications will vary based on factors specific to your newsroom and its current level of digital transformation. As mentioned earlier, you may want to tackle such skill requirements in waves or phases. Or you may be at a point where newsroom folks are in need, of and ready for, a full bore approach. The important thing is to intentionally do the work needed to clearly and granularly define needed skills for continuous digital first publishing.

Once you have clearly defined required skills, use the steps described in the chapter entitled "Shaping the right staff roles and skills for your newsroom" — including assessing newsroom folks current skills against those required, choosing ways to support folks trying to gain skills (use of specialists, training and so forth) and setting and holding folks accountable for performance results (e.g. traffic, engagement, etc.) that can only be achieved with the needed skills. In addition, you'll need to think through what and how to best work with folks who are not trying. The Shaping Roles and Skills chapter also provides guidance for how senior leaders of larger newsrooms should focus on skill gaps at the desk or team level while requiring desks and teams to focus on individual skill development.

2) Reposition producers and digitally skilled specialists to help others practice new skills while also being masters of enhanced storytelling and innovators

In general, three choices confront individuals or teams whose success depends on learning and practicing one or more new skills, behaviors, attitudes and ways of working with others:

- Do this myself
- Do this with me
- Do this for me

Say, for example, you wish to have a new kitchen table yet have no furniture making skills. You have three choices. You could have someone do it for you — buy a table at a furniture store or hire a carpenter. You could choose to learn furniture making with the help of a carpenter — that is choose 'do this with me.' Or, you could go buy books on furniture making or take other steps and 'just do it yourself.'

In many newsrooms, producers and other digital specialists spend nearly all of their time 'doing it for others' — that is, reporters, editors and others who lack needed skills hand the work over. Not only does this preclude the practice required to learn new skills — it also means the specialists spend far too much time doing basic tasks instead of the kind of enhanced story telling and innovation needed to serve and grow audiences.

Instead, senior newsroom leaders need to reposition how these experts spend their time and are evaluated. Here's a rule of thumb for newsrooms just getting started with digital transformation:

- **Skills developers (50% of time):** Doing skills work "with others" by providing coaching, workshopping, training and side-by-side support for developing digital skills across the newsroom. In other words, specialists have *the* key role in building "self-sufficiency" for digital publishing. Senior leaders should hold such specialists accountable for the progress in performance and learning of those acquiring digital skills. For example, if a digitally skilled producer works half her time over the coming 6 to 10 months with, say, 10 to 20 people in the newsroom, then the progress of those 10 to 20 against their traffic, engagement and other goals should be partly what is discussed at the specialist's own performance evaluation and review.

- **Skills innovators (20 to 30% of time):** Keeping abreast of developments in their own field of expertise; continuing to develop their own skills; identifying and spreading better practices across the newsrooms to refresh and advance skills; and working with groups across the newsroom on conducting and evaluating quick story-telling and platform use experiments to better serve audiences. Success here reflects some blend of identified and deployed new practices with audience and other metrics/goals accomplished as a result.

- **Skills masters (20 to 30% of time):** Working with reporters and editors on enhancing select, high investment stories where advanced skills can really make a difference in deepening audience engagement, expanding audience reach, and building audiences' recognition and perceived value of the newsroom's brand. Success here turns on the performance of such stories and projects.

In doing this repositioning, it's important to discuss with the individuals involved how their roles will be changing along with the rest of the newsroom and that they will be expected to carry all three roles going forward. Some individuals may be stronger in one role than another and take more of a lead in that area within the newsroom. But few if any should be allowed to just "do their thing" in isolation. In addition, these different duties, time requirements and success factors ought to get written in to job profiles for new specialist hires. And, finally, senior leaders in conversation with these specialists must monitor the progress of newsroom folks toward digital self-sufficiency. As this happens, the allocation of effort across the three roles should change with more time going toward innovation and master story enhancement.

3) Think in terms of "roles not positions" and shift traditional positions to combinations of roles

Digitally transformed, audience focused newsrooms are far more flexible than traditional print centric ones where reporters wrote text, photographers shot photos and copy editors edited copy. Instead of these highly fixed jobs, folks in transformed newsrooms can and do play several roles that themselves vary over the course of a day, week, month, quarter and year.

Here are examples of combinations of roles that emerge in digitally savvy, audience-focused newsrooms:

TRADITIONAL FUNCTIONAL POSITION	ROLES AND COMBO ROLES FOR AUDIENCE-FOCUSED CONTINUOUS DIGITAL FIRST PUBLISHING
Reporter	• reporter/producer/audience developer ("one-person workflow" capable) • member of an audience and/or minipublsher team (see Table Stake #1 and #7 for more)
Editor	• producer/editor/audience developer • digital story editor (all elements of the story, not just text) • digital hub "real time" producer/audience developer • digital hub shift editor/manager • leader of an audience, platform or minipublisher team (see Table Stake #1, #2 and #7)
Digital producer	• story enhancer (applying advanced skills to select stories) • skills developer and coach • story form creator (working with audience teams and producer) • skills innovator
Photographer, videographer or graphics designer	• visuals producer/editor/audience developer • visuals skills developer and coach • visual story form developer (working with audience teams, producers and tech developers)

TRADITIONAL FUNCTIONAL POSITION	ROLES AND COMBO ROLES FOR AUDIENCE-FOCUSED CONTINUOUS DIGITAL FIRST PUBLISHING
Audience developer	• audience development skills developer and coach • audience development opportunity identifier • audience development innovation/experimentation leader • audience or platform team leader/owner (see Table Stake #1, #2) • skills innovator
Tech developer	• story form developer (working with audience teams and producer) • technology coach and advisor (e.g., primers, cautions on breaking and hacking) • audience experience watchdog (e.g. load times, page/screen rendering)

Thinking and organizing around such role combinations rather than set positons makes for a stronger and more dynamic newsroom, especially from an audience perspective. The payoffs include:

- Greater staffing flexibility for serving audiences when and where they want to be served (e.g. for filling shifts in the "digital hub");
- An increased sense of total story ownership by individuals (versus responsibility for only certain steps in the workflow);
- More cross-newsroom collaboration and teaming as individuals learn and appreciate the roles of others and share their skills with others;
- A common focus on the audience as all roles are reshaped from a perspective of "what value are we providing the audience?" and "How are we monetizing that value?" In this sense, "audience development" is no longer the responsibility of just the person with that title.

In addition, work is more fulfilling for folks doing these combinations of roles — in part because the overall work is more challenging. Instead of working throughout a whole day on a narrow set of tasks, these folks operate across a multi-colored checkerboard of various roles played at various time throughout each day.

The exact role combinations you develop will depend on your circumstances (e.g. union or guild presence) and will shift over time as you move beyond Table Stakes. Specialization will always be part of the mix. This is true especially for a larger newsroom with the scale to warrant and support such specialization and benefit from the potential advantages that can come with it (greater focus, higher work efficiency, more accumulated experience, deeper skills, etc.).

d) Provide the tools to support better workflows and broader roles

In the course of the Table Stakes effort, two essential tools emerged as key to digital transformation: a universal budget plus a communications app for messaging, coordination and file access. In addition, a key role emerged (for an individual or team) related to being the 'tool master' who continually identifies tools that work and oversees the shared repository folks use to access and learn how to use the tools in that repository.

1) Create a complete and universally shared "budget" covering all digital publishing

The term "budget" is part of the print legacy's lexicon that, while still actively used, nonetheless has entirely different purposes, meanings and dimensions in digital publishing. Rather than allocating physical space within a daily print product, the digital budget is key to coordinating content publishing throughout the hours of the day and across multiple platforms on a continuous basis.

However, too few newsrooms have a universal budget that can do these jobs. Instead, newsrooms evolve a hodge podge of workaround efforts that too rarely get used by everyone or in similar ways. In some newsrooms, the digital budget remains a loose, after the fact plan made once the print budget is set (i.e., curating digital from print). Other newsrooms attempt to use the budget system of the print CMS even though it may only include content that will appear in print and has deadlines only by the day instead of hour. Perhaps most commonly, the digital budget exists in multiple spreadsheets, word documents and Google docs kept by different groups and individuals across the newsroom with no shared access or integrated view. One newsroom, for example, admitted to *24* different such efforts.

What's required is a "digital-native" budget system that's suited to achieving this Table Stake of matching your flow of publishing to the times when audiences are seeking content, a system that meets these requirements:

- **Basic data:** inclusion of all the data points needed to profile and track digital content across platforms, including but not limited to print (reporter, editor, slug, digital headline, visuals, deadline, status, publishing platforms, publishing time by platform, etc.);

- **Complete entry and continuous updating:** clear roles and responsibilities across the newsroom for entering all content items along with clear expectations for keeping the status as current as possible;

- **Universal access:** open access by everyone in the newsroom to the entire budget;

- **Easy access:** availability not just on desktop but also on mobile and via coordination tools (e.g. Slack);

- **Multiple publishing views:** the ability to sort and report the content in progress from key digital publishing perspectives: platform, time window, status, reporter, etc.;

- **Lead times and views:** inclusion of lead times for story elements where needed (e.g. complex graphics) and the display of those lead time dates within the time-based views;

- **Forward view:** the ability to go out a year in advance to forward plan date-pegged content (e.g. calendared events such as major holidays), major reporting initiatives, etc.

Such systems are available commercially, though they should be considered only once your requirements and selection criteria are clearly defined. Because such systems are essentially just a database, you can also get started with something as basic as a Google Sheet shared to everyone in the newsroom. This simple start can also be a cheap and easy way to test and refine your data needs and prototype entry and report formats before purchasing a system or developing one in-house.

The Dallas Morning News was considering a commercial system when in-house developers decided they could take on the project and quickly developed a version that the newsroom started using immediately. The system has continued to be refined and adapted to their digital publishing needs and Dallas has now licensed it to another newsroom and is sharing further development costs with them.

2) Adopt a readily available messaging, collaboration and file access app to coordinate continuous digital publishing

Hand-in-hand with the a universal budget is the need for a common tool for managing the cross-newsroom communications and coordination needed to produce the content in the budget. The all-too-common shortfall in newsrooms arise from a hodge podge of different messaging apps used in different ways by different groups to connect with one another and with stories/content under way. This multitude of email distribution lists and clutter of uncategorized emails generates ever more cumbersome sending, retrieving and organizing story assets that are nearly unmanageable — and make cross-newsroom collaboration nightmarish.

It's no surprise then that as the four initial Table Stakes newsrooms moved to digital first publishing across the day, they also adopted an integrated communications, coordination and file access app. Slack[2] was their favored choice as it is with many news organizations, though there are alternatives to consider (e.g., Azendoo, Bitrix24). Besides the expected uses for editorial planning, story development, breaking news coordination and the like, they also used Slack to support/advance other digital production uses such as headline workshopping.

Just as with the universal budget system, it's important to clearly define your requirements and selection criteria up front (e.g. full mobile functionality, integration with existing email and file storage systems, etc.). It's also essential to think how to introduce the tool, provide basic training, enforce universal usage, promote active use, and manage the tool going forward. For example, Slack channel proliferation is a common byproduct of success — and must be managed if frustration is not to set in[3].

---

[2]

The American Press Institute (API) offers a helpful introduction and detailed guide to using Slack, along with other resource materials based on news organizations that have adopted it.

[3]

Background information, a training module, documentation and interviews with several news organizations on adopting and using Slack are available from API.

3) Identify and create a shared repository of tools you expect newsroom folks to use to speed and ease continuous publishing tasks

Having easy access to the right tool for the right task dramatically increases the odds that folks in busy newsrooms use that tool. Even if a reporter, for example, recalls hearing about some tool someone else used, the odds of that reporter taking advantage drop like a rock if the reporter has to hunt down the tool. In contrast, if the right tool is available and the tasks take, say, 15 minutes, it's much more likely to happen. Of course, if the reporter has never even heard of the tool, she won't use it.

There's an ever expanding range of digital storytelling and production tasks and tools — a range that spans photo and video editing (on both desktop and mobile), chart building and other data visualization, video storytelling, interactive storytelling, social media searching, audio transcription, language translation and more. Fortunately, after more than 20 years of digital production there are many such tools optimized for defined functions, easy to learn, quick to use and often available for free or modest cost. And information, reviews and training webinars on such tools are readily available from various journalism support organizations and sites, including the Digital Tool Catalog developed by the Poynter Institute and API with Knight Foundation support, or by directly contacting Amy Kovac-Ashley, API's Senior Newsroom Learning Program Manager.

Given the ready availability and number of such tools, newsrooms need to designate one or more folks to play the role of tool masters who not only look out for new and/or better tools but also create, maintain and manage a repository where folks can access, learn about and share successes with the tools themselves. These tool masters should treat the repository as a product they manage — and the rest of the newsroom as their customers. They are responsible for identifying needed tools, finding the right tools, working with others to get them deployed, learned and used across the newsroom, being the resident expert on tool questions, and staying apprised of upgrades and better replacements. And they must continuously 'market' the repository to others.

In the course of its work to broaden digital production skills across the newsroom, the Philadelphia Media Network started building its own on-line "Knowledge Base" described as "a living interactive checklist for common publishing tasks." Along with basic guidance, this repository provides links to how-to articles and training materials. Philadelphia continuously updates the repository as workflows and practices change.

Creating such a "front-end" knowledge base for your own newsroom has the advantage of providing navigation based on your particular situation and then linking, as needed, to the wealth of outside articles and training resources that are available (e.g. the Philly Knowledge Base has top-line navigation based on the CMS and such choices as "Quick! Breaking News," "Standard toolkit" and "The works").

There is an upfront investment in time and basic tech development to create repositories that then are built out over time. The return on this investment comes from a blend of time, resources and money saved and better used along with faster, more engaging digital content that attracts, retains and monetizes users, advertising and other revenue opportunities.

e) Re-organize to be digital-first, print later and better

Print and digital platforms attract and serve differing user needs, expectations and habits. And organizationally print and digital have different publishing cycles and rhythms. It's not a surprise, then, that news organizations often created separate print versus digital newsrooms in the early days of the Web. That bifurcated approach is not likely to work today, though, because it inflexibly divides up labor instead of maximizing opportunities to serve audiences through adaptable and effective coordination. In addition, it perpetuates a losing either/or-ism, condemning news organizations to endless squabbling over whether "we're print first or digital first" — squabbles that bury the lede that today's legacy newspaper enterprises must be *audience-first*.

Such either/or-ism muddies and delays a key insight: continuous digital publishing provides real time story telling and story shifting possibilities that reflect *both what is happening to the story as well as how the audience is responding to the story*. After Prince died, for example, the Star Tribune's audience-driven, digital first approaches generated scores of stories and content pieces that the Strib folks curated into a much better printed paper. The newsroom folks recognized that, had they gone print first, they would have lost the opportunity for a better paper in large part because their print focus would have led to fewer pieces of content and far less engagement with audiences.

Three steps can guide your newsroom toward digital-first approaches that also lead to better, more audience-focused newpapers:

- Create a 'digital hub' to proactively manage digital publishing
- Form a print team responsible for curating the best possible paper from the digital content
- Over time, shift from audience and platform teams toward full minipublisher teams

Table Stake #7 provides guidance for the third step. This rest of this section describes actions to take for the first two.

1) Create a "digital hub" to proactively manage digital publishing

Digital hubs run by digitally-adept folks serve as the central coordinating point for continuous digital publishing. In particular, digital hubs:

- Bring together the skills and roles needed for publishing effectively across digital platforms;
- Guide and coordinate digital publishing done across the newsroom, particularly by audience teams (see Table Stake #1 and, as needed, specially skilled staff (e.g. visual journalists);
- Operate in real time with a constant eye on audience traffic and engagement
- Seize opportunities to serve audiences based on breaking news and trending stories;
- Are staffed in shifts to cover all the digital publishing windows through the day and night, each day of the week;
- Build digital skills in others by having reporters, editors, and producers "learn by doing" through set rotations of working in the hub.

All four Table Stakes newsrooms formed or strengthened their digital hubs. What they called the hubs varied — e.g. Philly called its hub the "Real time news desk" while Miami named its one the "Central News Desk." You can pick a name that suits your newsroom — though, as an aside, don't lose the opportunity to choose a name that reflects the cultural shift you're hoping to bring about. In this sense, "Real Time News Desk" is superior to "Central News Desk."

Benefits

In addition to increased audience reach, usage and engagement, a digital hub:

- Functions as daily innovation and learning lab where new digital skills are developed, new tools tested and new audience building opportunities spotted and worked in real time.
- Is the nerve center of the newsroom where data-driven monitoring of day-to-day patterns of audience habits and content interests emerge and get shared with the entire newsroom.
- Accelerates skill building because folks assigned part time to the hub spread digital writing, production and platform management skills to their regular desks back into their home areas, accelerating the overall development of digital skills across the newsroom.
- Enhances the quality, timeliness and audience-focus of content — for example, by putting the journalistic talents, accumulated knowledge and insights of experienced editors to better use in reaching and serving audiences.
- Ensures more work gets done earlier and across the course of the day in developing, testing, versioning and fully preparing stories for the benefit of the print platform and the crunch of print deadlines. In particular, curating a better print report from digital means the peak print workload is lowered, there's less need for evening and night staffing for print production and resources can get shifted to the hub.
- Adds energy to the newsroom. It's one place where the newsroom is alive throughout the day and night, and where staff gather together and interact with one another and with the real-time feedback of audience data, including data about small and large wins that fuel excitement and a sense of achievement.

Responsibilities

The digital hub's responsibilities tie back to the two types of audience-focused publishing windows and include:

FOR "WINDOWS OF AUDIENCE USAGE" (DAY-TO-DAY PATTERNS SUCH AS MIAMI'S "LUNCH BUNCH")	FOR "WINDOWS OF OPPORTUNITY" (BREAKING NEWS AND TRENDING STORIES)
— Choosing and naming the daily patterns/windows — Making sure the windows are reflected in the digital "universal budget" — Publishing to the digital "universal budget" and monitoring that others are publishing to the budget — Enhancing basic posts created by reporters/producers (e.g. advanced editing, adding enhanced video) — Producing morning and evening "round-ups" or "what you need to know" summaries of major stories — Aggregating content to supplement the budget — Curating wire stories for local interest and good reads — For aggregation and wire services, choosing and fine tuning the criteria for selection based on monitoring traffic results — Updating developing stories (in conjunction with reporters) based on story evolution and/or traffic results — Sharpening social and search headlines and social leads provided by reporters/producers — A/B headline testing — Providing in-the-moment feedback and guidance to reporters/producers on improvements (e.g. reworking a headline) and informally sharing tools, best practices, and production tips — Doing overall, real-time troubleshooting on publishing and poor traffic performance issues	— Monitoring for breaking news and initiating coverage — Covering breaking news until designated editors and reporters/producers take the lead; supporting and coordinating coverage throughout the event — Identifying stories with high traffic potential and giving advance attention to positioning and promotion — Monitoring trending stories and acting on opportunities to reposition, boost and promote stories — Aggregating the newsroom's own work and that of others on trending and breaking stories

Staffing

Staffing a digital hub will vary based on the size of your newsroom, current job configurations, and skills. In general, though, the configuration combines folks at the core who can tap into more specialized help as needed:

Illustrative Digital Hub Staffing

Visual specialists photo/video, graphics, interactives		**Audience engagement specialists**
	"Digital hub" • Digital shift editor (in overall charge) • Platform editor(s) for homepage, mobile, other • Social media editor/producer • Digital editor/producer • Visual editors/producer • GA reporter/digital producer	
Newsroom tech developers		**Analytics specialists**

    Ideally, the core digital hub staff operate in shifts providing 18/7 to 24/7 coverage. This ranges in difficulty depending on the size of your newsroom, the number of folks with required digital skills, and the demands of desk-by-desk coverage and print. The Table Stakes newsrooms most often found hub staff among the ranks of digitally savvy specialists, editing positions and reassigning night shift copy editors. You can increase your flexibility and options for staffing the digital hub by asking folks to play multiple roles instead of having fixed jobs. For example, a digital editor/producer slot in a shift might be filled by someone also dedicated to an audience team, or an audience/desk editor might take a turn at being the Digital Shift Editor.

    Finally, make sure to connect the dots between staffing your digial hub to similar steps you take to ensure folks in your newsroom start the day earlier and so forth. And, link both to what you learn from audience data and analytics. For example, over the course of 2016 to 2017, Miami iterated how they staffed their digital hub (the "Central News Desk") to reflect what they learned about audiences. They learned they were too thinly staffed on Sundays. Here's their schedule for Mondays (they set separate scheduled for other days of the week as well):

Miami Herald Central News Desk shift schedule for Mondays

Monday	AM									PM											AM		
	3	4	5	6	7	8	9	10	11	12	1	2	3	4	5	6	7	8	9	10	11	1	2	3
Editors																								
Day content																								
Night content																								
Reporters																								
Day Breaking GA 1																								
Day GA 2/Backup																								
Swing Breaking GA																								
Night Breaking GA																								
Overnight GA																								
Social media																								
Day social																								
Sports social/aggregator																								
Night social															New Hire									
Producers																								
Day producer/aggregator																								
Night producer																								
Night sports producer																								
Video																								
Day aggregator																								
Day aggregator																								
Night Aggregator																								

Note: Separate schedules are set for Tuesday-Thursday, Friday, Saturday and Sunday to optimize staffing to audience traffic flows. Each of the specialized groups (light orange areas in earlier "Digital Hub" picture) matter a lot. For example, audience engagement folks drive traffic and engagement, data and analytics folks help tease out what works versus what doesn't, and newsroom tech/code developers build the tools needed for success. And, given the ever growing visual content on digital platforms, visually skilled folks in your newsroom can make major contributions to the success of digital hubs. Miami, as described below, achieved a 10-fold increase in monthly video plays in 12 months.

2) Establish a print platform team responsible for curating digital first content into a better print product

Print matters — a lot! Instead of perpetuating lose/lose, 'print first versus digital first' battles, newsrooms must embrace audience-first, platform optimal[4] strategies that boost journalism quality and audience results by curating the best possible print papers from rich, continuous digital coverage, story telling, data and analytics. This means shifting away *from print being* **the** *platform driving the newsroom to* **a** *platform drawing from the newsroom.*

Print, just like other platforms (see Table Stake #2), needs a designated platform owner and team to produce the daily and Sunday papers from content produced by the newsroom for previous publication on digital platforms. In selecting and curating content, the print team should match what works best in print with the needs, interests, habits and expectations of print motivated, print preferred audiences.

In particular, print teams must:

- Be audience first: understand and respond to print-motivated audiences' preferences, needs and experiences
- Curate a better print product from the daily flow of digital content
- Participate in cross-platform planning for major stories and projects
- Innovate print as a platform

Newsroom leaders, in turn, must support print teams with information, coordination, and digital assets

Be audience first: understand and respond to print-motivated audiences' preferences, needs and experiences

This may be the print team's most challenging responsibility. While all platform teams have this same, core charter, only the print team must carry it out in the absence of a constant stream of detailed audience data and analytics about what audiences are actually reading and engaging with.

Nonetheless, the print team can find ways to understand and meet audience needs by:

---

[4] For sometime now, many journalists have talked of being 'platform agnostic' — that is, indifferent to specific platforms. The good news in this formulation arises from de-privileging print. But the bad news is such agnosticism inaccurately suggests that "all platforms are the same." Instead, each platform has differing strenths and weaknesses for serviing audiences. Hence, platform optimal better describes the job to be done.

- Making the most of audience feedback that is available (calls and emails), adding feedback mechanisms and tracking feedback systematically
- Forming print reader panels to test ideas and gather quick feedback on changes made
- Using user-centric approaches (often called 'design thinking') to identify jobs to be done for audiences from the audiences' perspective (not the newsroom's)
- Applying design-do and test-and-learn thinking and experimentation even if the feedback cycle times are longer and the quantity of feedback points smaller.

Curate a better print product from the daily flow of digital content

Within the overarching mandate to be audience-driven, print must switch from having the deadlines that drive all daily flow to the reverse: curating a better print produce from content already produced digitally.

First, the print team must monitor how audiences engage with stories in the flow of digital publishing throughout the day — and use that information to select, shape and place content in the paper for the print audience.

Second, the print team must pick the single best version of stories (content, visuals, length and so forth) based on:

- Different versions of the story in different digital contexts and platforms;
- The range of story perspectives and angles that can play out digitally;
- The addition of important sources who emerge from seeing the story digitally, including callbacks from earlier contacts;
- Incorporation of audience responses to the story;
- Having cleaner copy by the end of day as small things are caught and corrected through the day.

Participate in cross-platform planning for major stories and projects

Among the loudest complaints of digitally savvy folks at the beginning of Table Stakes was the failure of print-centric habits to welcome and incorporate digital folks at the beginning of major stories and projects. Instead, there was a "we'll get this done and then throw it over the wall to you digital folks" pattern.

As your newsroom moves to print curating from digital instead of the reverse, you must avoid the exact opposite problem: keeping the print team in the dark and throwing content over the wall to them.

Instead, when your newsroom chooses to pursue significant enterprise or investigative stories, series or other major content projects, you've got to maximize the return on that investment through early planning and ongoing coordination across the newsroom. Focus must be on where and when to publish the content across platforms, what special content needs to be produced (e.g. visuals), how to produce the special content most efficiently and effectively across platforms, and how best to cross-promote the content across platforms. Print needs to be part of this planning and coordination from the start, though not drive it. (Indeed, "hold for the paper" can only be advocated if there is a compelling, overall audience driven rationale and strategy — a likely rare occurrence.)

The need for early cross-platform planning and ongoing coordination extends to projects that are print-conceived and print advertising driven, such as print supplements. The key question is always: how can we deploy content across platforms to maximize audience reach, traffic, and engagement along with revenues and brand building? For example, the Miami Herald used content from a major "Neighborhoods" print supplement for an "exploring neighborhoods" vertical within the redesign and relaunch of Miami.com.

Innovate print as a platform

Possible print innovations can arise from better understanding the print audience's needs and desired experiences, including:

- **Building on digital successes and innovations**. New digital story forms that better serve audiences and are more efficient to produce may be adaptable to print as well — e.g. templated story forms for reporting on public meetings that provide quick-scan takeaways of what a reader needs to know. And thinking in terms of reader needs in moments of time (e.g. the 15 minutes in the morning with the paper) can lead to reconceiving whole parts of the paper. Such was the case with The New York Times' redesign of pages A2 and A3 in March of 2017 as a quick and engaging roundup drawing on the learnings

CASE ILLUSTRATION:
Realizing the opportunity of focusing visual specialist on continuous digital publishing.

As part of an initiative to increase video traffic, The Miami Herald reconfigured and consolidated existing photo-video staff to create a new video editor/producer position focused on working with their Central News Desk to bring more, smarter and faster video posting to their digital publishing. The person's work includes:

- Gathering video for stories - sourcing and verifying user generated video, securing surveillance, police and first responder and court evidence video;
- Quickly editing clips provided by reporters sent via Videolicious;
- Working with and providing tips to reporters on shooting "good enough" video;
- Adding related video to stories from the newsroom's video archive;
- Assigning, collecting and editing stringer video;
- Aggregating video on breaking news and trending stories from Facebook, YouTube, Twitter, Instagram and other social media sources;
- Watching the play through rates on video via Chartbeat to see what's working and what could be boosted by video additions.

The video editor/producer helped make "is there video?" a default question in story discussions, editorial meetings and performance expectations (e.g. expecting (and training) every reporter to shoot and send video clips via Videolicious). Miami Herald and El Nuevo Herald combined to achieve more than a 10x increase in monthly video plays.

and success of its mobile platform's Morning and Evening Briefings.

- **Developing and growing print related products with proven demand.** Consider the enduring qualities and attractions of the print experience — scanning and perusing, having a daily habit (time with the paper), the physical tangibility and artifact for remembering and reliving historic moments in time. The print team, in conjunction with business folks, can work back from these attributes to identify and experiment with enhanced or new products to revive and extend print as a profitable platform. Minneapolis' special print editions about the death of Prince, the Dallas Morning News' front page coverage of tragic shootings of police, and Philly's printed offerings related to the 2016 Democratic National Convention all extended print excellence. Even the e-edition might have increased revenues from advertising and sponsorship if seen more as an extension of print instead of just a digital oddity.

- **Creatively supporting print-to-digital subscriber migration strategies.** The print team must coordinate with others to implement any overall news enterprise strategy aimed at migrating print to digital users. This may include the development of transitional products (e.g. enhanced versions of the e-edition as above) and special offers and conversion support targeted specifically to the print oriented reader.

Newsroom leaders must support print teams with information, coordination, and digital assets

Newsroom leaders must provide new or enhanced coordination tools, roles and systems to help the print team operate efficiently and effectively. Key among these are:

- **The "universal budget."** As long as it is fully and continuously updated, the universal budget tool described earlier gives the print team a picture of which digitally published stories and story assets are available as well as the status and planned assets of pending stories.

- **Designated points of contact.** The digital hub must designate a "print coordinator" on afternoon and evening shifts to ensure the print team has all the content assets and story information needed, including updating any late-breaking stories. Likewise, each audience team or content group must have a role of coordinating with the print team in general and particularly in regard to larger or more complex story projects. All these coordinators are responsible for helping the print team work through any issues/challenges that arise.

- **Digital asset management.** A user friendly digital asset management system is needed to ensure the print team has ready access to all story assets. Just as important are clear roles and responsibilities for filing assets, along with 100% compliance by everyone creating assets. This includes clear guidelines on asset requirements and specifications (e.g. metadata to include and minimum photo resolution).

> **CASE ILLUSTRATION:**
> **Forming separate print production teams**
>
> In its newsroom redesign, the Dallas Morning News created a separate "Daily Team" to produce its daily and Sunday print editions. The team had new job descriptions that reflected responsibilities for getting the best print content from previously published digital efforts. Staff had to apply for these new positions. Also, when Philly combined the newsrooms of The Philadelphia Inquirer, The Philadelphia Daily News and Philly.com, they created a separate "dailies" team to produce the papers. In yet one more example, just prior to the Fall 2015 kickoff of Table Stakes, the Miami Herald formed a distinct print production group and has continued to adjust its staffing and refine it operations in line with changes in print deadlines and distribution practices.

f) Address the technology drags on digital publishing

Technology and tool issues, roles and skills and work and workflow all interrelate. Yet, technology challenges can be the most frustrating because of their drag on effectiveness and efficiency.

Some of these issues are easier to deal with than others — for example, replacing underpowered PCs or workstations that don't support simulataneously opening and working with multiple programs. Others take effort but are doable: for example, building a universal budget tool. But some are brutal — especially those related to large and complex content management systems, the bane of most print-legacy newsrooms versus digital only competitors.

1) Print-centric CMS drags

If your newsroom has a print-based CMS that exports for digital publishing, then you're stuck creating digital content in a "non-digital" environment. Such systems were originally designed to collect discrete print story inputs from the newsroom (story text, photos, etc.) for composition into print pages by expert print designers. And though much modified for digital publishing over the years, these print-centric CMSs still aren't designed for the "one person" workflow described earlier. They don't easily support all the elements needed for engaging digital posts (e.g., hyperlinks, image galleries, embeds, pull quotes, separate headlines for the main post, social post and SEO, etc.). Nor do they allow anyone to see and experiement with how various elements come together into a digital story (e.g. the placement of multiple photos and embeds within the text of the story or the use of pull quotes). Consequently, they require clean-up and fill-in of missing elements when the content is exported for digital publication.

2) Dual CMS drags

Using separate CMS' for print and digital generate another set of headaches that impede digital transformation. First, separate CMSs perpetuate the print versus digital divide separating reporters and editors who persist in using the print CMS as their primary or "originating" CMS from digital producers working in the digital CMS. It increases the likelihood that not all content gets into digital form because the print-oriented reporters and editors rely too heavily on digital producers to do that work for them. And, it seriously slows the speed at which reporters and editors gain the skills needed for the one person workflow plus the mindset of continuous digital first publishing.

You can improve this situation by flipping to the digital CMS as the "originating" CMS for the entire newsroom. If you do this, you must also explicitly require reporters and editors to work in the digitally native system first, which has an added benefit of expediting their skills and mindset toward the one person workflow. But this perpetuates the possibility of double work on the backend as content is taken from the digital CMS and put into the print CMS.

3) The costs of addressing and *not* addressing technology drags

Fully addressing complex technology drags such as those arising from CMS issues is costly — both in terms of hard dollars for cash strapped news enterprises as well as pain-of-change costs related to learning and implementation. There's a natural reluctance to act because, day-to-day, it's easier to continue to live with and work around technology limitations.

Too often, though, the costs of *not changing* go unconsidered. These costs are real and come in two forms. First are the "excuse costs" that arise when technology drags give the newsroom justifications for not moving faster to the one person workflow that empowers reporters to fully own their digital storytelling and audience engagement.

Second are serious inefficiencies — the costs in money and speed arising from added steps to daily work plus errors that arise and must get fixed (reworked). Such costs rise when high value folks do low value work (e.g., a talented and experienced editor reinserting hyperlinks). Too often newsrooms that delay action out of concern for costly new CMSs also fail to quantify and discuss these hidden inefficiencies and costs. For example, say you have a producer spending 2.5 hours a day at an hourly rate of $25 on tasks that would not be required in a good CMS environment. Multiply this by six producers in similar circumstances. Add to this the reporter who spends or loses 45 minutes a day on unproductive CMS-related tasks and other technology problems (again at $25 an hour). And, say, you have 50 folks in the same boat — so multiply by 50. Now add experienced editors who spend two hours a day of CMS-related "clean-up" and "fix-it" work at an hourly rate of $50 (based on a fully load annual salary of $80,000). Multiply this by eight editors. Add all this up and you reach an annual total cost of over $500,000.

4) The benefits of taking action

The case for action becomes clear when your newsroom accounts for and considers these "excuse" and staff time costs.

And, in addition to the costs of not taking action, there are a series of benefits that arise when CMS issues get addressed — though some of these are difficult to see until action Is underway. For example, Dallas converted to a digital-first CMS (called "Serif") that they developed with an outside firm for the launch of GuideLive (a standalone entertainment product). As part of the migration, Dallas first scaled the CMS and tested it for sports before expanding it across the entire newsroom.

Amanda Wilkens, Audience Development Editor, described the CMS conversion as a journey from "workflow" to "work with flow." She made clear "it hurt at first, but then we realized how much better life can be than what it was" which, in turn, she described this way (emphasis added):

> Using Serif has been **a career-changing experience for our reporters and editors**. There are so many ways to quantify the difference between our new way of working and our old way, but **the obvious victory** for us is this: We are **now coaching writers in article design rather than urging, pleading, begging them simply to upload photos or embed tweets**.
>
> **The ease of embedding rich media is a game-changer**; reporters don't need to know code or screen sizes any more. Add to that the streamlined method for importing photos and building galleries, and **the result is a newsroom that is energized in the way it seeks to better integrate all the tools digital storytelling has to offer**.
>
> **No firewalls, no coding, no wonky display. Now we are empowered by seamless, WYSIWYG interface.** Having gone through more than a half-dozen iterations of different systems over 20 years, I can attest that Serif's **user-centric design** and **simple, elegant focus on building solid, structured content** are unmatched in the news industry.

Her remarks go beyond endorsing Serif. They also speak to the great value realized by squarely facing up to and directly addressing the drags of non-digital CMS's on digital transformation.

7. Measures of success and tracking progress in closing the gaps

Three of measures of success arise from using digital first continuous publishing to better meet audience needs: 1) outputs achieved toward more continuous publishing; 2) outcomes achieved in audience growth by day part; and 3) capabilities built across the newsroom.

a) Tracking success at continuous plublishing outputs

These direct and controllable measures focus on the execution of plans for continuous as well as increased amounts of publishing. The output being measured is straightforward — more posts published in the targeted daypart. Consider, then, a simple scorecard for tracking this against, say, a targeted period of weekdays between 5am and 9am:

POSTING TARGETS SCORECARD

Illustrative

Target publishing period: M–F 5am–9am

	Base-line*	MON 3/1	TUES 3/2	WED 3/3	THURS 3/4	FRI 3/5	MON 3/8	TUES 3/9	WED 3/10	THURS 3/11	FRI 3/12
Target # of posts											
news.com	5	8	8	8	8	8	10	10	10	10	10
Facebook (main account)	2	4	4	4	4	4	5	5	5	5	5
Twitter (main account)	1	2	2	2	2	2	3	3	3	3	3
Actual # of posts											
news.com		6	5	7	8	9	8	9	10		
Facebook (main account)		3	4	3	4	2	4	5	5		
Twitter (main account)		2	2	2	2	3	2	3	3		
+/– target attainment											
news.com		–2	–3	–1	0	1	–2	–1	0		
Facebook (main account)		–1	0	–1	0	–2	–1	0	0		
Twitter (main account)		0	0	0	0	1	–1	0	0		
Week's average attainment over baseline											
news.com						40%					
Facebook (main account)						60%					
Twitter (main account)						120%					

*average for prior 3 months

Remember "what gets measured gets done." It's one thing to hear someone report, "I think we're doing better at publishing more in the morning" and another to know that over the past month the postings increased by 10% between 5 and 9 a.m. on weekdays.

b) Tracking success at audience outcomes by daypart

Increasing the targeted outputs for more continuous digital publishing is a key step toward achieving the real objective: namely, increased traffic and engagement arising from publishing fresh, relevant and engaging content during the times of day when audiences are seeking it. Think, then, about increased visits (sessions) across targeted dayparts. So, in addition to looking at audience numbers by day, week or month or by desk or reporter, a scorecard to monitor success at boosting publishing and visits during the Monday-Friday 5am to 9am morning daypart might look like this:

AUDIENCE GROWTH BY DAYPART SCORECARD

Illustrative

Target publishing period: M–F 5am–9am

	Baseline*	13 week target	% increase	Week: 1 — 3/1	2 — 3/8	3 — 3/15	4 — 3/22	5 — 3/29	>	13 — 5/24
Visits										
All visits (sessions) within time period	125,000	162,500	30%	128,123	131,587	133,002	140,045	138,125		
In market visits within time period	41,250	51,563	25%	42,098	43,567	43,897	44,990	44,702		
Attainment toward 13 week target increase										
All visits (sessions) within time period				8%	18%	21%	40%	35%		
In market visits within time period				8%	22%	26%	36%	33%		

* average for prior 3 months

Obviously, you can tailor this scorecard to focus on different days and dayparts (e.g. Sundays from 6am to noon). You might do something similar for time of engagement, frequency of visits by the same user, source of traffic (direct, organic search, social referral, and other referral), and more.

c) Tracking success at capabilities built in the newsroom

Continuously publishing where and when audiences show up requires newsroom capabilities that blend work, workflows, roles, skills, technology and tools. So, it is key to be as rigorous in setting and tracking capability goals as it is audience growth and engagement goals.

For example, suppose your newsroom sets this objective:

> Bring **every** desk to at least an 80% level of digital skills **attainment** and **use** for digital production "self-sufficiency"

You can devise a scorecard for this goal by:

1. Defining the specific skills required for "self-sufficient" digital publishing by reporters and others in your newsroom.
2. Naming the individual contributors on desks and setting a scale for proficiency at the required skills. Be careful not to make this scale too cumbersome — perhaps use 1 to 3 or 1 to 4. The illustration below makes the scale binary: either the individual has the skill ("1") or not ("0"). List all individuals on the desk that this scorecard covers.
3. Monitoring the actual usage of the skill in question. Audiences are ill served by folks who have the needed skills yet don't use them. The illustration has a 0 to 4 scale for usage. You can alter that however you like — but again, be careful to avoid too much complexity.
4. Summarizing the picture with overall scoring mechanisms. Add a section for "doing the math" by specifying the factors for scoring, determining the score for 100% attainment, and then calculating the current level of attainment towards the "at least 80%" target specified in the objective. As you'll see, the desk in question in the illustration does better on skill attainment (63%) than effective usage of those skills (40%).

DIGITAL "SELF-SUFFICIENCY" DEVELOPMENT SCORECARD

Skill use and competence

0 = not doing
1 = inconsistent / needs development
2 = inconsistent / competent
3 = consistent / needs development
4 = consistent / comptent

Description

Basic skill grasp / setup
1 = basic skill and/or is properly setup

Skill area / self-sufficient skills	NAME	NAME	NAME	NAME	NAME	NAME	NAME	NAME	NAME	NAME	NAME	NAME	NAME	NAME	NAME
Plan															
Audience needs and interests identification															
— social accounts setup and use (FB, Twitter)	1	1	1	1	1	1	0	1	4	3	1	4	2	1	0	1
— social listening points and practices	1	1	1	0	1	1	0	0	4	3	2	0	2	3	0	0
Audience news behavior understanding															
— drawings insights from audience data across all your stories	1	1	1	0	0	1	0	0	3	2	1	0	2	2	0	0
Multi-post planning															
— developing and feeding a story through multiple posts	1	1	1	0	1	1	0	0	4	3	2	0	2	3	0	0
Gather content															
Text															
— writing for digital	1	1	1	0	0	1	0	0	2	3	2	0	0	2	0	0
Visuals															
— photo shooting basics	1	1	1	0	1	1	0	1	3	2	1	0	2	3	0	3
— video shooting basics	1	1	1	0	1	1	0	0	4	3	2	0	2	3	0	0
— uploading photos/video from the field	1	1	1	0	1	1	0	0	4	3	2	0	2	3	0	0
— creating simple data charts	1	1	1	0	1	1	0	0	3	2	1	0	2	2	0	0
UGC															
— sourcing UGC	1	1	1	0	1	1	0	0	4	3	2	0	2	3	0	0
— verifying and gathering rights to UGC	1	1	1	0	0	1	0	0	2	3	2	0	0	2	0	0
Produce															
Text															
— composing in the CMS	1	1	1	0	1	1	1	0	4	3	2	0	2	3	2	0
— pull quote use and placement	1	1	1	0	1	1	0	0	4	2	2	0	2	2	0	0
— self-editing	1	1	1	0	1	1	1	0	3	2	1	0	2	2	2	0
Headlines															
— story headline writing for digital	1	1	1	0	1	1	0	0	4	3	2	0	2	3	0	0
— SEO head construction	1	1	1	0	0	1	0	0	2	3	2	0	0	2	0	0
Visuals															
— photo cropping and sizing	1	1	1	0	1	1	0	0	4	3	2	0	2	3	0	0
— video simple editing	1	1	1	0	1	1	0	0	4	3	2	0	2	3	0	0
— metadata tagging	1	1	1	0	1	1	0	0	3	2	1	0	2	2	0	0
— loading/searching in asset mgmt system	1	1	1	0	1	1	0	0	4	3	2	0	2	3	0	0
— placement in body text in CMS	1	1	1	0	0	1	0	0	2	3	2	0	0	2	0	0
— caption/narrative writing	1	1	1	0	1	1	0	0	4	3	2	0	2	3	0	0
— source crediting	1	1	1	0	1	1	0	0	4	3	2	0	2	3	0	0

Table Stakes #3 Produce and Publish Continuously to Meet Audience Needs

Links/embeds															
— hyperlinking in text	1	1	1	0	1	1	0	0	3	2	1	0	2	2	0	0
— tweet and YouTube embedding	1	1	1	0	1	1	0	0	4	3	2	0	2	3	0	0
Related content															
— content selection	1	1	1	0	1	1	0	0	4	3	2	0	2	3	0	0
— reference placement	1	1	1	0	1	1	0	0	4	3	2	0	2	3	0	0
Publish															
— publishing posts	1	1	1	0	1	1	0	0	4	3	2	0	2	3	0	0
— scheduling posts for later publication	1	1	1	0	1	1	0	0	3	2	1	0	2	2	0	0
Monitor traffic															
Audience monitoring															
— data access (desktop and mobile)	1	1	1	0	1	1	0	0	4	3	2	0	2	3	0	0
— metrics interpretation	1	1	1	0	1	1	0	0	3	2	1	0	2	2	0	0
— key metrics to watch	1	1	1	0	1	1	0	0	4	3	2	0	2	3	0	0
Follow-on publishing															
— updating and enhancing	1	1	1	0	1	1	0	0	4	3	2	0	2	3	0	0
— reversioning	1	1	1	0	1	1	0	0	4	3	2	0	2	3	0	0
— self-aggregating	1	1	1	0	0	1	0	0	2	3	2	0	0	2	0	0
Individual attainment score	35	35	35	1	30	35	2	2	122	97	61	4	60	91	4	4
Desk attainment score								175								443
Number of skills								35								35
Highest rating #								1								4
Number of reporters on desk								8								8
Maximum score								280								1120
Attainment %								**63%**								**40%**

Table Stakes
Number 4
Funnel Occasional Users into Habitual and Paying Loyalists

1. The Table Stake
Funnel occasional users into habitual and paying loyalists

Guide your audience through the stages of a funnel from random or occasional use, to increasing use, to habitual use, to paying for your content, products or services, to recommending your brand and content to others. Use the same step-by-step funnel approach to maximize the value of your audience to advertisers. Do this through the focused use of data and analytics, technology, content and platform tactics, multiple types and approaches of "offers" and "asks," and continuous testing.

2. Why this is Table Stakes

a) Audiences want and need well told, trusted local news and information — but have lost the habit of paying for it

People of all ages want and need the *local* news and information required to (1) be informed citizens in the places they live; (2) make good choices about the necessities in their lives (e.g. finding jobs, locating affordable homes or apartments, choosing among education options for their kids and/or themselves); and, (3) enhance the quality of their lives beyond necessities (e.g. where to eat, where to dance, where to play). Audiences also value well-told stories that provide context for staying informed.

This is true even of "millennials," a generation wrongly labeled apathetic and disconnected. In 2015, for example, API reported that 85% of millennials say keeping up with the news is important to them, 69% get news every day, and 45% say they follow five or more "hard news" topics.

Audiences still trust local news organizations. Pew, for example, reports in 2016 that 82% of folks say they trust the information they get from local news organizations, a number higher than national news organizations, friends and family, and social media news sources.

Yet, beyond the declining number of mostly older print subscribers, audiences have lost the habit of paying for news content. Too many consumers believe that 'if the news is important, it will find me.' Many (not all) consumers of all ages do understand that information is not cost free to create; and, that news enterprises need revenue to pay employees to create, produce, market, distribute, sell and otherwise support quality journalism. Many — again not all — express a willingness to pay for local news. And 40% of millennials do pay for some forms of news products and services. Still, today's audiences have zillions of choices — *including one another through social* — for where to get news. And, they have more than decade of experience of not having to pay.

b) Engaged audiences create more and better opportunities for higher value local advertising and sponsorship

High volume, scale strategies that convert digital dimes and mobile pennies into big revenue streams are not possible for metro, local or regional news enterprises who cannot escape their geographic footprints. But reaching *more* of the *relevant* people locally opens doors to more lucrative advertising and sponsorship. The ability to offer local businesses access to the specific, engaged audiences those businesses seek — especially when you can provide rich data about those audiences — is the central competitive advantage a metro news organization can provide when it comes to advertising.

One example: The Star Tribune's sponsorship package with TCF Bank for its special Vikings season subscription, which the Strib wove into its Vikings coverage, is a unique value proposition to TCF and delivered meaningful new revenue:

c) Revitalizing the habit to pay for content — as well as attracting and engaging the audiences advertisers seek to reach — are tough jobs in a media-scape cluttered with high numbers of options and platforms

Ben Thompson, who writes the *Stratechery* blog (link: https://stratechery.com/), illustrates the difference between yesteryear's simple market context for metros versus today's complex and difficult one:

Balcony View: From oligopoly to competitive market structure

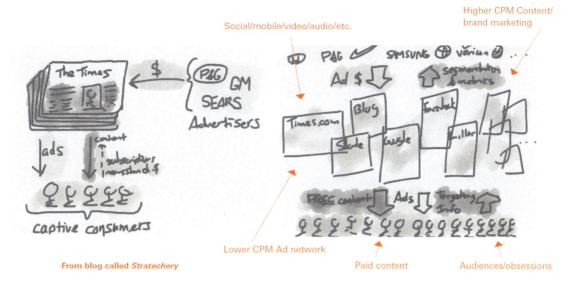

From blog called *Stratechery*

Pay particular attention to the ellipsis — the "…" — following the content providers Ben has in his sketched rectangles. That "…" is more than just "et cetera." It arguably indicates 'to infinity' because it is impossible to count the number of content providers vying for those seeking news and information.

On top of which, here's what's missing from Ben's picture: the myriad platforms and devices through which consumers get news and information as well as the rapid migration across those devices and platforms. Today, 72% of Americans say they get news via mobile devices and of those who get news on both desktop/laptop and mobile devices, more (56% to 42%) prefer mobile. Further, 62% of Americans get news on social media, dominated by Facebook. Digital news discovery is more push (it finds you) than pull (you seek it out). Similarly, consumers often have less loyalty to specific news brands.

The shift in news consumption dynamics is clear. Users have more options and more sources to get news, and *no longer have the same need to seek it out let alone pay for it.*

Moreover, in a social/mobile world dominated by powerful platforms (Facebook and others), it's more difficult than ever to connect user behavior to news enterprise economics. It's not just the shift to social/mobile — it is also the question of whether any particular user clicks on a link and goes to the news enterprise site — or doesn't click on that link and stays in, say, Facebook. Or, even more difficult, stays in Facebook or another platform because the platform's rules require that. If audiences don't leave Facebook/others, then how do creators of that news monetize content?

d) Only today's metro newsrooms in collaboration with technology and tool-building colleagues and partners can attract and retain the audiences that pay for content and are desired by advertisers — no one else can do this

In today's digital context, the objectives of circulation and distribution have moved into the newsroom. *They are now the newsroom's job to get done.* In the print era, circulation, marketing and distribution had the job of ensuring consumers paid for content. This is still true today for the platform we call 'newspapers.' But, all that changes when audiences seek digital as opposed to printed content. As described in Table Stakes 1, 2 and 3, metro *newsrooms — along with technology colleagues —* must hold themselves accountable for serving targeted audiences with targeted content (TS#1), publishing on the platforms used by chosen audiences (TS#2), and producing and publishing continuously (TS#3) to meet audience needs for local news, information and connectedness.

Even these three Table Stakes, though, are not enough to get in the game of today's multiplatform, digital realities. Newsrooms also must actively and aggressively hold themselves accountable for building new audiences, deeply engaging audiences they already have, and re-introducing audiences to the lost habit of paying for content. Yes, folks beyond the newsroom must join in this effort: marketing, publishers, and especially technology and so forth. Those efforts, though, cannot succeed in the face of newsrooms whose journalists fail to go beyond traditional notions of reporting and editing. Newsrooms must create such great local news experiences that local audiences are convinced to pay for (and recommend) their content and products, through delightful user experiences, valuable benefits/features/functions/utility, important community services and more. Further, newsrooms must play a key role in finding additional ways to derive revenue from the audiences they build as well as show local advertisers the added value (at a higher cost) of being associated with such engaged, loyal audiences.

e) Time — accelerated by deteriorating economics — is running out

No enterprise of any kind — no nonprofit, no governmental enterprise, and no private sector enterprise — can exist without cash to pay for operations as well as innovation. For metro, local and regional news enterprises this needed cash is declining at alarming rates

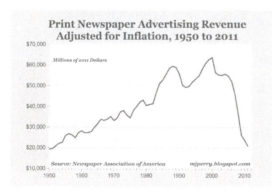 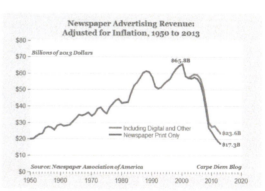

U.S. print advertising revenue plummeted from 2000-present (above left), and losses aren't close to being offset by digital advertising gains (above right). Further print circulation declines have been dramatic since the early 2000s (next page).

Source: Editor & Publisher, NAA
© Statista 2016

3. Assessing the gaps in your newsroom

Ask folks in the newsroom to use this assessment — then meet together to compare answers on individual items and overall scores.

		YES	NO
1.	Some of our newsroom staff believe the job of attracting and retaining paying users belongs outside the newsroom.		
2.	Some of our newsroom staff believe the job of attracting and retaining the audiences attractive to advertisers belongs outside the newsroom.		
3.	We have reporters and editors who do not understand the audience 'segmentation' and funnel methods for audience development.		
4.	We don't know how many total digital news consumers there are in our local market.		
5.	We do not know the total size of any audiences we are targeting that reach beyond our local market.		

	YES	NO
6. We do not know how many of our potential customers we reach currently.		
7. Less than all of our staff have easy, actionable access to the data and analytics needed to reach, attract, retain and engage our target audiences.		
8. We do not know how many users experience our products, services and/or content in any given month, and/or how that number is trending.		
9. We do not have a clear picture of how users find, use and experience our content, products and services.		
10. We lack a clear and shared definition for the loyalty of our digital audiences.		
11. We don't know how many of our digital audiences are loyal users.		
12. Not all of our reporters and editors understand and use tactics that are effective at making our digital content 'stickier.'		
13. We don't know the conversion rates for users — that is, what percent go from random to habitual users and what percent of habitual convert to subscribers. And we don't know how those rates are trending.		
14. We don't know whether (or to what degree) we're delivering the audiences most valuable to advertisers.		
15. Our newsroom lacks a continuous test-and-learn culture and related habits/skills.		
16. We do not routinely set and hold reporters, editors and others in the newsroom accountable for audience growth and engagement.		
17. We do not have a widely understood and practiced process for experimentation followed by implementation of ideas that work.		
TOTAL		

4. Why these gaps exist

a) In the print era, audiences had no choice. Now they do.

Audiences had limited choices among newspapers, TV, radio and magazines for news and information during the long history of the monopolistic (or oligopolistic) market positions of metro, local and regional newspapers. Now they have zillions of choices.

You know this. You know this from your own lives as consumers of news. You know this because you've watched a decade of explosive growth in choices available to news and information seekers. You know this because it has been written about and worried over for a long time now.

If you don't know this, you're living in a cave.

b) It is only now dawning on newsrooms that they and their technology and tool-building colleagues — not circulation — are accountable for building and engaging with audiences

Many metro news organizations have been late getting into the new game, and only now recognize how essential it is to build digitally based subscriptions and pay for content approaches. For them, building digital loyalty is a new thing.

Often, the role of audience development in the digital era has been no one's job. As digital has evolved, many people in many functions have grown concerned with pieces of the funnel but no one or no one group has clear accountability. It was simpler when circulation was a standalone function.

Yet, digital audience development is not something newspaper circulation people know how to do — or even could do if they did know how. Circulation folks are excellent at marketing, pricing, selling, renewing and otherwise serving print subscribers. Some of that experience is relevant to attracting and retaining audiences who pay for digital content — for example, marketing, pricing and renewal approaches and tactics. But only in the broadest sense because converting occasional digital users into habitual and paying ones doesn't happen through such tried and true circulation approaches like direct mail. Instead, it demands an every day, every moment engagement supported by data and analytics. And, that engagement is the responsibility of the newsroom — not circulation. Only the newsroom — the folks who create, publish and deliver the consumer experience — can succeed or fail at what spells the difference between usage and payment versus neither.

And, in some ways, circulation's experience and know-how can get in the way. Steve Yeager, Minneapolis' head of marketing, points out that the complex number of differing pricing and renewal options used for paper subscribers are entirely inappropriate in a digital context that must be user-friendly. He notes that the Star Tribune has dozens upon dozens of different offers compared to Netflix, which has just a handful.

c) Newsrooms lack the *basic orientation and language* of serving — and *selling* to — audiences first and foremost

The long history of the divide separating editorial and content from the business side enforced a clear division of labor in news enterprises. During the mid-to-late 20th century, generations of journalists learned — and conscientiously handed down to successors — a paramount principle that they were not and should not concern themselves with commercial matters.

This has shifted over the past decade. The walls are coming down. Younger journalists are more likely to understand that the difficult economics of journalism require everyone working together to figure out how to attract revenues to pay for their jobs. Still, the *required, basic orientation is new: serving audiences through identifying and delivering against audience needs is first, foremost and paramount*.

Decades of craft and practice militated against this orientation. It is no surprise, then, that part of the print legacy expresses itself through journalists who think and at times declare:

"We, not readers, know what's important, what constitutes news and what's necessary for democracy to function."

"We cannot and should not pander to audiences."

"I'm a journalist. Not a sales person."

"Audiences are, sad to say, stupid. Not always. But often."

Compare folks who work on American automobile assembly lines. Throughout the 1970s to 1990s, numerous books and articles pinned declining sales of American-made cars in part to worker attitudes — attitudes born and fostered from prior decades of oligopoly, of consumers just not having that much choice. Beginning in the 1990s, though, attitudes began to shift ("At Ford, Quality is Job #1") as workers realized their jobs and livelihoods depended on making cars that made customers happy.

The shift in autoworker attitudes was largely sufficient to the task at hand. For newsrooms, though, the shifts are more difficult because, unlike autoworkers, newsrooms directly serve and sell to consumers every day.

Along with rooting out and forbidding any commercial orientation, the church/state divide also precluded journalists from learning the basic language of service, sales and, indeed, the industry in which they work. Each of the four Knight Temple Table Stakes newsrooms, for example, had folks who did not understand what "CPM", "UX", funneling, A/B testing, EBITDA and other essential words and concepts mean.

In addition, sometimes the same word had a different meaning to the newsroom versus marketing and sales. For example, Robyn Tomlin of Dallas notes that 'product' means an advertising unit to ad sales while to some folks in the newsroom it means a content-tailored offering designed to meet specific needs of customers.

d) Newsrooms trail in having the *individual as well as institutional skills* to serve — and sell — to audiences

The Knight Temple Table Stakes effort — indeed, this entire report — address the gaps in newsroom skills — both individual and institutional — required to be in the game. It is worth teasing out the distinction between individual and institutional shortfalls. For an example of individual skills, look at the description for a fully skilled reporter in the Chapter entitled "Shaping The Right Staff Roles And Skills For Your Newsroom."

Institutional skills, in contrast, reflect capabilities required of the enterprise, not just individuals themselves. For example, news enterprises do not have a long or rich history at being institutionally skilled at fundamental innovation: experimenting in disciplined ways with identifying, testing and, if successful, rolling out dramatically new and different ways of doing things. This sort of fundamental innovation differs from continuous improvement — tweaks at the margins.

Institutional capabilities also reflect the blend of human effort with technology. Today's metro news enterprises, for example, too often make it difficult for audiences to be loyal. Slow, cumbersome load times, poorly designed, hard to navigate web or mobile sites, poor integration with social media: overcoming these depend on people and technology performing in ways audiences expect. And, as discussed throughout this report, newsrooms are only now building the data and analytics required for the organization to get good at attracting, engaging, retaining, and monetizing users.

Further, news enterprises have historically emphasized transactions over relationships and customer solutions. Print subscriptions are transactions — you pick the subscription package you want and pay for what you get. The same for print advertising — sell off the rate card for ad size and placement (and now programmatic which is purely transactional). Neither encompasses the kind of ongoing relationships and/or solution problem solving required.

And newsrooms in particular have historically ignored the customer experience. Newsrooms have gotten better thinking about user experience (UX) for a particular platform, but this is still a platform-by-platform approach and not the total customer experience across platforms and across time.

e) Newsrooms lack tech solutions to do it right

In addition to skill limitations, newsrooms have technology limitations that get in the way of using a funnel to convert random users into paying loyalists. Too many newsrooms have far less data about users — individually and in the aggregate — than is required. Tools — like those that help manage user identity (good registration systems across devices/platforms/products) or serve targeted messages (notifications, digital marketing, etc.) — are often inadequate. And most news organizations struggle to connect these various tools and user data into usable approaches (where print, email, registration, and site cookie data, for example, are all in one useful CRM/database).

5. What success looks and feels like

Systematically moving users through an audience funnel requires different skills and mindsets. Success looks and feels like the "to" side of the following:

FROM > TO view of success for funneling occasional users to loyalists

FROM	TO
We don't align business and journalistic goals	Everyone in our enterprise shares common measures of success including, for example, digital subscriptions and maximizing digital ad revenue via such things as higher average eCPMs

FROM	TO
We do not use any funnel approach at all	We have and use multiple variations on funnel approaches reflecting differing contexts and objectives
We use little or no data, or listen to the *wrong* data	Our newsroom is focused on useful, actionable performance indicators and we track progress over time We collect, utilize and routinely gain actionable insights about audiences: who they are, what they want/need, what makes them come back, what makes them tick (and click), and how to serve them best
We don't listen to users or use design thinking	Our newsroom embraces user feedback through usability testing, qualitative research (like focus groups and informal listening posts), and quantitative feedback like survey results Our newsroom understands and uses design thinking — an approach that puts the customer at the center in order to identify and solve customer problems
We have a "build it and they will come" mindset	Our newsroom is constantly building, tweaking, revising our product offerings, distribution models, outreach efforts, and how best to reach our target audiences
We don't test	Our newsroom has a rigorous and efficient test-and-learn mentality in everything we create
We don't integrate digital marketing and ecommerce thinking into the design, user experience and functionality of our products	Our enterprise functions less like Newspaper.com and more like Spotify: where programming, product, marketing and design work together in harmony to reach common goals
We perform below the minimum threshold required to meet digital audience expectations for such UX things as load times, site navigability and stickiness, etc.	We meet and exceed the minimum threshold required to meet digital audience expectations for such UX things as load times, site navigability and stickiness, etc.
We reach too limited a number of news and information hungry members of our community	We reach a significant portion of our prospective audience where they are and when they're there, including social platforms, other media, and our own products and services

FROM	TO
We do a lackluster job of encouraging loyalty among our audience(s)	We convert a significant portion of our audience(s) into heavily engaged and loyal users
We do a lackluster job of converting loyalists into paying digital subscribers Rates at which our richly engaged users convert to paying customers fall well below digital standards of 3 to 5%	Our newsroom successfully converts a significant portion of our heavily engaged users into paying subscribers Rates at which our richly engaged users convert to paying customers meet or exceed digital standards of 3 to 5%
We neither set — nor learn from — objectives for each stage of the funnel	We set goals for each stage of the funnel in order to convert our users to the next stage (and ultimately paying for content) as well as to maximize advertising revenues for each stage We actively review, draw out lessons and adjust goals based on those lessons for what works and why

6. Actions to close the gaps

This section describes the key steps required to funnel occasional users into habitual and paying loyalists, including:

a) Learn what the funneling approach is and how each step in the audience funnel is defined in terms of actions and objectives
b) Customize the funnel approach to your news enterprise's context, strategy and goals for different audience segments
c) Match the steps you take to the actions you hope the audience will take
d) Identify ways to seed/earn/increase revenue at each stage of the funnel, from the first stage to the last while also shaping/using different funnels for different purposes
e) Continually experiment to improve results
f) Recognize that, for any given user, the journey through the funnel may not be linear

a) Learn what the funneling approach is and how each step in the audience funnel is defined in terms of actions and objectives

The funnel approach is not new. Many industries and businesses use funneling to achieve marketing, sales and other objectives. While the specifics of particular applications vary, the essential steps in the funnel are a progression of *steps taken by the audience — by the potential customer/user*.

Here's a high-level and general example of a funnel based on the desired customer actions:

- **Awareness:** I have heard of the particular product/service/brand in question. I may not know everything there is to know about it, but I'm aware of it. Illustration: When asked if I'm familiar with a brand of mobile devices, I say, "Yes, I've heard of the iPhone."

- **Experience:** I have tried the product/service. Illustration: "I have used an iPhone."

- **Preference:** If I am given a choice, I choose one particular product/service over a competitor — or a similar product/service. Illustration: "I prefer the iPhone to Samsung Galaxy" — "I prefer using mobile devices to desktops."

- **Purchase/Loyalty:** I purchase and stick with a particular brand. Illustration: I own an iPhone. When new phones come out, I stick with iPhones. For example, when my cell plan ends and there's a three-week delay on getting a new iPhone — and Samsung is offering a 50% off sale today — I still wait for the iPhone.

- **Advocacy/promotion:** I actively promote the brand to people in my life. Illustration: I tell everyone I know about the superiority of the iPhone compared with any other device. In effect, I am an extension of Apple's public relations, marketing and sales folks.

Notice these stages describe a funnel — at each step, the number of people is higher than at the succeeding step. More people are aware of iPhones than have experienced them. More people have experienced iPhones than prefer them. More people prefer iPhones than purchase and remain loyal to them. And, more people are loyal to iPhones than actively advocate and promote them.

News enterprises need to adjust this generic industry funnel for the realities of digital contexts and audience behaviors. For example, iPhone users typically purchase before advocating and promoting. Ditto for cars, beverages, restaurants, insurance, mutual funds, bicycles, and on and on. In comparison, audiences who have great experiences with news and information — and make use of social platforms — regularly 'like' things without purchasing them first. Which means the last two stages of this generic funnel can happen in either order: that is, users might purchase and then recommend; or, they might recommend before purchasing.

The objective is to seek the highest possible yield from each step to the next. Also, note that the funnel approach does not stop with a purchase. In a world now dominated by social and mobile, brands must have as many advocates/promoters as possible while also worrying about the reverse — about folks who detract or bad mouth the brand, product or service in question.

For example, consider one of the most popular approaches to brand loyalty that's called a 'net promoter score' in which consumers are asked about the intensity with which they either promote or detract from a brand, product or service. In this approach, only the most intense responses count — the most positive ("promoters") and the most negative ("detractors"). The Net Promoter Score is calculated from research that asks one simple question: "Would you recommend (fill in the blank brand, service, or product) to a friend or colleague?" It's a 0-10 scale, with 0-6 being evidence of an active detractor, 7-8 being neutral, and 9-10 indicating an advocate. Typically, when calculated, the mid-range of responses is ignored. Instead, the number of intense detractors is subtracted from the number of intense supporters — yielding a number that is either positive because promoters outnumber detractors (good) or negative because detractors outnumber promoters (bad).

Your funnel approach must be specific to your strategy and context. You can start with this simple yet powerful set of objectives regarding digital consumers:

> Get them to come
> Get them to stay
> Get them to pay

With that in mind, you must tailor the funnel to your circumstances. For example, here is a slightly more nuanced funnel that builds on these basic objectives:

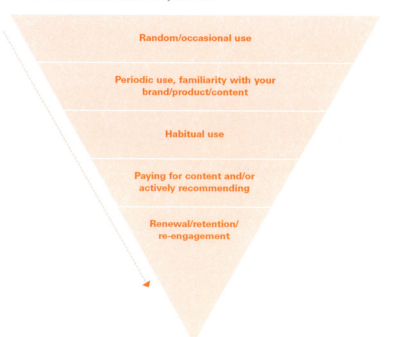

Note that the stages are described in terms of user actions:

- **Random/occasional use:** Users who visit your site(s)[1] for the first time, or from time-to-time.

- **Periodic use and brand familiarity:** Users who experience your site(s) periodically and have reasonable knowledge of what you offer.

- **Regular, habitual use:** Users who have developed a routine of visiting your site(s).

[1] Note that this funnel pertains to your site. You need to use the funneling approach broadly — that is, for sites, newsletters, apps, live events — or any product, service or set of desirable consumer/user actions.

- **Paying for content and actively recommending your content to others:** Users who subscribe, join, contribute or otherwise support you financially and/or advocate on your behalf.

- **Retention:** Long-term loyalty in the form of renewing and/or continually engaging over long periods of time

You and your colleagues should discuss and agree on the set of user actions you desire — then, the actions you can take to maximize the odds that those user actions happen.

b) Customize the funnel approach to your news enterprise's context, strategy and goals for different audience segments

Your newsroom along with others in your enterprise (e.g. marketing and technology) must apply the funneling approach to fit your unique context, strategy and goals for different audience segments.

Segmentation means dividing a broad group of your audience into sub-groups who have shared characteristics. It is essential to Table Stake #1's requirement to serve targeted content to targeted — that is segmented — audiences. Identifying the unique needs and interests of a different audience segment is enormously helpful to moving those segments through the funnel.

Minneapolis used behavior and usage patterns to identify four audience segments: grazers, test drivers, intenders, and subscribers[2]. They know what traits separate the segments (for example, referral source, page depth, how recent visits are, frequency of visits). They know how many users are in each group. And they use these segments to choose the actions Minneapolis takes.

2

Your segments may be different. And you might use Star-Tribune-like segments for subscriptions but different segments for a niche product or service such as events.

Audience: Segmentation strategy

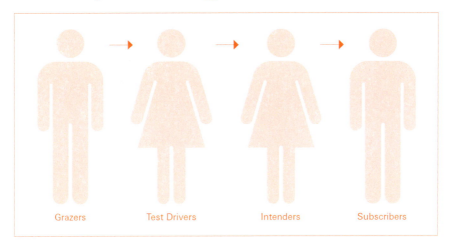

Minneapolis' objectives are: (1) to optimize user experiences at each stage of the funnel; (2) maximize the value to the Strib from user actions at each stage; and, (3) increase yields from one stage to the other all the way to the biggest payoff of all: digital subscriptions. Goals differ for different segments. For example, the objective with grazers is to monetize via advertising and recirculation (e.g. encouraging one more article view) while the objective for intenders is to convert them into subscribers.

Minneapolis works hard to continuously get better at figuring out what actions trigger desired user behaviors *within each segment*, especially those behaviors through which users progress through the funnel. These tactics included logins, newsletter sign ups, social follows, ad experience, what kind of content focus, and trial access. Dallas also uses newsletters in one of its funnel approaches. That effort, though, is directed at attracting and converting social users into digital subscribers.

User engagement funnel drivers

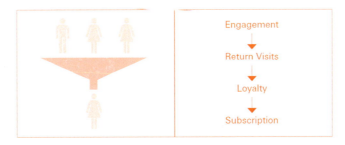

Here is how Robyn Tomlin of Dallas described this funnel approach:

1. When new users come to the website via a social referral — we prioritize the messaging they get on the article page to try to get them to "like" us on FB:

2. When users come back and visit the site a couple more times, we prioritize a request for a slightly deeper level of engagement — the newsletter signup.
3. When users sign up for the newsletter and/or continue to return, we prioritize a digital subscription pitch.

c) Match the steps you take to the actions you hope the audience will take

Like Minneapolis, you and your colleagues must get better every day at what makes the funnel effective. That means embracing a continuous cycle of choose-act-learn.

Here are steps you can take at each stage of a funnel to encourage users to move to the next stage of the funnel, and so forth. It's imperative that you discuss these in advance to (1) make sure the particular suggestions make sense for your context and strategy; and, (2) make sure you and your colleagues understand the nature and purpose of the steps themselves.

1) Random/occasional user

The first step in the audience funnel is 'to get them to come" — to attract to your site(s) as many potential users from your target audiences as possible (see Table Stake #1).

Begin by recalling Table Stake #1's requirement to focus on specific, target audiences as opposed to the 'general public.' Different approaches are required to attract different kinds of audiences to the top of the funnel. For example, steps that you take to reach high school sports fans and supporters will differ from those you use to reach luxury real estate buyers.

Users in your target audiences might come to the top of your funnel because (1) they know your brand; (2) they link through social platforms; (3) they link from search; and/or, (4) they come via distribution partnerships you have with others. Consider, then:

- **Social platforms.** First, revisit Table Stake #2 to explore choices for which social platforms to use as well as setting your objectives for the ones chosen. Remember to distinguish your own social platforms versus those controlled by others — and, within the latter, those that link back to your site versus those that don't.

  Once you have selected social platforms to use, here are considerations for using trial-and-error, test-and-learn approaches to attract users to the top of your funnel:

  — *Timing*: Time your posts to match user patterns and rhythms on the platform in question (versus, say, your print deadlines)

  — *Mobile*: Social and mobile go hand-in-hand. The form and style of your content must fit the mobile platform (versus, say, merely redirecting text from a print article)

  — *Visual*: Visuals often attract users better than pure text

  — *Tone*: Social content does better when presented in the language of the social medium — when the tone presents your brand with a distinctive social voice

  — *Platform specifics*: Each social platform has its own specific advantages and approaches. For example, on Twitter, you will attract more users by tagging influencers, geo-targeting, using mentions and hashtags, and joining into conversations when you/your site are mentioned. Meanwhile, social platform algorithms continually evolve and change. For example, in 2016, Facebook de-emphasized publisher posts in favor of those from friends and family — making it more important than ever to have your content be shareable while also thinking hard about encouraging others to post on your behalf.

— *Archives*: Many users appreciate and engage with the context made possible by your archives. For example: The Atlantic has had more than half of traffic in a given month come from using archival stories to put news into context

- **Search.** Search, dominated by Google, drives referral traffic. You can use search engine optimization (SEO) and search engine marketing (SEM) to make it easier for your target audiences to find your site(s):

    SEO

    — Know where you rank on key search terms, including the name of your city and any other important identifiers
    — Consistently improve your search standing with SEO best practices, including site speed and page load times, tagging, image quality, inbound and outbound links, etc.

    SEM

    — Use ongoing SEM to promote your brand and key products/services
    — Boost visibility during peak traffic periods (big breaking news, city events, major enterprise reporting projects, etc.)

- **Distribution partnerships.** You can partner with others to drive traffic to one another's site(s). For example, you might experiment with:

- Partnering with other sites in your market such as local businesses, trade groups, fan sites and more in order to increase the visibility of your brand as well as cross-linking. Such partnerships might range from simple link exchanges to full-scale joint marketing partnerships using shared email lists and co-promotion

- Sharing resources in ways that benefit one another. For example:

    - Putting your reporters on air via radio/TV partnerships with local outlets

    - Working together on projects and/or beats that deliver free promotional value to your organization

2) Periodic use and brand familiarity

Once you've attracted users to your site — you've got them to come — the next challenge is to 'get them to stay.' This requires constant test-and-learn efforts aimed at providing users compelling, easy-to-use experiences aimed at (1) keeping them on your site; (2) revisiting your site; and, (3) increasing the odds the users take actions that are useful to them and to you. Here are thought starters:

- **Deliver acceptable user experience (UX):** Consider, for example, speed. *Data consistently shows a wait time of three seconds causes a high abandonment rate.* Yet, most metro news sites are way too slow — for example, according to one report[3], the average load time for U.S. newspaper sites was 17 seconds. Audiences will not return to a site that's aggravatingly difficult to load, particularly on mobile devices. Fixing this problem can have a major effect on the retention step in the funnel. There's a direct correlation between page load time and business performance[4], in addition to the obvious benefits to the user experience. The Washington Post, for example, cut page load times by 85 percent and saw an immediate benefit to audience growth[5].

[3]

Barrett Golding, *"Need for Speed 3"*, Reynolds Journalism Inst (November 23, 2015)

[4]

Martin Lugton, "Why Page Load Speed Is Important", martinlugton.com (June 28, 2015)

[5]

Ricardo Bilton, "How The Washington Post Cut Its Page Load By Time 85%", Digiday (July 16, 2015)

- **Consider email because it is, in many ways, a perfect news delivery and marketing mechanism combined:**

    - It's personal. Delivered directly to you from a brand you know/trust.
    - You can adjust the tone — for example, make the emails conversational.
    - You have many options: daily digest, weekly summary, breaking/developing, topic-based (RSS or curated, always-on or story with legs), author-based, etc.
    - It's on-demand. The timing and frequency of use is in the consumer's hands.
    - It's flexible in terms of customer choices. For example, when a customer considers unsubscribing, you can provide options such as decreasing frequency or switching to another email product

- **Invest in conversations both online and off:**

    - Encourage comments and participate in the conversation online. Consider steps you can take to participate in and move conversations forward, perhaps using real identity rules to keep civility high, and (occasionally) curating comments/conversations to summarize and shed light on important topics and issues.
    - Connect virtual online dialogue to the real-world connections with live events built around news and/or issues or topics of interest to your target audiences.
    - Experiment and learn-by-doing with offering audiences access to conversations with newsmakers, topic-based panels, ideas, festivals — and other ways of using your brand's convening power.

- **Encourage registration and login:** Registration is key to success at funneling. Without registration, it's difficult to get accurate and actionable data about your users. With it, you can create a better, more personal experience and shape content of greater interest — all grounded in what you learn about users.

Registration also helps boost subscription conversion rates and the sale of more targeted, higher CPM advertising. Consider:

— Giving your audience reasons to register — such as access to better features like on-site personalization or in-person event attendance, standard features like commenting or email newsletters, new features like beta releases, or additional access like increased meter count for those with metered subscription models.
— Making registration frictionless by minimizing the steps and information/data needed (for example, perhaps require only an email address and (maybe) password).
— Defer additional data requests until later. Users tend to get more comfortable providing additional information (like title or address) after they gain more familiarity through more frequent use.

3) Regular, habitual use

Convert periodic users into regular, habitual users by engaging them to increase *how often* and *how deeply* they experience your content, products and services. *You want them to become hooked.* Here are thought starters:

- **Onboarding.** When users register, make sure their first post-registration experience — how they onboard — is rewarding. Welcome them as members of a club, introduce them to site/app features and functionality, and remind them about the amazing content and tools they now have at their disposal.

- **Navigation** techniques to keep users on your site. Whether users arrive at a story page (typically the case for social and search) or your home page, article-to-article linkages, your own or other users' content recommendations, and 'infinite,' easy-to-scroll actions are all supremely important.

- **Personalization.** The more you customize a user's experience to fit their needs and interests, the more likely they are to regularly use your site(s). The spectrum of personalization options range from simply highlighting/recommending stories based on a user's past consumption all the way to entirely customizing the content and options provided based in a blend of user stated preferences and past behavior/usage.

- **Notifications.** Remember that it's key for you to go to your audiences and not just wait for them to come to you. Notifications are a powerful way to do this. Whether through apps, the desktop, email or other means, make sure to alert registered users about trending or breaking stories as well as content or features that serve their interests and needs.

- **Interactivity** (including gamification/game mechanics). Interactivity by its nature keeps users engaged — such things as quizzes, data-driven discovery, prompts to 'learn more' and so forth. Indeed, you might ask users themselves to provide anecdotes or data as part of building/exploring an ongoing story. Games and gamification of content/experience are another form of this. To work, though, you must tailor content and approaches in ways that provide users a clear purpose and a goal to pursue and deliver value to users who participate/play.

4) Paying for content and actively recommending your content to others.

You have got them to come and got them to stay. Now you must get them to pay — to commit to, and become advocates for, your brand.

Here are thought starters:

- **Purchase/paying.** In contrast to attracting and retaining subscribers to a newspaper, the newsroom working with marketing and/or consumer revenue folks (not circulation) must convert users to payers. This is the case whether your news enterprise depends on digital subscriptions, newsletter subscriptions, crowd funding resources, event ticket sales or other means by which users of your content financially support that content.

    It also matters for more nuanced steps you need users to take — e.g. giving you data. Data is essential to a variety of revenue opportunities at *each stage of the funnel*, including advertising and subscriptions but also such things as events, special offers, convening and others. Data on a specific user, via registration or signing up for an email newsletter or pulling from a social graph, helps create a pipeline for revenue in other areas. Similarly, even non-registered users can have a wealth of data (via the site cookie) that can be useful for all sorts of monetization options. For example, knowing a user's site consumption patterns (reads a lot of stories about public education issues) and geography (lives in a certain part of town) can allow you to target that user with information about an upcoming education event in their area via on-site messaging.

So, you should stay aware that, even absent a pay model, data is a form of 'payment' you require in exchange for what you offer.

Whether it's money/payment or data, though, it is table stakes for the newsroom to hold themselves accountable for results. Marketing and technology play key roles. Through such activities as advertising and public relations, marketing folks can help communicate and sell the benefits users gain when they pay. Marketing folks can also help with pricing as well as A/B testing design. And, technology folks are essential to insure that your news enterprise delivers a user experience (UX) that matches or exceeds user expectations.

- **Recommending/advocating.** Content differs from, say, cars and mutual funds because your users who have great experiences — especially loyal, habitual users — can and will refer, promote and advocate to friends and others without necessarily purchasing. Word of mouth matters — and is more likely to happen when you create and deliver indispensable content and experiences that your users believe strongly help them connect with others. And, you might stimulate all this with various refer-a-friend tactics — for example, looking to your data to identify habitual users, then offering those users discounts or special deals or opportunities in exchange for friend referrals. You can and should also just ask: TheSkimm, for example, uses a tried-and-true fitness gym tactic, by creating a Skimmbassador program to acknowledge users who have signed up a certain number of friends as email subscribers.

Shares on social, of course, are an essential way to track who and how often your users recommend and advocate on your behalf. The net promoter score described earlier is an additional approach to measuring this.

5) Retention

Once you have folks paying for your content, you need to keep them doing so. This is common sense but also supported by research and experience in industry after industry: *the value of a paying customer far exceeds the value of a prospective paying customer.* The newsroom (along with help from marketing and technology) must focus on:

- **Renewal.** Ensuring that everything that can be done is done to convince paid supporters to continue paying. There are many tactical steps from a digital marketing and digital product perspective to consider (billing, customer service, save-the-stop initiatives, etc.) but also opportunities to provide new content/product/services as incentives to renew. For example: At The New York Times, the most loyal subscribers were offered access to beta products and insider events.
- **Re-engagement.** Ensuring that loyal users who show signs of disengagement are pulled back into the fold. For example: When data shows a user is trending down in email open rates or number of return visits to the site, a "come back to us" email message may be appropriate. The onboarding steps described earlier can apply when you're starting to lose a consumer, too. Use similar tactics to re-engage folks whose loyalty (based on frequency, page depth, etc.) is beginning to slip.
- **Reducing churn.** Churn is bad. It measures the turnover among paying users. For example, imagine a three-month time frame at the beginning of which you have 20,000 digital subscribers and at the end you have 21,000. If none of the 20,000 left, churn would be zero. If, on the other hand, 5,000 of those left, it means you had to gain 6,000 new subscribers just to have a 1,000

incremental gain. In that case, churn is way too high. It means your news enterprise is working far too hard basically just to stand still.

d) Identify ways to seed/earn/increase revenue at each stage of the funnel, from the first stage to the last, while shaping/using different funnels for different purposes

You and your colleagues need to tailor the funnel approach for the different strategic objectives of your enterprise. Do this in two ways:

- Make sure to maximize revenue opportunities at each stage of the funnel by connecting desired user actions to your strategy and economics. As mentioned above, for example, Minneapolis seeks advertising revenues from the actions of 'grazers' and digital subscription revenues through converting intenders into subscribers.

- Use different funnels for different purposes. Dallas has a funnel for users who arrive via social. Miami's "Food Inc" effort sought, among other things, to *get audiences to attend events*. And, Philadelphia's experiment with a data bridge sought to build shared understanding across the newsroom, marketing and sales as to which *audiences advertisers find most valuable* (that is, will pay higher CPMs to reach).

To illustrate this, consider a funnel aimed at increasing digital subscriptions:

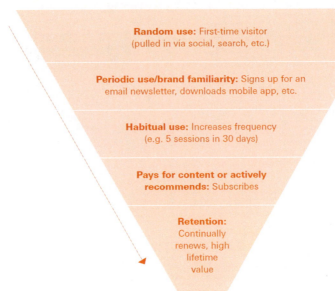

By contrast, here's what the funnel might look like for increasing the number of users who attend events:

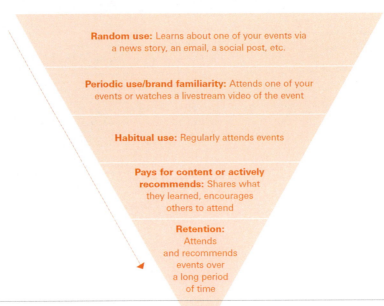

e) Continually experiment to improve results

You must identify and conduct well-designed *experiments* [6] aimed at increasing particular desired user actions that move those users through the funnel as well as link to your revenue strategies.

In Minneapolis, for example, grazers were shown higher density ad pages on mobile devices while a third-party tool (Keywee) was tested as a means to reach potential subscribers on Facebook.

> **① Audience: Funnel conversion tests**
>
> 1. "Grazers" article page on mobile and desktop: Higher density ad pages
> 2. Facebook test using KeyWee aimed at converting "test drivers" to "subscribers"
> 3. Newsletter prompt test on first visit

Dallas deployed different marketing messages linked to the number of articles a user had viewed (e.g., first-time viewers were shown "like us on social," more active users shown "sign up for an email newsletter," and heavy users shown "subscribe" calls to action.

[6] There are many tools that can help you experiment. For example, the Minneapolis Facebook test was administered by Keywee, A/B tests can be deployed via Optimizely, and subscriber messaging can be tested via Piano. There are, of course, many, many other tools and services to make your newsroom's testing possible.

f) Recognize that, for any given user, the journey through the funnel may not be linear

Users can (and often do) skip stages of the funnel, move backward, or move through the funnel at various paces. For example, some users at the top of the funnel might sign up for an email newsletter — or subscribe — even though they have limited experience with your brand or offerings. This was true at The New York Times, where, in the early days, a surprising number of digital subscribers hadn't even used the site in several months. Meanwhile, users can and do become enthusiastic recommenders at any stage. The linear path down the funnel grounds your tactics for optimizing results from linking goals for different audience segments to your strategy and economics. Still, remaining alert to non-linear user actions will help you refine and tune your strategies — and improve results.

7. Measures of success and tracking progress in closing the gaps

Funnels are their own scorecards! By setting, pursuing and monitoring performance against the specific goals for each stage of the funnel, you and your colleagues can track progress, learn what works and doesn't work, and iteration-by-iteration close your key gaps.

Performance is the primary objective of change, not change. Consider, for example, Miami's efforts to build newsroom skills. They set goals requiring all reporters to increase traffic by 7.5% — then provided the training and support to increase the odds that reporters succeeded. Dallas also made performance results (10% traffic increases plus gains in a specially designed engagement index) the primary object of skills training.

The same principle applies to funnels — and continually improving results that funnels produce. Don't just say, "Use a funnel." Instead, set and update specific goals at each stage of any particular funnel — and expect folks to learn what works versus what doesn't work through attempting to succeed at those goals.

Here, for example, are the initial goals — and benefits of those goals — that Minneapolis set for the funnel used to convert different audience segments into digital subscribers:

Segment goals

SEGMENT	GOALS	BENEFITS
Grazers	• Optimize ad revenue • Convert 5% to Test drivers	• Increased ad revenue • Increased visits/page views
Test Drivers	• Convert 5% to create a login, newsletter signup, or social follow • Convert 5% to Intenders	• 80k new login, newsletter, or social sign ups • Increased visits/page views
Intenders	• Convert 20% to create a login, newsletter signup, and/or social follow (30k) • Convert 5% to Subscribers (8k)	• 30k new login, newsletter, or social sign ups • 8k new subscribers
Subscribers	• Increase engaged time • Increase value perception • Convert 5% to additional subscriber benefits	• Increased retention • 6k new newsletter sign ups or social follows, etc.

For illustrative purposes, here's an example of a funnel that serves as a scorecard, from the nonprofit news organization CALmatters:

CALmatters digital audience funnel | Metrics to monitor

Total addressable market
- Market size: How many people should be CALmatters readers? (Ideal: one-time research; less ideal but still valid: estimate based on existing data)

Awareness: Users who know about CALmatters
- % target market unaided brand awareness (custom research, 1x/year)
- Total reach (monthly totals, print + broadcast + digital)
- Partner story pickups (volume)
- Social reach (FB + Twitter); mentions

Acquisition: Users who have experienced CALmatters
- Monthly calmatters.org users
- Segmentation by geography (in-market vs. out-of-market; within CA)
- Segmentation by referral source (search, social, partner, email, etc.)
- Relative performance analysis (what stories do "best" and why)

Activation: Users who have a "happy UX"
- New email subscribers; total email subscribers
- Event RSVPs; event attendees
- Sessions with > 1 PV; bounce rate

Retention: Loyal users (aka "stickiness")
- Habitual users (users with 5 or more sessions/mo
- Email addicts (users who open X emails/mo
- Repeat event attendees
- Social conversion rate (comments/followers × 100)

Referral: Advocates
- "Influencer" following (# of influencers in CA politics/policy who follow you)
- % of state media who publish your content
- Social amplification rate (shares/followers × 100)

Revenue: Users who contribute $$$
- Donors; repeat donors
- Revenue per user; revenue per habitual user

Mission impact
- Awareness of politics and policy issues (pre/post research)
- Civic engagement behavior score (custom research)
- "The CALmatters Effect" (impact of Capitol presence; anecdotal)
- Laws changed: Tracked policy changes due to reporting
- Lives changed: Tracked personal stories due to reporting

Through setting goals for each stage of the funnel and monitoring results, you and your colleagues will discover what steps work best for the audiences you seek to serve and the revenue and financial goals you wish to achieve. Folks at the Texas Tribune used continuous testing-and-learning, for example, to discover a strong link between event attendance and membership. When they looked at any one event in isolation, they observed only a single-digit percent of attendees became paying members. As an isolated data point, that might have caused them to conclude event attendees were not likely to join, or that there was an execution problem at converting event attendees to members. However when they looked closer at the data, *they saw that when the same folks attended at least three events, the propensity to become members rose nearly ten-fold*. This, in turn, led to a shift in tactics: Instead of a primary objective to convert one-time event attendees into members, the Texas Tribune folks instead worked hard to get those folks to attend a second — then a third — event.

Table Stakes
Number 5
Diversify and Grow the Ways You Earn Revenue from the Audiences You Build

1. The Table Stake
Diversify and grow the ways you earn revenue from the audiences you build

Innovate, test and develop as many ways as possible to gain revenue from the audiences you build, and the relationships you develop. Avoid the search for silver bullets — for *the* answer to *the* new business model. Do this by collaborating across all functions of your enterprise with a focus on innovating to grow consumer revenue and advertising as well as creating, testing and growing a range of new products, services and businesses of value to your target audiences and community.

2. Why this is Table Stakes

a) No business can survive without revenue and cash to pay for the work — an urgent challenge for metro news enterprises whose revenues and cash are declining

News organizations are not different from any enterprise in requiring cash to pay the bills. The cash coming in must equal or exceed the cash used to pay for (1) all expenses; (2) at least some investment in innovation; and, (3) any profit expectations of ownership. The same applies for nonprofit news organizations. When Philadelphia shifted to a nonprofit owner in January 2016, they eliminated profit expectations, but not the need for cash to cover expenses and innovation.

It has been a decade or more since the revenues and cash available to metros has been seriously declining.

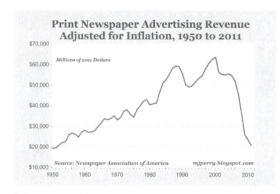
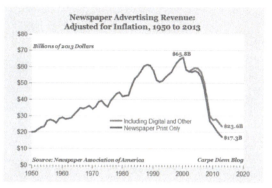

U.S. print advertising revenue plummeted from 2000-present (above left), and losses aren't close to being offset by digital advertising gains (above right). Further print circulation declines have been dramatic since the early 2000s (below).

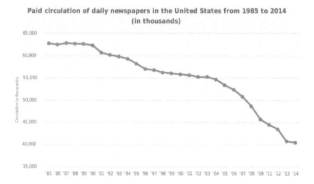

**Source: Editor & Publisher, NAA
© Statista 2016**

b) The lucrative subscription-advertising-classifieds economics of print *cannot* be duplicated digitally because of important differences in the nature and structure of digital markets, costs and revenues

Print dollars, digital dimes, mobile pennies is — or should be — well known in your news enterprise. In the print era, subscriptions, advertising and classifieds combined to produce large, unassailable pools of revenues because metro, local and regional news enterprises benefitted from oligopolistic or monopolistic market structures. They along with some others were the only game in town. People and businesses wanting to stay current with news *had few* choices but to subscribe. Businesses that wanted to advertise to local audiences *had few* choices. Individuals seeking to sell or connect with others locally through classifieds had *few choices*.

None of this characterizes contemporary, digitally mediated markets. Potential subscribers have *lots of choices* — so many indeed that they have lost the habit of paying for content. Businesses have *lots of choices* for reaching and communicating with local audiences; and, with the rise of digital data and analytics, businesses can choose more precisely and pay less for the specific audiences they wish to reach. Individuals wishing to sell something to — or connect with –others in the community have *lots of choices*, many of which are free (e.g. Craig's List).

Digital revenues, then, will never be as robust or unassailable as print revenues. *Ever*.

That is, unless any enterprise establishes a monopoly or oligopoly market position — an enterprise such as Facebook in social. Google has similar market power in search. Monopoly and oligopoly are lucrative. No surprise, then, that Facebook and Google have so quickly dominated advertising revenues.

These shifts in market structure are well documented. What is less understood are the differences between print and digital in

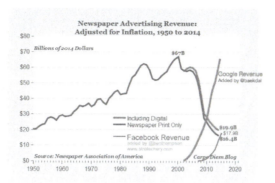

(1) the nature and structure of costs; and, (2) the relationship between cost and revenue.

Go back, say, to the late 90s and think about what folks in metro news enterprises knew at the beginning of each year regarding costs — namely, that it took a lot of money for printing plants, presses, and trucks as well as sizeable newsrooms filled with journalists and the circulation, distribution, marketing and sales staffs responsible for revenues.

The bulk of these costs were set. The challenge was generating enough subscription, advertising and classified revenues to pay for the set costs and generate returns to the owners — which, given strong market positions, was straightforward to do and do so profitably.

Costs were large, set and predictable. Revenues were large and predictable.

This changed with digital. *Digital revenues for metros fighting to compete with so many other players are tiny, fluid and unpredictable*. Yet, digital-related costs — e.g. for technology and tools — are not tiny. Though smaller than, say, printing plants, the costs for such things as content management systems are not trivial. They can be fluid and unpredictable though (for example, how often do you contemplate a new CMS with even better functions and features?)

Moreover, in the print era, *costs were newspaper-related and revenues were newspaper-related*. Profitability was simple to understand. Metros paid for costs that went into publishing the newspaper. Metros generated revenues from the newspaper. It was apples-to-apples: newspaper costs related to newspaper revenues.

Not so today. Consider the newsroom. In the web's early days, some folks imagined that digital teams would repurpose print content. Had that worked, the revenues of digital could have offset the extra costs for those who digitally repurposed content.

In other words, digital costs would relate to digital revenues in the same straightforward way as print costs related to print revenue: oranges-to-oranges (digital) to go along with apples-to-apples (print).

This didn't work out as expected. As the industry's experience and this entire report show, content for digital audiences cannot simply be repurposed from print. Instead, folks must work hard to create and publish content in ways that are tailored for digital audiences. The costs related to digital (oranges) and print (apples) are jumbled together. And revenues are as well (e.g. blended subscription offerings combining digital and print — apples and oranges).

"Is digital profitable?" has obsessed the industry only slightly less than "Can digital ever be profitable?" But, that is not a helpful question. It is a trap and a snare that diverts attention and effort away from the more critical, essential question: "How can we make our news enterprise profitable — or even financially and economically sustainable?"

Small, fluid and unpredictable digital revenues **cannot** cover large, set and predictable costs of print-oriented newsrooms. Digital economics cannot replicate print economics. The challenge today is how metro, local and regional news enterprises inexorably drawn into both digital and print can find as many sources of revenue as possible to pay for costs that are no longer simple to understand or manage. The only alternative to exploring and building multiple revenue sources is to *cut costs* — which eventually doesn't work.

c) Geographically circumscribed markets prevent metros from using scale-based digital strategies

Even tiny per-use, per-click digital revenues can, if multiplied across zillions of folks, add up to attractive economics. Facebook, for example, had more than 1.9 billion users in mid-2017. In contrast, Philadelphia's metros served a metropolitan area with just over 6 million people.

Six million sounds like a lot. But it's miniscule compared with Facebook. Consider any sort of yield — batting average if you will. Say, a digital effort can successfully monetize 1 out of every 100 users — a yield of 1%. Do the math. Philadelphia, even if it reaches all 6 million people, has a yield of 60,000. At a 1% yield, Facebook succeeds *19 million times*.

If the revenue generated is, say, 10 cents per success, Philadelphia reaps $6,000 while Facebook reaps $1.9 million.

Major metros such as Philadelphia, Miami, Minneapolis and Dallas have professional sports teams with fans spread across the nation. Might they pursue a scale strategy with those fans? Sure. But even if successful, they come up short in comparison with others such as ESPN that taps into unlimited digital scale because all fans of sports teams seek content at ESPN or Bleacher Report and so forth — enterprises for which geography is not a constraint.

Importantly, the benefits of social/mobile/web connectivity are available to any enterprise not geographically bound. For example, the award-winning single-topic enterprise Inside Climate News does not confront geographic barriers. Nor do *BuzzFeed, Huffington Post, the Marshall Project, CNN, NBC, ABC, The New York Times, Washington Post*, and a much longer list that grows every day.

There are exceptions for metros. Miami, for example, is the 'capital of Latin America'; and, during Table Stakes, Miami experimented with ways to take advantage of this digital scale and reach.

Importantly as described in Table Stake #6, news enterprises also can *find ways to partner with one another to reach beyond geographic boundaries*. To illustrate, imagine a handful of metros partnered on a product or service responsive to audience needs common to them — for example, say, an app that helped folks find housing. Zillow, of course, is a competitor. But, if metros partner together, they could reasonably aspire to digital reach and scale strategies that none of them alone could make happen.

Such exceptions aside, metro, local and regional publishers have no choice but to *find as many ways as possible to generate revenues locally through strategies not dependent on large digital reach and scale*.

d) Cost reductions and/or industry consolidation do not eliminate the need for revenues and cash

Revenues must exceed costs[1]. This is true even for nonprofits: unless the donations, income on endowments, major gifts along with any commercial revenues exceed the costs, the nonprofit will go out of business.

One way to ensure revenues exceed costs is to cut costs. But, you cannot cut costs to zero. At some point, costs are rock bottom and the only choice remaining is to generate revenues.

This same inexorable logic applies to industry consolidation. As Penny Abernathy reports in *"The Rise of a New Media Baron and the Emerging Threat of News Deserts,"* private equity, hedge funds, and other corporations buying up news organizations have a standard playbook of aggressive cost cutting combined with financial restructuring. For Wall Street investors, this promises attractive gains. In practice, it also can lead to what Abernathy calls 'news deserts': formerly robust newsrooms hollowed out and bereft of revenues needed to do their work.

Low-cost strategies, then, have limits. There is, though, another crucial point. Knight and Temple initiated the Table Stakes effort out of concern for the role local journalism plays in preserving and advancing democracy. That purpose demands strategies grounded in creating value for customers. Yes, value within responsible cost structures. Value-based approaches, though, require revenues and cash linked to value as opposed to relentless cost cutting.

e) The profound disruption of the early 21st century provides opportunities for metros to reinvent the value they create and reap — opportunities to generate revenues in ways that include

---

[1] The seeming exceptions to this truism are companies that seduce the capital markets into subsidizing annual losses in the hopes of reaping a big payday from selling stock. See Uber.

but go beyond subscriptions and advertising.

Solving the revenue side is *the* challenge facing metro, local and regional news enterprises in search of economic and financial sustainability. A part of the solution lies in putting audiences first — particularly local audiences — in search of as many ways as possible to attract, engage, and retain audiences who generate revenues through paying for content and/or advertising.

Digital subscriptions and advertising, though, will not suffice to cover print era costs — including the size of print era newsrooms — for metros, locals and regionals confined to geographic markets that preclude digital reach and scale strategies.

That's the bad news. The good news arises from the many opportunities emerging from the ways metro, local and regional publishers might respond to the consequences of how digital disruption has combined with widespread industrial consolidation, globalization, deregulation and other powerful forces to reshape — even blow apart — local economies and communities and how folks approach the problems and challenges of their lives *locally*.

Where do I find a job? How do I make do on a fixed income? Should we send our kids to charter schools? What are my options to get home at rush hour today? How can I help my aging parents understand Medicare options? What are my rights and my landlord's obligations to remove lead paint? What is the quality of our local water? I'm new in town and love jazz — where are the best places? My boss runs the local ACE hardware outlet and has asked me to come up with a social/mobile marketing plan. We're part of a global bank whose brand has been hit hard by a settlement for mistreating consumers — how can we overcome the negativity locally? Our hospital has to figure out how to work with folks locally to reduce the adverse effects of such social determinants of health as food deserts, poor transportation options, and little time for exercise in our schools.

These are but some of the *local* problems metros might help solve for people and organizations. For people, problems fall in five categories (1) help me/us be informed citizens in the place I/we live; (2) help me/us solve the necessities of my/our lives; (3) help me/us enhance the quality of my/our lives beyond necessities; (4) help me/us work with others to make the places we live together better; and, (5) help me/us have the confidence that you are holding powerful people and institutions accountable.

Meanwhile, enterprises from all three sectors (private, nonprofit and government) confront *local* problems across a broad range from how best to reach, market, sell and serve customers all the way to figuring out how to fulfill obligations to local communities (e.g. hospitals, schools, local government agencies and so forth).

Note in particular a major problem arising from the disruption of local communities and economies: *the deep need people have to connect with one another, especially in real life.*

The explosive growth of social media responds to the *hunger for relationships* — for *connectedness* with other people. Yet, as important as social media interactions are, they still happen virtually and not in real life. For example, Philly's chosen vision to be 'the local leader in news, information and connectedness" embraces how best to connect folks in Philadelphia to one another through shared information and news (traditional), virtual interactions (social media) and in real life.

Metros that figure out how to solve local problems confronting people and enterprises — including the need for connectedness — create value. Creating value, though, is a necessary but not sufficient condition for success. *Metros, locals and regionals also must figure out how to reap value from the value created.* And that means monetization.

Monetization must include more than the two standard solutions of legacy mindsets: consumers who subscribe to our news offerings and/or advertisers who pay to reach customers. Dallas, for example, is part of Belo's intentionally constructed ecosystem aimed at generating revenue from audience development, content marketing, events, digital optimization and other services. Miami's "Food Inc" experimented with ticket sales to attend celebrity chef prepared meals. Minneapolis sold commemorative editions when Prince died. Philadelphia got cash from local foundations to support a "Next Mayor Project." The *New York Times* doubled down on revenues from affiliate links with the purchase of Wirecutter.

These illustrate a new mindset — one that conscientiously avoids limiting revenue *types* to subscriptions and advertising — and instead considers as long and *creative* a list as possible of other approaches: product or service sales, commissions, membership, joint ventures, referral fees, ticket sales, licensing, business-to-business services, contributions, major gifts, endowments, software and/or technology sales/licensing, fundraising and more. The question is: *What are the many ways we the metro, local or regional news enterprise can find to generate the cash that we need?*

3. Assessing the gaps in your newsroom

a) Gap: How long do you have?

Do the math comparing cash coming in to cash going out.

You might start with the cash needed to pay for the work of your newsroom. To illustrate, imagine a 250-person metro newsroom with an average cost per person of, say, $100,000 (this average cost should include at least salaries and benefits).

That's $25 million. Now, say that print subscriptions plus advertising generate $30 million. Great! And, say this metro currently has digital revenue of $2 million growing at 5% per year.

Today, this metro is okay as far as the newsroom expenses are concerned. It has $32 million of cash coming in; and, $25 million going out. That leaves $7 million to pay for folks in the rest of the enterprise (marketing, technology and so forth), a pool for reinvestment and innovation, and, if there's money left over, returns to the owners.

Imagine, though, that print revenue is declining at 10% per year. So, next year it'll be $27 million instead of $30 million. And the year after that it'll be $24.3 million. In the third year out, it'll be $21.9 million.

Now, add the growing digital revenue of $2.1 million, $2.2 million, and $2.3 million. By year 3, this metro's revenue has dropped to $24.2 million — not enough to cover the $25 million for the newsroom's work. (And, if newsroom costs rise because of inflation, the picture is worse.)

This illustration is limited to the newsroom. Including costs for marketing, sales, technology, finance, HR, and so on — as well as any ownership profit expectations — make the shortfalls come faster. In this example, if there are just 70 additional employees averaging $100,000 per year, the enterprise is at breakeven with regard to personnel: $32 million coming in and $32 million going out. Of course, that means the enterprise is losing money when non-personnel costs are accounted for.

When you and your colleagues do this math, you could factor in cost reductions — e.g. downsizing the newsroom and/or other departments. As you'll see, depending on the rates of print related revenue declines, digital and other revenue growth, and current size and cost per person, the math is likely to paint a challenging picture. Your metro must either find new revenues or confront the brutal math of downsizing.

b) Gap: How many "whole P&L" products, services and businesses do you operate?

The *newspaper* has a 'whole P&L' — that is, it has *newspaper* revenues and *newspaper* costs that, when combined, provide a *newspaper* P&L. Similarly, Minneapolis has a whole P&L that matches revenues from what it calls tent-pole events to expenses from tent-pole events. And, when Dallas created GuideLive, they used a whole P&L to monitor results.

Use the following table of possibilities, to identify products and services you operate that have their own whole P&Ls:

WHOLE P&L?	PRODUCT/SERVICE/BUSINESS
	Newspaper (whole report)
	Print niche report(s) (e.g. guide books)
	Print magazines/books
	Digital (whole report)
	Digital niche report(s) (e.g. entertainment)
	Events
	Newsletter
	Email
	Podcasts
	Videos

WHOLE P&L?	PRODUCT/SERVICE/BUSINESS
	Licensing
	Consumer service(s): list out if more than one
	Business service(s): list out if more than one
	Data service(s): list out if more than one
	Other?

The fewer you have, the greater the gaps. Why? Because the more 'whole P&L" products and services you have, the more likely it is that leaders of those efforts can experiment and innovate in diversifying revenue.

c) Gap: In how many ways does your news enterprise approach revenue generation?

Use the following to assess the ways your news enterprise goes about — indeed, even considers going about — creating value and generating revenues.

REVENUE TYPE			YES / NO?	APPROXIMATE REVENUE $$
Revenue from consumers (Remember: businesses, nonprofits and governmental organizations can be consumers that pay for content)	Subscriptions	Metered		
		Fremium		
		Hard wall		
	Memberships	One-time donations		
		Recurring		
	Crowdfunding			
	Micropayments			
	One-time payments			
	Events (ticket sales)	News		
		Marketing		
		Social		
		Experiences		
		Banquets		
	E-commerce (merchandise)	Direct		
		Branded		
	Packaged content			
	Niche/standalone content	Features		
		Utility		
Revenue from advertisers and other businesses	Direct sold (can be site social, email, video, mobile, etc.)	CPM		
		CPC		
	Third-party	Network		
		Programmatic		
		Content Recommendations		
	Native	Custom		
		Automated		
	Sponsorship/ underwriting	Display, events		

REVENUE TYPE			YES / NO?	APPROXIMATE REVENUE $$
Revenue from advertisers and other businesses	E-commerce (affiliate)			
	Deals			
	Classifieds, directories			
	Site intercepts			
Revenue from other	Philanthropy	Foundations		
		Major individual gifts		
	Education/training	Training other news orgs		
		Training the public		
	Services	Advertising		
		Marketing		
		Content		
		Technology		
	Licensing			
	Research	General		
		Custom		
	Data			
	Job boards, networking			
	Paid content/ syndication/ distribution	To other news orgs		
		To academia/research		
		To third-party platforms		
		To other media		
		To businesses/ enterprises		
			TOTAL	

Table Stakes #5 Diversify and Grow the Ways You Earn Revenue from the Audiences You Build

d) Gap: Shortfalls in enterprise orientation, skills, disciplines and coordination

Ask folks in the newsroom to use this assessment — then meet together to compare answers on individual items and overall scores:

		YES	NO
Revenue sources	1. We define our challenges as print vs. digital.		
	2. The best way for us to succeed digitally is by generating huge amounts of traffic.		
	3. We don't have a clear sense about whether or how to identify and pursue opportunities that go beyond our geography.		
	4. We don't focus on actively connecting people and entities in our community in ways that go beyond our content.		
	5. We don't have goals aimed at revitalizing our local community and economy.		
	6. We only make money via subscriptions and/or advertising.		
Revenue responsibility	7. We ensure strong journalistic values by keeping the business side and newsroom separate from one another.		
	8. We believe the newsroom should not play a role in generating revenue.		
	9. Our newsroom folks lack an understanding of our current financial performance and what explains it. Newsroom staff don't understand business concepts/terms such as EBITDA, CPMs "product," etc.		
	10. The newsroom doesn't share goals with other departments around audience, product, or revenue.		

		YES	NO
Revenue responsibility	11. The newsroom typically introduces new features or products without involvement by other departments (or vice versa).		
	12. We have not had many initiatives led by a combination of editorial and business staff that sought to establish and achieve audience development and revenue targets		
Innovation investment & discipline	13. We don't have a specific innovation budget (time and/or money).		
	14. We remain unclear and uncertain about the criteria to use for choosing how and when to try new things and how to judge whether they worked.		
	15. We aren't clear about the difference between continuous improvement and fundamental innovation and whether we're doing either of them well.		
	TOTAL		

4. Why these gaps exist

a) Culture, habit, language, inertia and orientation hinder people across the entire news enterprise from embracing shared risk taking and accountability for economic sustainability

Church-versus-state. Edit side versus business side. This division of labor worked during the monopolistic/oligopolistic print era. Today, it cripples metros through perpetuating a strong belief that "X" or "Y" is not my job. It's their job.

When journalists shroud themselves behind this veil ("church-versus-state"), they idealistically, reflexively, fearfully or cynically close their minds to the basic economics of their enterprise as well as holding themselves accountable for contributing to those economics.

Newsrooms, though, are not alone in this self-defeating habit. Too many ad sales folks remain stuck in taking orders for print ads as opposed to working with potential advertisers in ways to help them solve the difficult problems they face today — problems that demand coordination with the newsroom —and, like newsroom folks, learning and practicing new ways of doing their jobs. Publishers, marketers, technologists, controllers and others also can see themselves in ways that favor 'what our role has been' versus 'what we together must do today.' The deep habit, for example, of limiting revenue possibilities to subscriptions and/or advertising arises from enterprise habits tied to outdated conceptions of who does what jobs.

b) Impossible to meet criteria block risk taking and experimentation

Senior leaders who use print economics to judge whether to move forward with investments in digital and other experiments disserve themselves and their enterprises. This is the 'fumbling the future' problem that takes its name from the book recounting how Xerox fumbled away the opportunities in personal computing created at Xerox PARC because Xerox executives could not see a fast or immediate path to replicating copier financial performance with a technology whose uses were still being discovered and whose economics remained uncertain.

Reviving metro financial sustainability — and especially sustainability built on creating and reaping value as opposed to cost cutting — demands a broad portfolio of approaches, no single one of which will reproduce print economics. No single digital effort will do this. And no single new service or product with non-subscription, non-advertising revenues will do so either. Yet, if senior leaders insist on looking only for ideas that will replicate attractive print economics, their enterprises will fail to find ideas that, while smaller today, can alone and together move the enterprise toward sustainability.

c) News enterprises do not set aside enough resources for innovation

Hard-pressed by eroding economics, too many metros, locals and regionals fail to invest in fundamental innovation. While this pattern is understandable, it nonetheless trades off near-term financial results for medium-to-long term economic sustainability. Fundamental innovation is not the same as continuous improvement. Both matter. It is essential, for example, that metro newsrooms get continuously better at driving traffic and engagement through an audience-first orientation supported by excellent data and analytics while also reaping maximum revenues by funneling random users into habitual and financially attractive loyalists (see Table Stake #4).

That's necessary but not sufficient. In addition, metros must take risks — be willing to spend valuable financial and human resources — to discover fundamental new ways of creating and reaping value. When Belo purchased SpeakEasy, CrowdSource and other companies necessary to their ecosystem strategy — just as when they asked a team to spend time creating GuideLive — they were attempting fundamental innovation as opposed to experimenting at the edges of continuous improvement. The same describes the Minneapolis effort to build a multi-layered, strategically driven events business.

Innovations like these are fundamental because success or failure turns on figuring out serious uncertainties about the existence, needs and responsiveness of customers as well as whether the metro can blend required technology and capability to deliver on the necessary promises. While disciplines exist for minimizing the cost of failure for any single effort, an entire portfolio of efforts demands levels of investment and risk that legacy metros find difficult to make. Limiting the revenue side of such efforts to subscriptions and advertising unnecessarily raises the bar — and jeopardizes the resources — for innovation.

d) News enterprises lack institutional disciplines for innovation

Traumatic declines in print subscriptions and advertising are just that: traumatic. While understandable, the desperation produced too often fuels a blend of cost cutting and random 'moon shots' instead of a careful, strategic and disciplined portfolio of revenue generating efforts grounded in a dedicated pool of financial and human resources.

This pattern is at odds with one of the best capabilities of the print era: capital budgeting. Newspaper companies regularly confronted capital-intensive choices related to new plants and equipment. They used well-understood capital budgeting analysis and problem solving to make those choices. That kind of rigor, though, has yet to mirror itself in the new and different challenge of innovation. As a consequence, news enterprises have yet to build, practice and get good at the innovation disciplines required to move forward with confidence.

e) News enterprises suffer from too little imagination regarding new and different ways to solve civic and economic problems that arise from the disruption of all things local

Local is broken. How people — as well as private, nonprofit and governmental organizations — function and relate locally bears little resemblance to what prevailed when metro newspapers flourished in the mid-to-late 20th century. At an abstract level, people and enterprises confront problems not dissimilar to earlier times. But, the much more concrete ways in which they go about solving such problems locally has undergone tectonic shifts caused by digital disruption, widespread industry consolidation, winner-take-all economics, extremist politics and more.

This provides a blank canvas for local news enterprises that embrace the opportunity and responsibility to lead. Consider, then, the elements of the following syllogism:

1. We live in an age of information.
2. Metro, local and regional publishers have trusted brands for local information
3. Therefore: (You fill in the blank)

The conclusion — and the myriad opportunities arising from it — ought to be clear. Yet, taking advantage demands mindsets open to possibilities beyond providing general news to general audiences in return for subscriptions and advertising.

Think, for example, about membership. Many nonprofit news enterprises use membership as a pathway to financial sustainability. Moreover, the range of meaning — and opportunity — for membership tap into several problems: (1) the need for a sense of belonging locally; (2) the need to have purpose(s) shared with others locally; (3) ways to connect with others locally; (4) sources of local information vetted by providers and other members; and, (5) economic value provided in return for regular participation locally.

When folks in news enterprises say and hear the word "membership" only as a slick or fluffy way to repackage 'subscriptions' — say, with tote bag gifts — they miss out on reimagining their own purposes, roles and ways of contributing to the revitalization of local.

5. What success looks and feels like

FROM > TO view of success in maximizing revenue from the audiences you build

FROM	TO
A small number of 'whole P&L" products, services and businesses	A large number of 'whole P&L" products, services and businesses
10% or less of revenues from non-print based subscriptions and advertising	Both overall revenues growing and at least 20% come from revenues from non-print based subscriptions and advertising
Saying no to any experiments/innovations that cannot demonstrably replace print economics soon	Saying yes to experiments/innovations as long as they meet criteria aimed at solving uncertainties about customer need, market readiness, enterprise and/or partner capability and technology feasibility/workability
The news enterprise dedicates less than 5% of its human and financial resources to fundamental innovation	The news enterprise dedicates at least 15% of human and financial resources to fundamental innovation
There are neither established nor widely shared and understood criteria by which innovation efforts are selected and advanced or stopped	There are established and widely shared and understood criteria by which innovation efforts are selected and advanced or stopped
Our news enterprise's mission and purpose does not embrace revitalizing the local community and economy as a primary focus	Revitalizing the local community and economy are at the heart of our enterprise's purpose
The newsroom is not involved in — and the organization doesn't generate — new types of revenue, particularly those outside advertising and subscriptions	The newsroom is a key player in setting the strategies and executing on the tactics the organization employs to generate revenue; the company makes money from a wide variety of sources, including those outside advertising and subscriptions.

6. Actions to close the gaps

This section describes the key steps required to diversify and grow the ways you earn revenues from the audiences you build, including:

a) Dedicate a pool of financial and human resources for innovation and name a cross-functional team to guide innovation across the enterprise
b) Distinguish and communicate how the enterprise will approach both continuous improvement and more fundamental innovation
c) Force yourselves to explore and consider the full range of revenue possibilities for the products, services and businesses you're in or might begin
d) Drive both continuous improvement and fundamental innovation efforts from a customer-first perspective built on answering, "What problems are we solving for the customer?"
e) Establish, monitor and use whole P&Ls for each distinct product, service and business

a) Dedicate a pool of financial and human resources for innovation and name a cross-functional team to guide innovation across the enterprise

You cannot transform yourselves in the absence of innovation and change. Doing so requires shifting your strategy, work, workflow, roles, skills, technology, tools and organization and culture in ways that embraces the Table Stakes described throughout this report — including this Table Stake #5's mandate to find new and different kinds and sources of revenues.

It is highly likely that folks across your enterprise from leadership to the front lines already know innovation is a watchword for moving forward. What's less likely is that your top management approaches innovation in the manner they would any other crucial strategic imperative: *by allocating a specific pool of human and financial resources to the challenge of innovation and asking across that functional team to run the effort with regular updates to top management and the rest of the enterprise*.

In dedicating a set pool of resources to innovation, top management must figure out:

- **How much time folks ought to be expected to spend on innovation.** Consider the mini-publishers described in Table Stake #7, "Incs," obsessions or desks, audience developers and social media editors, technologists and tool makers, newsroom leaders such as the executive and managing editor, folks from marketing, sales and communications — and so on. The mandate to innovate might differ for different folks. What's key, though, is to declare and then hold folks accountable for some allocation of time and effort — whether that's 10% of their time, 20%, or whatever. In doing this, avoid self-delusion. Anything less than 10% is a fantasy. Finally, if there are some folks (e.g. on the innovation team) who should dedicate full time — or all but full time — make that clear.

- **What specific performance and learning goals to set for teams and individuals working on innovation.** It's key that top management — ideally with the input of the innovation team along with, if relevant, HR — put explicit innovation goals into individual and team performance plans. Progress against these goals should be monitored through: (1) regular team reviews; (2) innovation initiative reviews; and, (3) personal performance reviews.

- **How much financial resource to budget for innovation.** This is the most difficult decision — especially for metros, locals and regionals hard pressed by shrinking revenue and other constraints. Innovation is not cost free. Consider the Dallas team that innovated GuideLive. Yes, much of the bet turned on dedicating the team's time and effort. Yet, they also needed access to money to pay for work with the local partner who helped create Serif, the CMS that later was adopted by the newsroom as a whole.

In putting together an innovation team, top management should:

- Pick folks based on innovation skills, experience and perspective along with cross-functionality and seniority
- Keep the team small (e.g. 3 or 4 folks instead of 7 or more)
- Either establish — or ask the team to establish — an aggressive purpose/vision for the effort along with the outcomes or results that answer, "What success looks like?"
- Ask the team to come back within 3 to 5 weeks with a proposed plan for leading and managing innovation across the enterprise

b) Distinguish how the enterprise will approach continuous improvement and more fundamental innovation

Continuous improvement efforts must pervade the entire enterprise. Given the 'from/to' challenges described throughout this report, everyone has to find better, more effective ways to build the skills, roles, work and workflows, technology, tools and habits and culture required for audience-first approaches that respond to today's digital realities.

Continuous improvement, though, differs from fundamental innovation because of the nature of the risks and rewards involved. To use an analogy, consider the famous "Fosbury Flop" — the fundamental innovation Dick Fosbury made for high jumping. Prior to Fosbury, high jumpers went over the bar stomach first. Fosbury innovated this to back first. The risks he confronted had more serious unknowns than, say, the continuous improvement efforts of stomach-first high jumpers who tried out different diets, exercise regimens and so forth to keep getting better. Think only, for example, of the risk of injury when Fosbury shifted to back first.

Getting to Table Stakes requires both continuous improvement and fundamental innovation. Table Stakes #4 and #5, though, are likely to encompass more fundamental risk taking than, say, many of the actions needed to serve targeted audiences with targeted content (Table Stake #1), publishing on the platforms used by your targeted audiences (Table Stake #2) and producing and publishing continuously to meet audience needs (Table Stake #3).

Consider moving to a meter — which can be key to success at Table Stake #4's mandate to convert random visitors into habitual, and paying, loyalists. During Knight Temple Table Stakes, Dallas made its third attempt at a meter — an experience fraught with serious uncertainties about whether folks in Dallas would pay for content. Or, think about Philadelphia's effort to build shared data as a bridge through which PMN might focus on, attract and build audiences with greater value to advertisers.

Similarly, experiments in building new kinds of revenue beyond subscription and advertising have significant uncertainties more akin to fundamental innovation than continuous improvement. How might your metro, for example, embrace — and monetize — the challenge of revitalizing local connectedness among folks? Similarly, reimaging the role and value of classifieds, building eCommerce businesses, exploring membership, creating and selling new consumer services — these and other possibilities confront serious unknowns regarding such things as whether a market exists and, if so, is it large enough to be attractive, whether or not your news enterprise has, can build or can partner for the needed capabilities, and whether the technology and tools exist to deliver on promises you'll make.

Your innovation team has to ensure widespread shared understanding about the distinction between continuous improvement versus fundamental innovation across your enterprise — and, design and lead a coherent overall effort that embraces, guides, and regularly monitors progress against both. In doing that, the innovation team must ensure that:

- All continuous improvement efforts have performance and learning objectives, and use clear, established criteria for selecting or rejecting efforts (including one criterion related to 'We have and will commit the resources required.').
- All fundamental innovation efforts are selected (or rejected) against a clear set of criteria. The team must identify the uncertainties to be tested, figure out how to test those uncertainties as speedily and cheaply as possible and, for innovation efforts demanding significant resources or risks (e.g. brand risks), use/follow a "phases and gates" approach.

c) Force yourselves to explore and consider the full range of revenue possibilities for the products, services and businesses you're in or might begin

It's essential for your habits of mind to shift from automatically limiting revenue possibilities to subscriptions and advertising to consistently, comfortably and confidently considering, exploring and testing additional possibilities. The innovation team must guide itself and everyone else toward practices that are more inclusive.

One way to begin is to use this table (also included earlier) as a checklist and prompt:

REVENUE TYPE			YES / NO?	APPROXIMATE REVENUE $$
Revenue from consumers (Remember: businesses, nonprofits and governmental organizations can be consumers that pay for content)	Subscriptions	Metered		
		Fremium		
		Hard wall		
	Memberships	One-time donations		
		Recurring		
	Crowdfunding			
	Micropayments			
	One-time payments			
	Events (ticket sales)	News		
		Marketing		
		Social		
		Experiences		
		Banquets		
	E-commerce (merchandise)	Direct		
		Branded		
	Packaged content			
	Niche/standalone content	Features		
		Utility		
Revenue from advertisers and other businesses	Direct sold (can be site social, email, video, mobile, etc.)	CPM		
		CPC		
	Third-party	Network		
		Programmatic		
		Content Recommendations		
	Native	Custom		
		Automated		
	Sponsorship/ underwriting	Display, events		

REVENUE TYPE			YES / NO?	APPROXIMATE REVENUE $$
Revenue from advertisers and other businesses	E-commerce (affiliate)			
	Deals			
	Classifieds, directories			
	Site intercepts			
Revenue from other	Philanthropy	Foundations		
		Major individual gifts		
	Education/training	Training other news orgs		
		Training the public		
	Services	Advertising		
		Marketing		
		Content		
		Technology		
	Licensing			
	Research	General		
		Custom		
	Data			
	Job boards, networking			
	Paid content/ syndication/ distribution	To other news orgs		
		To academia/research		
		To third-party platforms		
		To other media		
		To businesses/ enterprises		
			TOTAL	

Generally speaking, any product or service or business you might pursue can earn revenues in a full range of ways. Consider, for example, eCommerce possibilities such as selling products and services directly or through referral. You might monetize through one or more of the following approaches:

1. Single unit sales in the manner of most consumer goods
2. Commissions and/or referral fees for sales
3. Membership dues for access to an ongoing set of offers
4. Selling data to third parties
5. Fees for group purchasing discounts

d) Drive both continuous improvement and fundamental innovation efforts from a customer-first perspective built on answering, "What problems are we solving for the customer?"

As mentioned above, the innovation team must establish criteria by which experiments/efforts are selected to pursue (and, as part of that, garner the necessary human and financial resources). A key criterion for all such efforts should require identifying the specific problems potential customers confront that will get solved (or attempted to be solved) through the effort at hand. Here, 'customer' can mean individuals, families, groups, and communities as well as private, nonprofit and/or governmental entities.

Here's one illustration teams might use:

We wish to pursue X because X is something people:

- Must have to be *informed citizens* in the places they live
- Need to make *effective choices* for the necessities of their lives in our geography
- Want to enhance the *quality of their lives* beyond necessities in our geography

- Need/want to *connect locally* with others in meaningful, purposeful ways that make the place they live together better
- Want or need well *beyond our geography in ways that our enterprise can build a sustainable competitive advantage through digital scale and reach*

With respect to any proposed product, service or business reaching beyond your geography (the last item on the above list), make sure the criteria for consideration include the following:

- How many users/customers might this innovation reach in theory?
- What yield on that potential number is required to make this worth our while?
- Are there competitors against whom we must succeed in order to achieve the required yield?
- What basis do we have for believing our offering is superior to those of the competitors?
- Do the competitors have related/additional products/services/businesses that make it less costly for them to serve the audiences we seek?

In making the case for X, the folks proposing any innovation should at least hypothesize how many customers there might be who share the needs described as well as the proposed pathway to monetization. Once such hypotheses are stated, the innovation discipline ought to require stating the level of confidence that such things are or will be proven correct (e.g. very confident all the way to 'no clue but worth figuring out').

Use an analogous logic for proposing, choosing and pursuing innovations in how to serve enterprises that need to reach, connect with, sell and/or service local audiences. What specific problems do such enterprises have that your news organization can solve? How many such enterprises have that need? What promises might you make to solve those problems? Do the technology and tools exist to meet those needs? Does your enterprise — either alone and/or with partners — have the capabilities to fulfill the promises you'll make?

e) Establish, monitor and use whole P&Ls for each distinct product, service and business

Your news enterprise must manage distinct products, services and/or businesses from the whole enterprise perspective. This requires establishing and monitoring economic performance with 'whole P&Ls' — that is, setting, pursuing and monitoring progress against financial goals that match revenues and costs for the products, service and/or businesses at hand. A key role in all this is the product/service/business owner (a role for an individual or team). Your enterprise must ask and expect such product owners to set and pursue revenue and cost goals that contribute to overall enterprise financial success and sustainability while simultaneously succeeding at non-financial goals related to audiences, innovation, skill building, partnering and more.

7. Measures of success and tracking progress in closing the gaps

a) Monitoring progress against the overall cash picture

Your metro, local or regional news enterprise must put together a picture — or, if you will, a model — that portrays a small number of scenarios for where, when and how you'll generate the cash needed to be financially sustainable and/or attractive. The key measures in this picture relate to trend lines — and the rates of change — for cash coming in from key sources, cash going out to pay for major categories of expense, and the cash needed for ongoing innovation and change.

Essentially, your senior management must project the *rate of change* for:

- Print subscriptions
- Print advertising
- Digital subscriptions
- Digital advertising
- All other revenues of new and different kinds (events, eCommerce, etc.)
- Major expenses categories (e.g. the newsroom and other key functions)
- A pool for investment in innovation and change

You can include any profit expectations — or, you can look at the implications of the above cash picture first and layer in profit expectations after that.

The trick in all this relates to what rates of change you'll project — what assumptions you'll make for shifts in the amount of cash coming in and going out. Don't drive yourselves nuts with too many scenarios and so forth. Even a 'best case', 'worst case' and 'most likely case' set of assumptions will illuminate just how long and under what circumstances your news enterprise must get to and monetize Table Stakes.

b) Converting uncertainty into certainty

The measures for monitoring uncertainty and risk are qualitative judgments that get tested with intentional actions. Consider, for example, ways your news enterprise might partner with Meetup to establish and grow local connectedness — connectedness informed and enhanced by the information and news you cover.

To illustrate, imagine your focus is on folks who wish to connect with one another to better understand where and how to plan for retirement. To work, such an innovative service must build successfully on a number of assumptions (here, all described as things we will do successfully):

- We can identify discrete retirement based needs/problems.
- We can conceive of solutions to these problems.
- We have the technology, tools and capabilities to deliver these solutions.
- We can use membership as the vehicle for participation.
- We can charge a membership fee.
- We can attract enough folks to pay the fee and regularly participate.
- We can partner with MeetUp to use its technology in ways that get us into this game sooner and better.

Each of these assumptions must play out well if the new retirement service/business is to succeed. Yet, in all likelihood, the folks leading the effort at your news enterprise will have a range of confidence about each of these assumptions. For some they'll be certain or near certain. For others, they'll be quite uncertain.

By asking the team to evaluate their level of confidence — from certainty to uncertainty — the team is then in a position to test all of the aspects and especially those for which they are least confident.

c) Scorecard for revenue diversity

Use the Table for different revenue types (see pgs. 272–273) as a scorecard for monitoring the diversity of approaches as well as shifting actual amounts and share of total revenues your enterprise uses.

d) A product/service/business whole P&L

It's essential to increase the number of folks across your enterprise using a 'whole business/whole enterprise/general management' perspective. This cannot be over emphasized. The absence of a deep bench of general managers is one of the most crippling legacies of the print era's church/state division. Just when the tsunami wave of digital disintermediation hit news enterprises broadly — just when those legacy enterprises most needed leaders who could 'see' across the enterprise and embark on innovative strategies accordingly — there often was but one such leader: the publisher. This is why, for example, Table Stake #7 emphasizes mini-publishers.

A product, service or business whole P&L need not be complex. What's key is that it include revenues generated by the product, service, or business along with costs directly incurred related to those revenues.

Table Stakes
Number 6
Partner to Expand Your Capacity and Capabilities at Lower and More Flexible Cost

1. The Table Stake
Partner to expand your capacity and capabilities at lower and more flexible cost

Use partnerships, third-party services, shared resource arrangements and flexible staffing to expand your capacity and capabilities across all areas of your enterprise: content creation, marketing and distribution to target audiences, new services and products, access to needed skills, technologies, tools and data, and more. Do this in ways that lower investment requirements, reduce and add flexibility to your cost structure, increase speed, and better share risks compared with doing it on your own.

2. Why this is Table Stakes

a) Metro, local and regional legacy news enterprises cannot afford to do everything themselves

Newspapers were extremely profitable when they had oligopoly or monopoly market power. Thirty to forty percent or more of revenues went to the bottom line. Newspaper companies could and did pay for every aspect of the enterprise. Moreover, the range of required investments and related risks were well known: printing plants, equipment, trucks, zoned editions and so forth.

Today, metro, local and regional news enterprises generate much lower profits — which means less cash. They face a new and riskier range of required investments. Corporate chains do retain more flexibility to self-fund than family owned or otherwise independent news companies. That, though, underscores the point: chains are but one approach to sharing resources. And, even corporate chains have limits unlike a few decades ago. Going it alone is not a feasible option.

b) Shared resource approaches expand what's possible for resource constrained local news enterprises

Shared resource approaches allow metros, locals and regionals to use clean sheet of paper thinking with regard to *every* aspect of what they do. That means exploring such possibilities as:

- Lowering and making costs more flexible through aggregation, use of freelancers, automated reporting tools, outsourcing all or parts of print, using open source software approaches, tapping into students at colleges and universities, pooling back office functions and more
- Pooling risks and resources in pursuit of new products, services and revenue/business models
- Recognizing and acting on the insights that 'not all of us need to do everything alone' as well as 'some of us are really good at something and can do that for the rest of us'

c) Better solutions often arise from working with others

Metro, local and regional legacy newspaper enterprises face fragmenting audiences and ad markets, relentless technological disruption, geographically imposed competitive disadvantages, significant skill and capability shortfalls, and deteriorating economics. It makes no sense for news enterprises to isolate themselves with 'not invented here' habits. Indeed, quite the opposite is true: metro, local and regional news enterprises *must* tap into expertise, creativity, fresh perspectives, needed capabilities and additional resources wherever and with whomever they can.

The Knight Temple Table Stakes effort itself illustrates this. By sharing their respective market contexts, strategies, performance results and challenges, Miami, Dallas, Minneapolis and Philadelphia partnered in tackling key initiatives to help each get to table stakes. Over the course of a year of collaboration, many positive gains happened, including:

- Collaboratively defining what's needed (roles, skills, work flows, technology and tools)
- Crafting, deploying and learning from methods aimed at closing gaps (e.g. skills assessments, workshopping and training approaches, timing and purpose of daily meetings, newsroom design and build out, use of mini-publisher and "Inc" approaches, how best to deploy/use Slack, and more)
- Establishing and growing informal and trusted relationships (e.g. the social editors regularly tap into one another for ideas, insights and best practices — and that's just one of several similar informal and productive groups)
- Holding each other accountable in supportive and caring ways.

d) News enterprises are technology-dependent companies

Metro, local and regional news enterprises are primarily news and information companies. And news enterprises are not technology companies in the sense of Facebook, Google, Oracle or IBM. Still, technological capacity and capability is a *sine qua non* for news and information: *if your enterprise is not "tech enough" you cannot be in the game*. You must have the hardware, systems, software, applications, technology architecture — *and the technology talent* — demanded. Furthermore, the hardware, software and "wetware" (the tech talent) must integrate with, and effectively support and enhance, all the core work and workflows of news enterprises. Yet, no metro, local or regional news enterprise — even those part of larger chains — can be 'tech enough' alone. This is self-evident: consider only the role played by vendors who provide technology to many enterprise customers.

e) Investments in technology, publishing platforms and technology-related capabilities carry significant risks

Consider the anxiety and frustration you expend on content management systems. Much of this arises from difficult tradeoffs demanded by print and digital requirements. It also arises because established print CMS providers themselves must balance print versus digital customer requirements against current and prospective revenue streams. They wish to preserve big accounts and print related cash flows while transitioning to digital realities. Put differently, CMS vendor interests conflict with your interests — at least in part.

Yet, content management systems are but one example of risk-filled technology choices you confront. Social, mobile, communications (e.g. email, Slack, etc.), customer relationship management (CRM), apps, ad tech, data, analytics, coding, hosting — these and other technology capabilities and requirements weave themselves through everything your enterprise does. And all of them carry risks. Finding ways to share those risks with others reduces potential costs and losses while, importantly, increasing the nature and number of risks you can take.

f) Partnering generates revenue and financial resource opportunities

Your metro, local and regional news enterprise must maximize every opportunity to attract cash (see Table Stake #5). Partnering is a different way to diversify revenues through building the kind of local ecosystem that Dallas/Belo has done through acquisition. Content marketing, search engine optimization and marketing, analytics and data management, events, and other services and products all might generate more revenues for your enterprise and a partner enterprise together than either of you could do alone. And revenues are not the sole form of cash. Philadelphia, for example, used partnering to attract foundation funding — *cash* — to support the "Next Mayor's Project."

g) Partnering creates possibilities that otherwise will not happen

Innovations and strategies that demand cross-functional coordination have lower odds of success if the only option is for Function A of the enterprise to work with Function B of the *same* enterprise — as opposed to Function A finding a partner organization to provide what B does. For example, imagine that a mini-publisher "Inc" type effort (see TS#7) shapes a revenue strategy that includes selling sponsorships for events. If the ad sales force declines (whether explicitly or implicitly) to sell the sponsorships, the plan fails. Partnering disciplines and processes help the mini-publisher explore how other entities could do sponsor sales. True, senior management might choose to say no to what the mini-publisher proposes. In the absence of partnering disciplines, though, the option of working with outsiders never even arises.

3. Assessing the gaps in your newsroom

Take the following quiz for a quick read on where your efforts stand vis a vis this Table Stake. *Please note: these statements are phrased so that a 'yes' answer indicates your efforts have gaps — that is, fall short of the requirements of this Table Stake. And, the more yesses, the more gaps you face.*

It is worth having many folks take these quizzes, including people in the newsroom as well as from technology, marketing, sales, HR, finance — and top management. Compare and discuss your respective responses and where you have agreement or not. Use these discussions to identify and highlight the most significant partnering gaps you face.

	YES	NO
1. We do not consider partnering regularly as an option along with make versus buy.		
2. Partnering rarely works for us because our situation and needs are unique.		
3. We worry that we will lose control when we partner with others.		
4. Our newsroom limits collaboration to efforts related to content/stories.		
5. We see ourselves strictly as competitors and not partners with other news enterprises.		
6. We do not routinely think about partnering and collaboration as avenues to lower costs, increase revenues and reduce risks.		
7. Partnering always requires top management involvement and approval.		
8. We lack a shared understanding of the distinction between a vendor versus a partner.		
9. We do not have criteria for determining when and why to choose partnering as a path forward.		
10. We do not have any executive or team/committee overseeing partnering.		
11. We lack a defined step-by-step process for partnering.		
12. Partnering with others beyond our organization rarely happens at the desk and/or other front line levels of our enterprise.		
13. Few if any partnering arrangements have results-based commitments that we and our partners regularly monitor for success.		
14. We have few, in any, partnering arrangements in technology.		
15. We lack significant partnering arrangements that help us do the following: (1) address needed capacity; (2) add required capability; (3) increase speed; (4) reduce or share risks; (5) increase revenues; and, (6) lower or share our costs, or make them more flexible.		
16. We have few, if any, partnering or joint venture revenue-focused arrangements with companies that provide content management, search engine optimization, events, marketing, or other services and products that meet needs of local customers and enterprises.		
TOTAL		

4. Why these gaps exist

a) The legacy of high margin, autonomous businesses

When newspapers were extraordinarily profitable cash machines, owners and senior executives did not need to consider partnering as a *standard* strategic option. "Do X ourselves" was the assumed best option. Going it alone maximized financial returns and conferred control over the entire newspaper value chain — the step by step, function by function effort linking everything together (acquiring paper and ink, operating printing plants, distributing the paper, subscriptions, the newsroom, selling ads and so forth). When executives did have to make financial tradeoffs, the risks related more to just how much money would get made versus more existential realities such as the possibility of financial and economic collapse. Autonomy and control eliminated any reason to have an automatic, habitual orientation to explore partnering.

b) Limited experience and skills in partnering

Metro news organizations do have histories of working with others — just in narrow ways that have not extended across the edit/business divide or involved confronting unfamiliar risks *together*. Working with the AP to access non-local content, for example, goes back to the mid-19th century. Negotiating the best possible deal with the AP mattered. But, those deals did not rise or fall on how effectively metros and AP partnered to solve *existential* problems like those faced today. And the same can be said of working with local TV and radio outlets to cover weather or breaking news. Joint operating agreements focused on maximizing profit margins through operating efficiencies as opposed to adding new and different capabilities required to stay in business.

The church/state divide was mirrored in such arrangements. The newsroom worked with AP, local TV and radio; operations worked with others on operations. News enterprises that did not even partner internally across church/state had no experience partnering with others across the entire enterprise either. Nor did metro, local and regional news enterprises engage in the give and take of open-ended collaboration and partnering where (1) neither of the parties knows what will or won't work but (2) the future of both depends on figuring that out. When Miami's "Food Inc" team decided to partner with Yelp, for example, they and Yelp together had to agree on what each wanted from the arrangement and how best they could collaborate to achieve those goals.

c) No established management responsibility, process or criteria for partnering

In 2015, Philadelphia designated an executive to oversee partnering. That's rare. Most metro, local and regional news enterprises don't have the role. Nor do they have a cross-functional, whole enterprise management process for surfacing possible partnering opportunities; qualifying and testing them out against agreed upon criteria; and, for those that make sense, moving forward and monitoring results. In the absence of specific executive oversight plus a whole enterprise, criteria-based process, partnering cannot become a strategic competency.

5. What success looks and feels like

This Tables Stake requires you and your colleagues to probe every single aspect of work — every thing your enterprise currently does or might do — by asking, "Must we do this ourselves? Or, in how many ways might it be wiser to have others do this for us or partner to do this together?"

Success looks like the 'to' side of the following from/to statements that demand a range of from/to shifts.

FROM > TO shifts for partnering

	FROM	TO
Mindset and habits	Make vs. buy vs. partner choices happen randomly, if at all in our enterprise	We routinely consider make/buy/partner choices
	We rarely think about partnering with others as an option	We always consider buy/partner as options
	When we get together with peer enterprises, we limit our discussions to sharing best practices	We actively seek opportunities to partner with peer enterprises
	We do not set objectives and goals to be achieved through buying/partnering	We have annual as well as strategic goals for partnering
	We limit make/buy choices to cost concerns	We consider buy/partner as key alternatives for achieving specific capacity, capability, speed, risk, revenue and cost objectives
	We have a narrow set of arenas or kinds of work (e.g. only for content and technology) where we consider buy/partner choices	We subject every aspect of work to make/buy/partner choices
	Our front line teams lack authority to choose to buy/partner as options	Teams and leaders from top to bottom of our enterprise have well-defined authority for when they can choose to buy or partner
Partnering discipline, practice and authority	We have no framework for choosing among make/buy/partner options	We have a widely understood and used framework for make/buy/partner choices
	We lack criteria for choosing among make/buy/partner	We have established and shared criteria for make/buy/partner choices that we use, learn from and adjust
	We neither have an executive in charge of partnering nor a senior partnering team/committee	We have elevated the strategic importance of partnering by designating a senior executive to oversee partnering and/or a partnering team/committee
	We only randomly or episodically set objectives to be achieved through buy/partner options	Our strategic plans as well as annual plans include specific SMART outcome goals that we will achieve through buy/partner options

	FROM	TO
Partnering discipline, practice and authority	While we may have service level agreements with key vendors, they typically spell out the work to get done but not the specific SMART outcome based goals to be accomplished	Our service level agreements with vendors spell out every element of how we'll work together, toward what purposes and what success looks like in terms of SMART outcome based goals
	To the extent that we partner with other enterprises, we typically do so based on handshakes and/or loosely agreed upon terms	We always have detailed, purpose and performance-driven memoranda of understanding with our partners
Number and purposes of shared arrangements	We don't partner with other enterprises in ways that require their content/edit/tech/business folks to work together with our content/edit/business folks	We have partnerships that span content/edit/tech/business
	We rarely if ever have partnering arrangements at the desk or other front line team level	Our desks and other front line teams actively make buy/partner choices as key parts of getting their work done
	We have no strategy for building a network of local services (such as Belo/Dallas' ecosystem) that offer customers multifaceted ways to do business with that network	We use partnering to build and sustain a local service network that benefits from cross-selling and cross-delivery of products and services

6. Actions to close the gaps

This section describes the key steps required to partner to expand your capacity and capabilities at lower and more flexible cost, including:

a) Design and use a framework for identifying, analyzing and comparing make versus buy versus partner choices
b) Grow partnering as a discipline and practice across your entire organization from top to bottom
c) Structure — then manage — buy/partner arrangements for success
d) Put a senior executive or management team in charge of partnering, and hold them accountable for results

a) Design and use a framework for identifying, analyzing and comparing make versus buy versus partner choices

You and your colleagues must design — then use — a framework for identifying and evaluating options for how best to achieve (1) capacity, capability, speed, risk, revenue and cost objectives by (2) doing aspects of required work through (3) possible working relationships with others as opposed to yourselves.

Take a moment to reflect on the following situation. You want a new dining room table. You have a range of objectives: functional (e.g., number of seats), aesthetic (e.g. style), and economic (price). Work has to happen: design, construction, and placement. And, you have three options for getting the work done:

1. Buy the table (that is, have someone else *do it for you*)
2. Engage a carpenter to help you build the table (that is, have someone *do it with you*)
3. Build the table yourself (that is, *do it yourself*)

Your make/buy/partner choices are similar. For any aspect of work, you could[1]:

- Do it yourself — as you have been doing for so many decades
- Do it with others through partnering arrangements
- Have others do it for you through contracting and outsourcing

The following diagram illustrates the interplay among the three components of the required framework.

---

[1] Note there is one more option: stop doing the work. See Table Stake #1.

For this work (describe):

	OUR CAPACITY OBJECTIVES	OUR CAPABILITY OBJECTIVES	OUR SPEED OBJECTIVES	OUR RISK PARAMETERS
Make				
Buy				
Partner				

	OUR REVENUE OBJECTIVES/ REVENUE DRIVERS	OUR COST OBJECTIVES	OTHER OBJECTIVES
Make			
Buy			
Partner			

Table Stakes #6 Partner to Expand Your Capacity and Capabilities at Lower and More Flexible Cost

You can subject any and every aspect of work to this analysis: target audience service, growth and monetization, content creation and distribution, platform management, marketing, sales, brand building, innovation, technology and tool management, talent management — and more.

The range of objectives to pursue for any identified aspect of work might include:

- **Capacity.** Consider, for example, news coverage beyond your metro region or even the U.S. The first question to ask is, "How much capacity for this coverage is needed to serve the target audiences we seek to grow, serve and monetize?" Or consider server capacity to ensure that your digital operations do not break down when news events generate huge traffic. The point here is that, for any given element of work, you and your colleagues must identify how much capacity is needed, and how best to assure it.

- **Capability.** Capability refers to *institutional skills* not capacity. *The Washington Post*, for example, has dozens of coders in the newsroom, providing strong institutional capability they believe is key to mastering the challenges ahead. None of the four metros in Table Stakes could afford that number of coders. So, the question becomes: How do those — or similarly constrained — metros ensure they have the minimum coding capability demanded to be in the game? Options include:

    — **Make:** We hire X number of coders for our newsroom

    — **Buy:** We purchase coding capability — or the tools and approaches that arise from that capability — from third parties

    — **Partner:** We form a coding collaborative with other news enterprises (indeed, perhaps, even non-news enterprises)

- **Speed:** Speed matters. Whether it's reducing load times, decreasing the time for events from conception through execution, the rapidity of adoption of a new product, platform or capability — these and other critical requirements might best happen through buying and/or partnering as opposed to doing them yourselves.

- **Risk.** For any given aspect of work and initiative, what risks to you face? How might you reduce those risks? How might you share the risks? How might you defer the risks? How might you make risks less costly? How might you make risks more rewarding? How might you take more risks? These and other objectives must be part of your make/buy/partner framework.

- **Revenue.** What are the revenue requirements for your metro? How will you achieve them? What are the drivers of revenue? For example, what audience volume, engagement and sharing numbers are needed to achieve those revenues? What advertising, sponsorship and other sources of revenue are required?

- **Cost:** Metro, local and regional legacy newspaper enterprises must lower costs, make costs more flexible[2], and share costs. Buying services from others as well as partnering with others are options that might reduce your costs or make those costs more flexible.

- **Other:** Your efforts might have additional objectives. For example, the U.S. presidential election in 2016 brought concern over fake news to a boil. Metro, local and regional legacy newspaper enterprises — like other reputable news enterprises — need to figure out a range of strategies and approaches to navigating the adverse effects of fake news and constructive, positive effects of building trust in news. Okay. How might you set and achieve those objectives through identifying and weighing options among: (1) do this ourselves (make); (2) have others do this for us (buy); and/or, (3) do this with others (partner)?

---

[2]

Flexible means easier and faster to adjust down or up. Using freelancers instead of full-time employees, for example, is a well-known tactic for cost flexibility.

b) Grow partnering as a discipline and practice across your entire organization from top to bottom

Partnering must become a strategic capability for metro, local and regional news enterprises.

You know the old joke:

Question: How do you get to Carnegie Hall?

Answer: Practice.

So:

Question: How can you and your colleagues turn make/buy/partner into a strategic capability pervading your news enterprise?

Answer: Practice

Specifically:

1) Top-down practice

In annual, strategic as well as more ad hoc planning efforts, your enterprise's senior management team should require make vs. buy vs. partner choices. Indeed, it is good practice to set specific enterprise-wide objectives to be achieved through buying and/or partnering with others.

This discipline includes:

- Crafting enterprise-wide objectives for capacity, capability, speed, risk, revenue and cost
- Asking/expecting senior leaders to engage colleagues in proposing approaches to meeting those objectives through buy/partner alternatives
- Establishing *criteria*[3] for evaluating make/buy/partner alternatives. For example, imagine you're evaluating whether to make X yourself, buy X from others and/or partner with others to do X. Criteria for weighing each of those options turn on whether and to what extent each make/buy/partner option might best:

---

[3] The thoroughness with which you evaluate the criteria should fit the context, needs and risks at hand. For example, outsourcing all newsroom coding to a third party demands more care than, say, experimenting with local celebrity chefs in an effort to build audience, revenue and brand value for food coverage. Outsourcing all newsroom coding — much like, say, outsourcing printing for the paper — requires careful due diligence by a team comprised of the newsroom, technology, marketing, ad sales, audience development, finance and legal. Experimenting with any particular celebrity chef might only require gauging food team (probably including marketing folks) confidence that Chef A will attract enough of the desired audience at a price that's affordable.

- Expand our capacity to get X done
- Add/tap into a core capability related to X that we do not have
- Increase the speed with which X happens
- Reduce, share or otherwise manage the risks related to X that we face in moving forward
- Increase revenues and/or diversify sources of revenues related to X
- Reduce or share costs or make costs more flexible

- If buying or partnering emerges as the best choice, then using criteria for choosing among the enterprises (or individuals) from whom you might buy or with whom you might partner. These include gauging if and how any particular vendor or partner:

  - Has the skills and track record to deliver what is required
  - Commits to specific performance results as well as dedicating sufficient resources to deliver on those results
  - Will devote the management time and attention to deliver on the promises made
  - Will commit to pricing and/or risk sharing that are tolerable/affordable
  - Does not pose any unmanageable brand or mission problems

2) Bottom-up practice

Establish the expectation that make vs. buy vs. partner becomes routine for teams at every level of your enterprise. Ask teams to tailor the framework criteria to fit their particular contexts and to use them persistently (e.g. mini-publishers might analyze make/buy/partner options once or twice a year as well as whenever some new or different approach is being considered). Yes, it is important to establish parameters for what kind and how much risk front line teams can and cannot take absent senior management approval. But do not make these so stringent as to choke off the opportunity for everyone in your enterprise to learn about make/buy/partner through actually doing make/buy/partner choices.

c) Structure — then manage — buy/partner arrangements for success

[4] Remember that for any given aspect of work, an additional option is to stop doing it. That is, determine the work is not necessary.

For any given aspect of necessary[4] work, the choice to buy differs from the choice to partner. *Buying* means you decide to have others *do the work for you*. *Partner means you decide to have others do the work with you*.

Case Illustration: All four Knight Temple groups chose to work with API Metrics for News over the course of the year. Because API tailors Metrics for News to fit and serve each client, the arrangement is a choice to partner as opposed to buy. In addition, API works hard to share learning across their clients. As a result, API becomes a *shared resource* — a repository and set of relationships through which a network of partners learn from one another about the most effective data and analytics while each user's approach gets tailored to their unique context and situation.

You must structure each of these approaches for success. Here's how:

Service level agreements for choices to buy should include:

- **Purpose:** Name the purpose(s) and broad objectives for the work the service provider contributes — and why both the service provider and your organization care.

- **Results/performance:** Name the specific performance results that the service provider commits to deliver.

- **Work:** Describe the work the service provider agrees to do.

- **Handoffs:** Identify the handoffs — critical workflow points where the service provider hands off work to your enterprise. Detail and describe the requirements for timeliness as well as understanding — that is, steps necessary to insure your folks understand what they are getting from the service provider and how it fits into any work or effort to follow.

- **Information:** Describe any information, metrics and data the service provider will share.

- **People:** Name the people in the service provider who (1) are directly on the line to do the work and deliver the results; and/or, (2) responsible for sharing needed information, metrics and data.

- **Monitoring updates:** Describe the dates and/or time frames for regular meetings in which the performance of the service provider will be reviewed as well as the scorecard to be used.

- **Consequences:** Describe the consequences (and how those consequences will be determined) for failure and/or suboptimal performance by the service provider.

- **Financial arrangements:** Describe any financial arrangements (e.g., the schedule and amounts of any payments to the service provider).

- **Signatures:** Make sure that the service agreement is signed by the people delivering the work as well as the most senior executives.

Partnering memoranda of understanding (MOU) should include:

- **Purpose:** Name the purposes and broad objectives that you and the other partnering organizations are committing to achieve together. Describe why it matters to each organization, including each organization's mission.

- **Results/performance:** Name the specific performance results that the partnering organizations commit to deliver.

- **Enterprise names/term:** Make sure each partnering organization is named along with the most senior person involved and describe the term (length) of the agreement.

- **Need for collaboration:** Describe why it is necessary for the partnering organizations to work together in real time to succeed — and why the purpose and goals are not possible through individual organization effort alone.

- **Work:** Describe the work each organization will do, including work that will be done collaboratively.

- **Information:** Describe any information, metrics and data that the partnering organizations agree to share.

- **People:** Name the specific people in each organization who (1) are directly on the line to do the work and deliver the results; and/or, (2) responsible for sharing needed information, metrics and data.

- **Monitoring updates:** Describe the dates and/or time frames for regular meetings in which the performance of the collaboration will get reviewed. Identify who will attend, what will be reviewed and discussed and the scorecard to be used.

- **Consequences:** Describe the consequences (and how those consequences will be determined) for failure and/or suboptimal performance by any of the partnering organizations.

- **Partnership termination:** Describe in advance the circumstances and criteria under which the partners will discuss and decide to end the partnership entirely.

- **Financial arrangements:** Describe any financial arrangements among the partnering organizations (and, if relevant, third parties).

- **Governance:** Describe critical governance[5] issues and the governance arrangements related to them.

- **Signatures:** Make sure the partnering memorandum of understanding is signed by the people delivering the work as well as the most senior executives.

You and your colleagues also should use service level agreements or partnering MOUs to capture agreements between or among divisions or companies that are part of the portfolio of your corporation. Recall that, in addition to Dallas Morning News,

---

5

Governance issues arise when partners must resolve questions that go beyond the nature of the work they are doing together. These include such things as whether or under what circumstances to invite other organizations to join the partnership, how best to utilize any assets owned by the partnership, fundamental shifts in the purpose of the partnership and so forth.

for example, Belo owns companies that do content marketing, events, social media management, data and analytics, and mixed marketing (e.g. T-shirts, coffee cups and so on). Belo will get better and more mutually beneficial results by requiring these companies to use service level agreements and/or partnering memoranda of understanding depending on whether one company is doing the work for another, or they are partnering together.

d) Put a senior executive or management team in charge of partnering, and hold them accountable for results

In 2015, Philadelphia asked a senior leader to oversee partnering for the enterprise. In doing so, Philly simultaneously elevated the strategic importance of partnering and set in motion the resources and discipline needed to make that practice real. Your enterprise may lack the resources to dedicate a senior executive to the full-time job of overseeing partnering. You might, though, make that responsibility a key role for a senior executive even if not the full-time job. Or, you might designate a team for the same purpose. Absent taking one of these steps, though, make/buy/partner is not likely to happen with the rigor, discipline and repetition required.

Whether you choose to have a senior executive with a full-time job as head of partnering, or designate that as a role alongside other job requirements for an executive and/or establish a team or committee to guide partnering, those in charge of partnering should:

- Develop and recommend a set of make/buy/partner objectives for inclusion in strategic as well as annual plans
- Be accountable for delivering on the objectives and recommendations accepted and put into strategic and annual plans
- Work with newsroom leaders to ensure make/buy/partner gets included and practiced bottom up by desks, mini-publishers and others

- Establish and guide the regular monitoring and review sessions in which make/buy/partner efforts are managed and adjusted — including both when/how your enterprise monitors the objectives set as well as how particular service level agreements and partnering memoranda of understanding are performing (see below)
- Periodically report on make/buy/partner performance results, progress and shortfalls to senior enterprise management as well as staff more broadly

7. Measures of success and tracking progress in closing the gaps

Three types of scorecards can help you measure the success of your make/buy/partner choices as well as monitor progress toward closing partnering gaps:

a) Enterprise-wide scorecards
b) Front-line team scorecards
c) Service level agreement and memorandum of understanding scorecards

a) Enterprise-wide scorecards

The senior executive or team in charge of partnering should use a scorecard to manage and monitor performance results. This scorecard should focus on enterprise-level objectives that arise from the basic framework described above. Essentially, you:

- Convert capacity, capability, speed, risk, revenue, cost and other enterprise level buy/partner objectives into specific goals
- For each goal, identify the specific buy or partner approach chosen

- For each review period, discuss current results against goals to be achieved
- Use green, yellow, red to indicate acceptable progress versus caution versus danger of failing

b) Front-line team scorecards

Front-line teams — desks, mini-publishers, marketing, ad sales, technology and tool teams and so on — can use an approach similar to enterprise-wide partnering scorecards — that is, convert choices made into scorecards by:

- Converting capacity, capability, speed, risk, revenue, cost and other team level buy/partner objectives into specific goals
- For each goal, identify the specific buy or partner approach chosen
- For each review period, discuss current results against the goals to be achieved
- Using green, yellow, red to indicate acceptable progress versus caution short versus danger of failing

c) Service level agreement and memorandum of understanding scorecards

Scorecards are essential to ensuring buy as well as partner choices actually deliver the results and capabilities desired. Look again at the elements in an effective service level agreement as well as partnering memorandum of understanding. In each case, you'll see the agreement spells out the results to be accomplished, the approach to monitoring against performance promises, and the consequences for falling short. In this sense, the agreements themselves encompass and become the scorecards.

Table Stakes
Number 7
Drive Audience Growth and Profitability from a "Mini-publisher" Perspective

[1]

The term "mini-publisher" is drawn from the tradition of the publisher being the person in a news enterprise where the editorial and business sides — and the revenues and expenses — all come together. It may be that in your organization the term mini-publisher could be problematic — for example, carrying negative, unhelpful meanings that get in the way. If so, pick a different term. Several media organizations, for example, use product manager. But whatever term you choose, make sure the meaning of that term is clear: the person in this role along with her/his team is accountable for the P&L, audience, brand and other performance goals that, in turn, require the team to blend together all — not just some — of the needed functions.

1. The Table Stake
Drive audience growth and profitability from a "mini-publisher" perspective[1]

Drive growth and profitability in your chosen target audience segments and key publishing platforms by developing cross-functional "mini-publisher" teams and team leaders who use a general management perspective and strong sense of ownership and accountability for performance. Expand the scope of these teams' responsibility beyond content creation, content distribution and audience development to include revenue generation, financial contribution and brand development.

2. Why this is Tables Stakes

Mini-publishing responsibilities are the logical extension of the prior six Table Stakes

Several critical accountabilities emerge from the previous six Table Stakes, including responsibilities for:

- Serving target audiences (Tables Stake 1)
- Using key platforms (Tables Stake 2)
- Continuously publishing (Table Stakes 3)
- Converting random users into habitual, paying ones (Tables Stakes 4)
- Identifying/pursuing a wide range of opportunities to earn revenues from the audiences developed (Table Stake 5)
- Partnering with others to grow capabilities and capacity while lowering costs and making them more flexible (Table Stake 6)

This seventh Table Stake blends these responsibilities together in the role of a "mini-publisher" and mini-publisher team. There are two types of mini-publishers: mini-publishers for audiences and mini-publishers for platforms. Mini-publisher audience teams drive the work of Table Stakes #1 while mini-publisher platform teams drive Table Stakes #2. Both work to make Table Stakes #3 happen.

Mini-publisher audience teams coordinate with mini-publisher platform teams to implement Table Stakes #4 and #5 — namely, delivering the best possible financial contribution to the enterprise by generating revenue from target audiences and platforms in concert with managing and getting the most out of costs. Finally, mini-publisher teams work with senior leaders and others to optimize the use of partnering (Table Stake #6) and to extend and enhance the enterprise's brand(s).

a) The competitive challenges confronting metro, local and regional news enterprises demand general management perspective and skill across the newsroom.

As the table stakes — and the experiences of Philadelphia, Dallas, Miami and Minneapolis — make clear, metro, local and regional legacy newspaper organizations must do things new and differently to get in the game of 21st century news and information. *None of that will happen in the absence of significantly more general management thought and action throughout the newsroom.*

For decades prior to the 21st century, news enterprises were operationally and functionally excellent. Strong, functional leaders provided what was needed in terms of journalism, printing, distribution, marketing, finance, HR, technology and customer service — as well as continuous improvement. Which was fine because few if any of the challenges confronting news enterprises throughout the decades prior to the 21st century demanded a 'whole enterprise' perspective.

Consequently, news enterprises did not have many true general managers — leaders accountable for the performance of the entire enterprise or 'whole businesses, products or services' within the enterprise. Indeed, the publisher was often the sole true general manager.

Today, though, newsrooms are in fact accountable for essential aspects of the entire news enterprise: journalism of course, but also in key ways marketing, 'circulation,' distribution, technology, customer service, product management, and new product and service innovation.

Moreover, newsrooms must 'connect all these dots' in the face of unprecedented disruption, financial pressure and risk.

Meeting such intense challenges simply cannot happen in the absence of more folks understanding what general managers do — and getting a whole lot better at that.

The idea of the mini-publisher, then, comes directly from the concept of the general manager — a leader who is responsible for blending together all aspects of a business (or product or service) in ways that optimize results for the enterprise as a whole, not just a function.

In classic industrial businesses, general managers oversee product development, manufacturing, distribution, marketing, sales, and customer service. This contrasts with functional managers who lead only one slice of the business such as a VP of Manufacturing or Head of Sales. Unlike functional managers, GMs bring an integrated view of how all aspects of a business (or product or service) can best deliver results against a focused, defined segment of the market (e.g. Gap vs Gap Kids) — and do so at a more agile and manageable level than the entire enterprise as a whole (The Gap as a whole enterprise versus Gap and Gap Kids).

Though news differs from, say, clothes, cars or cereal, there are direct, informative parallels between a classic GM's scope of responsibilities and those of a mini-publisher.

Illustrative comparison: responsibilities of a "Classic GM" roles and a mini-publisher

GENERAL MANAGER RESPONSIBILITY	AUDIENCE BASED MINI-PUBLISHER	PLATFORM CLUSTER BASED MINI-PUBLISHER
Market research	Paying attention to emerging needs, interests of audiences and the problems audiences need solved	Paying attention to users, uses and user experiences arising in new platforms as well as new features and functions of existing platforms
New product development	Identifying and experimenting with new ways to use content, experiences and/or story forms to serve audiences	Identifying and experimenting with new approaches/new uses of existing and new platforms that better attract and serve audiences

GENERAL MANAGER RESPONSIBILITY	AUDIENCE BASED MINI-PUBLISHER	PLATFORM CLUSTER BASED MINI-PUBLISHER
Product manufacturing	The core work of using targeted content plus data and analytics to attract, serve, retain and monetize target audiences through producing and publishing continuously	The core work of publishing on the platforms used by target audiences — including platforms you own, platforms owned by others but that send audiences to you, and platforms owned by others where audiences stay Using data and analytics to optimize results on all three types of platforms
Distribution	Figuring out the best/optimal ways to make sure target audiences see and have access to content at the time and places they want. Audience teams must coordinate with platform teams	Figuring out the best/optimal ways to make sure target audiences see and have access to content at the time and places they want. Platform teams must coordinate with audience teams
Marketing	Shaping, articulating, and communicating the value proposition for the targeted audience: what benefits the audience receives and what actions (including payment and provision of data) they are expected to do/make. Put differently: shaping the give/get of what you give audiences and what you get from them	Managing platform delivery on the platforms you own to optimize results from the range of value propositions shaped/articulated by the audience teams Maximizing value your enterprise derives from (1) increasing audiences who come to your sites from platforms owned by others that send audiences to you; and, (2) optimizing brand and other value from audience experiences on platforms where the audiences stay
Sales	Using the funnel of TS#4 supported by data and analytics to convert random users into habitual and paying loyalists Working with advertising/sales to maximize revenue from advertisers seeking the valuable audiences being built	Coordinating with audience teams in funneling random users into paying ones — all supported by data and analytics Working with advertising/sales to maximize revenue from advertisers seeking the valuable audiences being built
Customer service	Using data and analytics to coordinate/work with technology and tool makers to optimize the user experience through (1) meeting minimum standards of what audiences expect (e.g. acceptable load times); and, (2) exceeding audience expectations in ways that surprise and thrill audiences	Using data and analytics to coordinate/work with technology and tool makers as well as target audience teams to optimize the user experience through (1) meeting minimum standards of what audiences expect (e.g. acceptable load times); and, (2) exceeding audience expectations in ways that surprise and thrill audiences

b) The competitive challenges confronting metro, local and regional news enterprises demand that senior newsroom leaders rebalance their focus and effort away from day-to-day matters — otherwise, serious medium- to-longer term challenges will go un-led

Too many Executive Editors, Managing Editors and other senior newsroom leaders spend far too little time and effort on the most critical aspects of their jobs: transforming their newsrooms — and news enterprises — to get in the game of 21st century local news and information. It is no longer the primary job of senior newsroom leaders to get the paper out — or even to get the digital report out. Yes, of course those must happen. But transforming metro newsrooms requires senior leaders to focus much more of their time and attention on:

- Guiding newsrooms to put the table stakes in place
- Reshaping work and workflows to the audience-first, digital and platform optimal[2] approaches demanded for success
- Ensuring newsroom folks overcome gaps and shortfalls in skills, behaviors, attitudes, and working relationships
- Teaming up with technology folks to do the best possible job of providing newsrooms the tools needed for success
- Working with other senior leaders in the news enterprise to make the enterprise financially sustainable through generating revenues, lowering costs and making costs more flexible, and investing in/finding innovations.

Squarely put, senior newsroom leaders must themselves transition from being functional managers to general managers.

---

[2]

Note the phrase "platform optimal." One unfortunate misunderstanding in too many newsrooms lies in the contrasting phrase "platform agnostic." You do not want to be agnostic about platforms. Instead, you need to understand what different platforms do well versus not so well for audiences — and then optimize your efforts accordingly.

Yet, this cannot happen if senior newsroom leaders are forced into day-to-day matters as a result of too few newsroom general managers — too few mini-publishers — on whom senior leaders can depend and to whom they can delegate the day-to-day work.

3. Assessing the gaps in your newsroom

a) Gap: Shortfalls in general management skills, disciplines and accountability

Ask folks to use this assessment — then meet together to compare answers on individual items and overall scores.

	YES	NO
1. If asked, most folks across our enterprise would say we offer two main products to our audiences: print and digital.		
2. While our newsroom is more aware of audiences today than before, we rarely collaborate across our entire enterprise about which specific audience segments we can serve well.		
3. We do not have general managers who oversee audiences or platforms as businesses.		
4. We have a clear separation between editorial/content and business — and very few positions span both sides.		
5. We operate largely/mostly within siloes — for example, desks keep pretty much to themselves as do sales, marketing and other departments.		
6. While we have some good examples of collaboration among individuals, we do not routinely use teams with a shared set of goals to which they hold themselves mutually accountable.		

	YES	NO
7. Who is responsible for what products, services or businesses is not clear –other than the publisher being responsible for all of what we do.		
8. Our enterprise essentially operates under a single P&L for which the publisher is responsible.		
9. We do not match revenues to expenses for specific audiences or platforms — or, if we do, I am not aware of that.		
10. We have few folks with real experiences as general managers who have responsibility for ensuring revenues exceed expenses — possibly only the publisher.		
11. We have few folks with strong, deep experiences as product or project managers.		
12. Most people in our enterprise work as individuals reporting to bosses as opposed to teams with shared goals and mutual accountability.		
13. Our senior newsroom leaders focus most of their time and attention on the daily to weekly challenges of ensuring the best print and digital content.		
14. Financial budget discussions in our newsroom focus only on expenses; revenues are not part of what is discussed or, if discussed, only cursorily.		
15. Few, if any, of our newsroom leaders have ever put together a business proposal or plan that includes projections for revenue, expense and profitability.		

b) Gap: Current versus optimal mini-publisher approach

The mini-publisher concept for key audiences and platforms is an end game toward which to evolve. The following spectrum provides markers along a continuum. Note that it is cumulative — that is, each stage builds on the prior ones.

You and your colleagues should use the spectrum to identify where things stand today versus the end game of fully operational and accountable mini-publisher audience and platform leaders and teams.

Spectrum of development of mini-publisher audience and platform teams

AUDIENCE-based mini-publisher teams

	CURRENT NEWSROOM	STARTING AUDIENCE TEAM	WELL-DEVELOPED AUDIENCE TEAM	AUDIENCE-BASED MINI-PUBLISHER TEAM
Organization unit/staff	• Conventional beat, desk or vertical structure	• Core newsroom team with audience-first focus supported by platform and other newsroom specialists	• Core team as described with working relationships with business-side	• Cross-functional core team with full P&L responsibility for target audience
Charter, Work, Accountability	• Story focused • Cover institutions, organizations related to beats • Deliver on assignments	• Audience-first focus • Serve targeted content to targeted audience • Accountable for audience growth and engagement across platforms	• Convert/funnel occasional users into habitual, monetized loyalists • Wide distribution in concert with platform specialists • Content partnership development • Audience revenue experiments	• Audience growth (all dimensions) • Revenue growth • Cost management, including average content cost through blending hi and lower cost approaches (e.g. aggregation) • Net financial contribution (attributable revenue minus expenses)

	CURRENT NEWSROOM	STARTING AUDIENCE TEAM	WELL-DEVELOPED AUDIENCE TEAM	AUDIENCE-BASED MINI-PUBLISHER TEAM
Success metrics	• Meeting deadlines • Some overall traffic numbers	• Traffic, local vs non-local uniques by platform • Reporter- and story-level traffic performance	• Local audience engagement and loyalty measures • Attributable revenues from funneling	• P&L performance • Performance of partnerships
Knowledge, skills and tools	• Beat reporting editing	• Understanding audience needs and interests • Audience focused story telling • Audience engagement skills • Access to basic data and analytics	• Understanding of specific problems being solved for audiences • Story form and platform experimentation and learning • Content partnership development • Customized data and analytics	• Partnership development and management • ROI thinking; contribution management • Project management
Key relationships	• Other folks on the desk and/or in the vertical • Sources within institutions, organizations being covered	• Platform, audience, social and other specialists • Tech/tool providers	• Platform teams • Business side colleagues • External partners	• Senior enterprise leaders

Note: all dimensions are cumulative; each level builds on the foundation of the prior level

PLATFORM-based mini-publisher teams

	CURRENT NEWSROOM	STARTING PLATFORM OWNER	WELL-DEVELOPED PLATFORM OWNER	PLATFORM CLUSTER MINI-PUBLISHER TEAM
Organization unit/staff	• Audience developers in a separate, specialist unit	• Individual platform owners	• Platform ownership group that divvies up platforms, holds each other accountable and coordinates with key folks from audience teams as well as business side	• Cross-functional platform teams responsible for P&L of clusters/ groups of platforms
Charter, Work, Accountability	• Day-to-day platform posting and upkeep • Spend most of their time 'doing things for' others instead of with them in ways that grow skills across the newsroom • Expected to keep up with platform developments and share tips	• Platform audience growth (local market) • Platform skill building through shift in time from mostly 'do it for' others to 'do it with them' plus training • Expected to communicate implications of platform developments to how newsroom must do work	• Platform-driven audience growth and engagement • Funnel audiences from random users to habitual, monetized loyalists • Speed of adoption and implementation of platform developments • Taps widespread platform skills in the newsroom	• Audience growth and engagement for platform clusters • Conversion rates through funnel plus revenue • Platform revenue growth • Platform P&L and financial contribution to enterprise • Platform innovation
Success metrics	• Traffic on platform	• Overall platform traffic performance, with particular attention to local audiences • Speed and effectiveness of adjustments required by shifting platform landscape	• Platform loyalty and engagement measures • Conversion rates through the funnel • Performance against competitor benchmarks • Demonstrated platform skills in newsroom	• Platform audience measures • Local market platform rank/ share • P&L and financial contribution • Number and quality of innovations • Platform-driven successes of audience teams

	CURRENT NEWSROOM	STARTING PLATFORM OWNER	WELL-DEVELOPED PLATFORM OWNER	PLATFORM CLUSTER MINI-PUBLISHER TEAM
Knowledge, skills and tools	• How-to's of using the platform • Various best practices • Rudimentary data and analytics	• Core understanding of keys to success on the platform • Training and coaching others in the effective use of the platform • More customized and actionable platform data and analytics	• Deep understanding of platform dynamics and audience behaviors • Advanced platform data and analytics	• Understanding of revenue flows and opportunities within and across related platforms • Partnership development and management with external platform owners
Key relationships	• Desks • Senior newsroom leaders • Industry colleagues	• Audience teams • Tech and tool builders • Key vendors	• Business side leaders	• Senior enterprise leaders

Note: all dimensions are cumulative; each level builds on the foundation of the prior level

Here is how Miami, for example, tailored a picture to assess their migration toward audience-based mini-publisher teams:

INC. formation stages — phase 1

Steps		FOOD INC.	CUBA INC.	LOCAL GOVT INC.	LAW & ORDER INC.
Committed team	Team leader	●	●		
— Core team would be reporters fully or primarily dedicated to the INC.	Core team				
— Extended team would be identified reporters who contribute content at some level on an ongoing basis	Extended team				

Can use Harvey Balls to indicate degree of progress from none to fully accomplished

Steps	FOOD INC.	CUBA INC.	LOCAL GOVT INC.	LAW & ORDER INC.
Clear target audience				
Clear content strategy				
Audience scorecard (cross platform)				
Regular rhythm • Weekly check-points • Short design/do sprints				
Rolling work plan (writing it down; keeping track)				
Innovations underway • New story forms • New distribution & promotion • Content partnerships				

INC. formation stages — phase 2

Steps	FOOD INC.	CUBA INC.	LOCAL GOVT INC.	LAW & ORDER INC.
Significant increase in audience traffic (50%+ from baseline)				
Business partner on team				
Clear INC. revenue strategy (integrated editorial & business)				
Revenue innovations underway (subscription, sponsorships, events, revenue sharing partnerships, etc.)				

Table Stakes #7 Drive Audience Growth and Profitability from a "Mini-Publisher" Perspective

4. Why these gaps exist

Two related sets of reasons explain why newsrooms have organized themselves in ways that produced too few general managers. The first are unique to the newspaper industry; the second common to any industry whose legacy players thrived under oligopolistic market structures only to get disrupted in serious ways.

a) The historic divide between editorial and publishing

This historic divide goes way back. In the late 19th and early 20th century, American newspapers moved away from their political origins into a more democratized and market-driven era. Eventually, standards of professional journalism emerged and, as is well known, the organization structures with high walls between the editorial and business functions served to protect the integrity of the editorial content from commercial and political interests of the enterprise (i.e. the influence of advertisers or people in positions of power). Under these structures, the two parts of the enterprise came together only at the top of the organization with the publisher — who was the single general manager of the enterprise.

Several assumptions underpinned this sharp divide between editorial and business:

- Editorial cannot operate independently in the absence of strong boundaries cemented by organization structure, the physical separation of people, and the functional division of planning and decision-making.
- The same degree of separation must apply to all types of newsroom content.
- The credibility and brand reputation of the enterprise depends on the public's perception and belief that this editorial separation and independence exists.
- The edit and business functions can be separated without impeding the economic viability of the enterprise.

These assumptions worked in an era of high profits. The enterprise could afford the organizational costs –both monetary and in terms of lack of speed, flexibility and responsiveness. But today, the costs of internal separation have risen while revenues have plummeted making the **structural** division of edit and business highly questionable, even suicidal. In the current era of competitive digital publishing and loss of local market dominance, inflexible, unresponsive, slow and uncoordinated church/state structures condemn instead of sustain metro news enterprises. And do so needlessly because there are less crippling approaches for maintaining the editorial integrity on which audiences still depend for trusted, quality journalism.

b) The common issues confronting legacy organizations in fundamentally changing industries

From the mid to late 20th century, newspaper companies evolved in ways similar to other industries that had oligopolistic or monopolistic market structures. While the business-editorial separation was unique to newspapers, the *functional organization structure* was not. Like other large firms in stable industries having limited competition (for example, industrial and consumer goods, transportation, and telecommunications), common characteristics included:

- Managing the whole enterprise as "one big business" without any customer or product focused segmentation (for newspapers this meant providing general news for general audiences);
- Organizing along functional lines with functional positions (for newspapers: the business and editorial siloes further functionalized into circulation, distribution, and ad sales on one side, and splits such as reporters versus copy editors and separate desks for separate content on the other);
- Operating under one big P&L in which no one below the CEO compared costs and revenues (for newspapers: the publisher).

Many industries operated this way for decades (roughly from the 1950s through 1980s/90s). People in such situations got habituated to cultures in which everyone was:

- Used to operating within fixed functional structures, none of which had the 'whole picture'
- Given to set ways of doing things grounded in an orientation toward functional and operational excellence
- Unfamiliar with working horizontally across the organization
- Deeply experienced in working vertically up the hierarchy of the organization as well as deferring to hierarchical decision-making
- Focused on accountability solely for functional responsibilities rather than any 'whole business' outcomes

These habits ill-served enterprises in industries disrupted by deregulation, globalization, technology, shareholder activism, financialization, socio-demographic shifts and the other forces that changed the rules of the game. Increasingly, senior management knew their enterprises had to shift course to overcome inflexibility, lack of responsiveness, ignoring the customer, inabilities to innovate and more.

One central response *that happened across every single one of these industries* involved reorganizing into business units focused on specific customer groups and/or products and putting general managers in charge. As a result, enterprises:

- Increased the number of general managers who paid greater attention to customers and/or product segments;
- Gave these GMs authority to 'connect the dots' of the functions needed for customer and product responsiveness and innovation
- Debottlenecked the enterprise so that planning and decision-making happened at lower levels in the organization closer to the customer;
- Integrated revenue and expense (P&L) accountability at a greater number of points in the enterprise
- Increased the use of cross-functional teams within and across operating units for both special projects and ongoing responsibilities
- Expanded and made more flexible the number and kind of roles for individuals whose personal development and

career paths toward general management demanded a greater range of functional perspectives, skills and teaming experiences

Legacy newspaper organizations have been late to make such changes. Yet, all the benefits of shifting to more general managers and business units — customer focus, smaller cross-functional organizational units, decentralizing decision-making and accountability, and fostering a sense of ownership and entrepreneurship within a larger organization — are now essential to survival.

5. What success looks and feels like

Success demands shifting your news enterprise away from the church/state functional structure of the newspaper past to a portfolio of general manager led, audience-first, and platform-driven businesses — all of which are guided by senior leaders whose time and attention is rebalanced toward medium and longer term transformation requirements.

Success looks and feels like moving through the stages of the spectrum described above until reaching fully operational and accountable mini-publisher audience and platform leaders and teams.

It also looks and feels like the 'to' side of the following:

FROM > TO shift for Table Stake #7

	FROM	TO
Leadership and organization	We only have a few general managers (perhaps just the CEO/Publisher)	We have many general managers
	We only have a few businesses, products, or services that use P&Ls	We have many businesses, products and services using P&Ls
	Our senior newsroom leaders spend more than 70% of time on day-to-day matters	Our senior newsroom leader spend no more than 25% on day to day matters

	FROM	TO
Core competencies	We are excellent at the operations required to make, market and deliver printed newspapers	We are excellent at serving targeted content to targeted audiences as well as distributing our content to those audiences on the platforms they use
	We have very limited experience in taking risks and/or making investments in doing things differently	Our culture is marked by serious risk taking and investment in doing things differently
	Several folks in our newsroom know what's best for our readers	Our newsroom is outstanding at learning from and responding to audience needs
	We have two key audiences: print and digital	We have a clearly defined set of targeted audiences
Shared understanding, experiences and values	The majority of folks in our news enterprise remain largely unclear about how their work blends with the work of other functions to deliver value to audiences as well as monetize that value	Lots of folk across our enterprise share an understanding of the business and journalistic basics demanded for success
	Our newsroom and business folks don't speak or use the same language	We have fostered across our entire enterprise a shared understanding of the basic language needed for success
	Less than half of the folks in our news enterprise have participated in cross-functional teams	Most of the folks in our enterprise have performance-and-goal based team experiences working cross functionally
	We continue to err on the side of a strict divide of edit versus business to preserve editorial integrity	We use shared beliefs and values along with various managerial processes to ensure editorial integrity
Performance and accountability	Our enterprise has a cost versus revenue picture only for the paper, 'digital' and (perhaps) events	We compare revenue and cost at much more specific levels than just the paper or just digital.
	Only our business folks are accountable for revenue generation	Our newsroom as well as business folks hold themselves accountable for generating revenue and ensuring our news enterprise is financially sustainable
	We do not have an explicit budget of money and/or people's time for innovation	We have and use an explicit budget for innovation
	We are not willing to lose money in pursuit of innovation and learning what works	We don't like losing money in pursuit of innovation — but will do so in order to learn what works

6. Actions to close the gaps

This section describes the steps required to drive audience and platform growth and profitability from a mini-publisher perspective while rebalancing senior leaders away from day-to-day matters toward the medium-to-longer term challenges that spell the difference between success and failure. These steps include:

a) Get going, ideally with audiences and platforms that have (1) the greatest revenue potential; and, (2) the leaders and teams who are most ready and passionate — but in any event, get going!
b) Ask a senior leader team to manage your mini-publisher audience and platform teams
c) Help your mini-publisher audience and platform teams build foundations for success
d) Shift the time and attention of senior newsroom leaders away from day-to-day matters in favor of the medium to longer term challenges of newsroom transformation

a) Get going, ideally with audiences and platforms that have (1) the greatest revenue potential; and, (2) the leaders and teams who are most ready and passionate — but, in any event, get going!

Look again at where your newsroom sits on the spectrum of development of mini-publisher audience and platform teams. It is imperative that your newsroom commits to moving toward the full mini-publisher approach on the right-hand side of that spectrum.

In other words, where ever you are now, pick some audiences and platforms and get going!

Use criteria for choosing which audiences and which platforms to begin with. The criteria should combine assessing the audiences/platforms with (1) the greatest revenue potential and (2) the most readiness. Leader and team readiness, in turn, reflects a blend of (1) capability (having key Table Stakes in place); and, (2) passion/will (leaders and teams who are excited about the mini-publisher approach).

This section provides guidance first for audience teams, then platform teams. In each case, you might select audience or platform leaders and teams just on a gut feeling about revenue potential and readiness — or you might ground the choices in facts, data and analytics about revenue potential and readiness. The latter alternative (facts, data, etc.) turns on just how much you know today and/or how much time and effort you think is necessary to develop facts you might not have today.

Remember this though: deferring 'getting going' in favor of analysis runs a risk of not getting going soon enough. And, mini-publisher leaders and teams learn a lot by 'just doing it' — by learning about mini-publishing by being mini-publishers.

1) Audience Teams

Use the logic in this matrix to assess mini-publisher audience opportunities against two sets of criteria:

Matrix for assessing audience teams to develop into mini-publisher teams

Audience team readiness (skill + passion)	Hi	Get going because you have strong audience teams contributing to primary revenue models	Get going with these mini-publisher ready audience teams
	Lo	Hold off while these possible audience teams move further to the right of the spectrum	Get going while providing support for leader/team skill development
		Lo	Hi
	Revenue potential		

Here are three ways you might make choices:

- Senior leaders use a blend of gut feeling and available data to pick some audiences and just get going
- Senior leaders ask for a small number of volunteers to just get going

- Senior leaders shape a sort of contest or competition in which potential mini-publisher teams make their case using the criteria of revenue potential and readiness

2) Revenue potential

Evaluate revenue potential by:

- Estimating how much revenue your mini-publishing efforts could generate from moving the target audience in question through the funnel of Table Stake #4 — whether the funnel produces digital subscriptions, ad revenue and/or other revenue types such as events.
- Estimating how much revenue your mini-publishing efforts could generate through Table Stake #5's approaches to diversifying revenue — using the table in TS#5

Considering more qualitative indicators of unique revenue opportunities that, absent a mini-publisher approach, will be lost. For example:

- The team has successfully bootstrapped revenue initiatives but needs further support from beyond the team to develop those further, e.g.:

    — A newsletter that's attracted a respectable number of subscribers with a high open rate
    — A couple of events that have attracted good-sized, engaged crowds but have been one-offs where the good buzz dissipated.

- The team has identified promising revenue producing ideas but has lacked the capacity or needed backing to pursue them beyond the conceptual stage.
- Leadership somewhere in the organization has developed a revenue producing idea that hasn't gotten traction but fits well with the team's audience and the team could really run with it and own it, given the right support.

3) Team readiness

Assess teams against these characteristics drawn from Table Stake #1.

Audience Team development and mini-publisher readiness assessment

AREA	READINESS INDICATORS	RATING 1 LO – 4 HI
Team identity, passion and behavior	• The team's composition is clear and members personally identify themselves with the team.	
	• The team members work as a team. They communicate well, actively collaborate, develop skills together and share accountability for the team's audience performance.	
	• The team coordinates well with platform teams as well as social editors, audience developers, technology/tool folks, and marketing and ad sales.	
	• The team is passionate about succeeding as mini-publishers.	
Audience focus and data/analytics	• The team thinks "audience first" and asks what audience needs and interests are served by every piece of content produced.	
	• The team can describe the problems it is solving for its target audience.	
	• Audience data is routinely used to better understand what content actually attracts and engages readers and viewers.	
	• The team has a clear mental profile of the audience being served and a deep understanding of their needs and interests and the audience's problems the team is solving.	
	• This audience profile is articulated and documented so it can be shared with others (e.g. advertising sales) and used to guide decision-making.	

AREA	READINESS INDICATORS	RATING 1 LO – 4 HI
Testing and learning	• The team routinely conducts quick experiments in coverage focus, story-forms, content partnerships, distribution platform or other areas to figure out what works and what doesn't.	
	• The team operates on a rhythm of short sprints (2-5 weeks) to focus on and achieve specific improvements in areas such as skill development, tool use, consistent best practice use, workflow streamlining or technology fixes.	
	• From its learning and experience the team is developing a "playbook" for winning with its target audience, ensuring that this institutional knowledge is not lost and can be imparted to new team members and other teams.	
Performance focus and accountability	• The team has created an audience scorecard that captures key measures of audience traffic, reach and engagement across the platforms used.	
	• The team holds itself both individually and mutually accountable for achieving its goals.	
	• The team regularly reviews performance against the scorecard and actively uses reviews to identify opportunities and plan improvement actions.	
	• The team has actually succeeded in making significant gains in audience growth (e.g. 30+% in local market uniques within six to nine months).	
	• The team understands and connects team and individual performance goals to the skills and training the team and individuals need to succeed at those goals.	
	• The team regularly reports progress in closing skill gaps.	
	• Senior newsroom leaders regularly review the progress of the team against the team's performance and skill goals.	

   Teams scoring threes and fours on most of these indicators are ready to take on the full scope of being a mini-publisher team. Teams scoring mostly twos and threes with maybe a few fours need more time (say, a few months) to fill in the gaps. If a team scores mostly 1s and 2s, but has a team leader truly ready to be a mini-publisher, ask that leader for a plan to get the rest of the team ready as soon as possible. Finally, senior newsroom leaders should direct teams scoring mostly 1s and 2s to take the steps required to fill gaps and otherwise prepare for mini-publishing.

4) Platform teams

Whereas target audience teams own enterprise-wide performance for audiences, platform mini-publisher teams own enterprise wide performance for platforms — for the critical distribution channels on which your metro, local or regional rises or falls.

Platform-based mini-publisher teams must take a whole business view of:

- Developing and managing platform specific revenue opportunities, which may include working and negotiating with outside parties.
- Growing revenue and audience on the platforms you own by coordinating with audience teams to maximize audience growth and engagement, funneling random users into habitual, paying loyalists, and maximizing ad and other revenues
- Growing revenue and audience on the platforms you own by bringing in outside partners or B2B customers, e.g.:

    - Partnerships with local entities to provide content for a new vertical within the platform — in effect, inviting the content partner to use you and your reach as their distribution platform
    - Service arrangements by which you license/provide access to local enterprises to use your platform technology or practices for their own publishing

- Investing (or recommending such investments to senior management) in more platform specific technology that demands mini-publisher attention and accountability for outcomes
- Aligning and optimizing the varying interests, competing priorities and potential conflicts across the newsroom's audience teams sharing the platform

You should form mini-publisher platform teams around clusters of platforms. For example, you might form teams around the three fundamental types of platforms described in TS #2:

- Platforms you own where audiences come to you
- Platforms owned by others that feed audiences back to your platforms
- Platforms owned by others where the audience stays on their platform

You might further tailor teams to align with the audience funnel stages and tactics outlined in TS #4:

Platform mini-publisher teams based on the audience funnel

BRAND AWARENESS BUILDING PLATFORMS	MOBILE/SOCIAL PULL PLATFORMS	PUSH PLATFORMS	CORE LOYALISTS PLATFORMS
• Instagram • Pintrest • Snapchat (general)	• Facebook • Mobile/responsive web	• Newsletters • Notifications • Twitter	• Websites • Apps

Note: particular platforms could be placed in different clusters depending on your current strategy for using the platform. They could also be moved to different clusters over time as your strategy for the platform shifts.

You will likely need only two to four platform teams. Indeed, too many teams risk fragmentation of focus and effort. As said, begin with putting Table Stake #2 in place: publishing on the platforms used by your target audiences. Individuals will emerge as platform owners; and, once they do, you can broaden their roles and responsibilities into mini-publishers.

Use the same two sets of criteria described above: capability and readiness of the platform team compared to the revenue potential of the cluster being considered:

Matrix for assessing platform teams to develop into mini-publisher teams

Platform owner readiness	Hi	Strong platform owners focused on growing platform reach and engagement and supporting existing platform revenue generation (if any)	Mini-publisher ready platform owners to focus on significantly growing existing and developing new revenues in a platform cluster
	Lo	Platform owners to develop further and/or re-evaluate	Priority platform owners to develop further and move up
		Lo	Hi
	Revenue potential of the platform cluster (size and uniqueness)		

b) Ask a senior team to manage your mini-publisher audience and platform teams

Legacy metros, locals and regionals have too few general managers overseeing too few businesses, products and services. Mini-publisher teams help close that gap. Still, mini-publisher teams are front line groups focused on the performance of audiences and platforms. Their success demands the support and guidance from — and 'feet to the fire' accountability to — senior leaders who themselves need to embrace and practice the general management perspective.

Executive Editors and Managing Editors are not general managers. Nor are heads of marketing, ad sales, or technology. Building general manager experience, skills and perspective among senior leaders, then, is just as important as it is in the mini-publisher teams.

Consequently, you should form a cross-functional senior team whose objectives and responsibilities include:

- **Mini-publisher team chartering and formation:** The senior team should charter and staff the mini-publisher team as well as select the team leader(s). The senior team must also guide audience and platform groups across the spectrum toward readiness for the mini-publisher approach (see above).

- **Reporting relationships:** Mini-publisher teams should report to the senior team. Senior leaders might consider divvying up more particular oversight responsibilities in order to balance workload and/or respond to variations in strategic importance of some teams versus others.

- **Performance management:** The senior team should define success and expectations for the mini-publisher teams. In addition, they should review progress by holding monthly review sessions to assess performance, raise and resolve issues, and identify needed support and next steps. (See below for more on progress reviews)

- **Capability development:** The senior team should advise and coach the team leaders on their leadership; work with the team leaders to assess team skills gaps and develop skill development plans; and, assess the case for investment in new team hires with needed capabilities and/or technology or other initiatives.

- **Technology and data support:** The senior team should work with team leaders to assess technology, tool and data needs; make the case for enterprise-level investments; and, ensure needed ongoing technology and data analytics support from across the enterprise.

- **Coordination and integration across mini-publisher teams:** The senior team must ensure strategic alignment across the portfolio of audience and platform teams; help develop partnership agreements that span more than one team and/or parts of the organization; and, resolve inter-team issues that involve enterprise-wide concerns and priorities.

- **Coordination and integration with the rest of the newsroom:** The senior team and particularly the senior newsroom leaders must ensure mutual support among the teams and other parts of the newsroom (e.g. a central news desk), prioritizing use of shared specialist resources where necessary.

- **Brand development and integrity:** The senior team should work with team leaders to make sure that any brands that emerge (e.g. among audience teams) comport with the overall enterprise brand strategy. If new branding approaches emerge to extend reach to new or different audiences — especially ones that spawn radically different or 'off brand' approaches, the senior team must help make sense of it all in ways that avoid brand damage, dilution, or confusion.

c) Help your mini-publisher audience and platform teams build foundations for success

Take four key steps to position mini-publishing efforts for success:

1) Give mini-publisher teams basic charters and ask the teams to put together operating plans needed for team success
2) Regularly review and manage team performance
3) Require mini-publisher teams to use the team discipline for performance
4) Provide mini-publisher teams with the background and support they need to master "economics for journalists" basics

1) Give mini-publisher teams basic charters and ask the teams to put together operating plans needed for team success

The senior team should charter audience and platform mini-publisher teams with core direction and expectations, including: (1) the purpose/vision for the team; (2) why and how the team's efforts matter to the future of the enterprise; and, (3) what success looks like in terms of audience and/or platform growth, engagement, innovation, revenue generation and financial contribution. The time frames for team charters might vary from, say, 1 to 3 years depending on how the teams fit in your enterprise strategy.

The teams should take these charters and come back to the senior team with detailed plans for how the teams will succeed. Team plans should reflect at least two time frames — the longer time frame of the charter as well as a shorter, say, 2 to 4 month time frame that captures what and how the team expects to progress immediately.

Operating plans must include the following elements:

Elements of a mini-publisher team operating plan

AUDIENCE-BASED MINI-PUBLISHER TEAMS	PLATFORM-BASED MINI-PUBLISHER TEAMS
• **Target audience** profile, needs and interests, content focus, etc. (see TS#1, sec. 6) • **Distribution platforms** used to reach the audience (see TS#2, sec. 6)	• **Publishing platforms** included under the team • Target audiences for each of the platforms included (see TS#2, sec. 6)
• **Team organization:** core and extended membership, leader(s), reporting relationship(s)	
• **Service vision:** overarching objectives for serving and growing the target audience	• **Service vision:** overarching objectives for developing the platforms and serving and growing audiences through them
• **Revenue opportunities:** existing and new ways to earn greater revenue from the target audience (see sec. 6 in both TS#4 and TS#5)	• **Revenue opportunities:** existing and new ways to earn greater revenue from the platforms (see sec. 6 in both TS#4 and TS#5)
• **Strategies:** the key means by which the service vision and revenue opportunities will be realized	
• **Goals:** specific objectives for audience growth and revenue attainment within one year and three-year time frames, stated as SMART goals (see Focus on Performance chapter)	
• **Partnerships:** key existing or planned partnerships, including content, distribution, technology and revenue opportunity partnerships and their ties back to the goals and strategies (see TS #6, sec. 6)	
• **Capabilities:** key capabilities to be developed within the coming year, including skills, process/workflows, tools and supporting technologies	
• **Budget:** resources provided to the team, including: staff, shared service commitments, and discretionary cash budgets	
• **Resources and investments:** reallocated or new resources needed from the enterprise in the coming year, including the type, amount, timing, and strategies/goals supported	
• **Assumption and uncertainties:** key aspects of the plan that are most uncertain at this point and how they will be tested to gain more certainty	

2) Regularly review and manage team performance

The senior team should regularly review the progress of mini-publisher teams. These operating reviews might happen monthly, bimonthly or quarterly. In the beginning, shorter cycle times (monthly) make most sense. Depending on the number of mini-publisher teams, such operating reviews might include all teams together — or subsets. At least quarterly, though, all the teams should gather to hear updates on their respective progress and challenges. The senior team should invite the CEO, publisher and others to attend (that is, if those folks are not part of the senior team).

The purpose of review meetings is twofold. The first to conduct a business review whose standing agenda includes:

- Reviewing performance against commitments for the period;
- Discussing issues and lessons learned related to successes as well as shortfalls in meeting targets;
- Identifying any needed enterprise-level support and cross-enterprise issues to be resolved;
- Discussing and setting commitments for the coming period (e.g., month, quarter) while adjusting any longer term objectives as needed;
- Logging identified follow-up action items including who is responsible and over what time frames for the next steps.

The second purpose is to collectively step back and assess the insights being gained and potential opportunities emerging from the work across the whole portfolio of mini-publishers. A part of this includes how best to apply what is working in some teams to the others as well as to other parts of the newsroom and/or other units of the enterprise.

3) Use team discipline

Mini-publisher teams are just that: teams. It's been a quarter century since folks across all three sectors of the economy (private, nonprofit and government) have understood that the discipline and approach to team performance differs from the more familiar boss-subordinate discipline for individual accountability and performance[3]. Here's how the two disciplines compare:

---

[3]

For more, see *The Wisdom of Teams* and/or *The Discipline of Teams* — each co-authored by Jon R. Katzenbach and Douglas K. Smith

BOSS/INDIVIDUAL: SINGLE LEADER DISCIPLINE	TEAM DISCIPLINE
• Boss in control	• Small number (less than 7 or 8 is best)
• Boss makes and communicates decisions.	• Complementary skills and perspectives
• Boss sets goals and decides individual roles, contributions, and individual work products.	• Common/shared purpose
• Boss sets pace and chooses how the group will work together.	• Common/shared SMART outcome-based performance goals
• Boss evaluates results and makes adjustments.	• Commonly agreed upon working approach, including collective work products
• Boss establishes benchmarks and standards.	• Both individual and shared/mutual accountability for results
• Number only limited by boss' attention span.	

Here's how to apply the team discipline to mini-publisher teams:

ELEMENTS OF TEAM DISCIPLINE	MINI-PUBLISHER AUDIENCE TEAMS	MINI-PUBLISHER PLATFORM TEAMS
Small number (typically 7 or fewer)	• Avoid large numbers of folks assigned to a team	• Avoid large numbers of folks assigned to a team
Complementary skills and perspectives	• Assemble team members who bring skill and perspective reflecting audience, content, platform, marketing, ad sales, and/or technology/tools as demanded for the team's performance.	• Assemble team members who bring skill and perspective reflecting platform, audience, content, marketing, ad sales, and/or technology/tools as demanded for the team's performance.
Common purpose	• To grow, engage, innovate, serve and monetize specific, targeted audiences	• To optimize and innovate how platforms are best used to serve and monetize audiences

ELEMENTS OF TEAM DISCIPLINE	MINI-PUBLISHER AUDIENCE TEAMS	MINI-PUBLISHER PLATFORM TEAMS
Common goals	• Specific measureable goals/outcomes for size, growth, engagement and monetization of target audiences • Manage the P&L for the target audience	• Specific measureable goals/outcomes for the quality of the user experience plus competitive functionality as well as traffic, engagement, brand and monetization goals tailored for platforms you own versus platforms you don't own that send you traffic versus platforms you don't own that do not send you traffic • Manage the P&L for the platform group/cluster
Commonly agreed upon working approach	• The work the team needs to do to succeed • How the team divvies up and reviews progress against that work • How the team will coordinate with folks who are not part of the team • How team members will problem solve together when they face uncertainties and/or get stuck	• The work the team needs to do to succeed • How the team divvies up and reviews progress against that work • How the team will coordinate with folks who are not part of the team • How team members will problem solve together when they face uncertainties and/or get stuck
Mutual accountability for purpose, goals and approach (in addition to individual accountability)	• How the team will go about building a shared understanding for blending what's needed for success from each team member and that team member's functional perspective • How the team will ensure that only the team can succeed or fail — that is, move toward a 'we' orientation as opposed to just a sum of individual best performance	• How the team will go about building a shared understanding for blending what's needed for success from each team member and that team member's functional perspective • How the team will ensure that only the team can succeed or fail — that is, move toward a 'we' orientation as opposed to just a sum of individual best performance

The team discipline is particularly needed because more than a decade of shrinking revenues, downsizing and diminished market power have left the legacy newspaper metro, local and regional news enterprises that are still standing with starkly fewer and more constrained resources. At the same time, metros, locals and regionals must get much more done than ever before if they are to navigate the demands required for financial sustainability and success in the midst of fragmenting audiences using multiple and constantly changing platforms to access news and information from numerous and growing numbers of competitors and other sources (including the audiences' friends and followers).

All of which means: Many more challenges requiring much more work that must get done by a lot fewer people with access to more limited resources. Legacy metros, locals and regionals no longer have the luxury afforded by vast newsrooms and business staffs with the capacity to assign work/jobs to different functions and individuals within the functions. So, metros and others must get good at teaming. There is no alternative.

Yet, these constraints requiring more teaming also raise specific questions and dilemmas to address in forming and guiding mini-publisher teams, including:

- **Do all mini-publisher team members need to be full-time?** No. Each team member, though, must have 'skin in the game' and give the team her/his full attention. In addition, you need to make each person's participation and contribution to team success an explicit part of personal performance plans and evaluation.

- **How many teams can an individual be on at the same time?** Probably no more than 3.

- **Is team membership the only way to tap into expertise?** No. Individuals with expertise might also be occasional resources to the team — whether as advisors and/or implementers of specific tasks. For example, audience teams can and should implement directions from platform teams. Tech/tool makers might fulfill team needs without being team members. Marketing and ad sales folks might provide ongoing advice to teams. If this approach is used, teams must work hard to ensure these experts have a shared understanding of the team's purpose and goals and how they can contribute to team success.

- **How should team members bridge responsibilities to the team with responsibilities to their 'home' functions?** For reporters and editors on audience teams, team participation *is* participating in the 'home' function. This question pertains to folks from technology, marketing, sales, finance and other functions — as well as reporters/editors who might participate in platform teams.

In approaching the question, first avoid a trap: team members must not see themselves as representatives of their home function whose job is to be a watchdog protecting their function's interests. That is a path to failure. Team members are not on the team to protect their home functions. They are there to hold themselves individually and mutually accountable with other team members for overall team success.

Instead of protecting home functions, such team members should act as bridges between the team and the function to optimize success for both through: (1) keeping key leaders and others in the home function updated on the team's purpose, goals and progress; (2) advocating on behalf of the team in home function discussions and choices that affect team success; and, (3) obtaining home function human and financial resources, data, analytics, and needed workflow or other changes critical to the team's success.

- **How can teams build the cross-functional shared understanding demanded for success?** Members of a mini-publisher team must build a shared understanding of how and why their respective skills, experiences and perspectives matter to achieving the purposes and performance goals of the team. Given the legacy of church/state and functionalization within church/state, mini-publisher team members must work quickly to educate one another in ways that break down walls while building shared appreciation for what each other do and how that matters to the team.

- **Who should be the team leader?** The team leader might be anyone from any function — whether edit or business side. It is likely, of course, that team leaders emerge from the newsroom for audience teams and from digital specialists for platform teams. You might also consider having co-team leaders — one from the edit or platform side, one from the business side.

What matters most in a team leader, though, is less about functional expertise and more about an individual's experience, proclivity, orientation and beliefs regarding:

- The general manager and whole business perspective
- A personal desire to own and drive the success of a business, product or service (Note well: folks with this kind of drive are also most likely to leave your enterprise if not afforded the chance to lead a mini-publisher team)
- The networking abilities to build the personal relationships and organizational connections within and beyond the enterprise demanded for team success
- An external orientation that includes a natural interest in audience needs and interests as well as market opportunities
- A willingness to take personal accountability for achieving results
- A strong belief in team, especially that only a team can succeed or fail together

4) Provide mini-publisher teams the background and support they need to master "economics for journalists" basics

Newsroom team members must master the basic business understanding of the market dynamics and business side efforts aimed at sustaining the enterprise. This means learning basic business concepts, digital media revenue sources and flows, and the fundamentals of sales processes and cycles. Much of this understanding will emerge from putting Table Stakes #1 through #6 in place.

Conversely, business side team members need to understand the basics of journalism practices and ethics, the mission and community service ethos of journalists, the connections reporters and editors have into the community, and the rhythms of news cycles and content production workflows of the newsroom.

Building this mutual understanding and broader base of perspective is not a one-shot thing. It happens over time — and should be an explicit part of each mini-publishing team's agenda. Suggestions include:

- Shadowing fellow team members. For example, a reporter/producer might attend the weekly sales meeting while a sales team member might observe a reporter pull together and publish a story
- Having team members give primers on a specific topic they know well (e.g. 10 minutes on the revenue flow behind the video player during a team meeting)

- Having team members bring guests to meet with the team to exchange perspectives (such guests might include outsiders as well—for example, a digital media buyer from a leading local ad agency).

d) Shift the time and attention of senior newsroom leaders away from day-to-day matters in favor of the medium-to-longer-term challenges of newsroom transformation

Today, *the* most important job of senior newsroom leaders is to transform their newsrooms by putting the Table Stakes in place. Absent this, the newsroom — indeed, the news enterprise — cannot escape decline into irrelevance and even extinction.

Newsroom transformation happens over a range of time frames:

- Near term of 2 to 3-ish months:
    - Win the day throughout the day
    - Win targeted audiences
    - Win on platforms being used
    - Win trust

- Medium term: 4 to 8-ish months:
    - Best talent
    - Best platforms
    - Best technology, tools, data and analytics
    - Best partners
    - Best innovation

- Longer: From 10-20-ish months to 2 to 3 years
    - Winning audience/content choices

- Winning economics/financial performance
- Winning products/services
- Winning brand(s)
- Winning ecosystem

Senior leaders must deploy themselves across these challenges and time horizons. The Focus on Performance chapter provides an overview of these different time horizons, the kind of performance objectives to set and how senior leaders can think through who is accountable for those results.

Problems arise when:

- Senior newsroom leaders spend too much time directing, approving and inspecting day-to-day work.
- Front-line reporters, editors, digital specialists and others never think beyond getting through the day or end of the week and just keep churning out the same output.
- Mid-level leaders don't give enough attention to setting targets for medium term performance and putting together initiatives to get there.
- Senior leaders react to the latest fads and launch hurry-up efforts that disrupt plans and approaches already in place without first thinking through and involving those affected to at least discuss whether and, if so, how, such shifts might or might not make sense.

The result can be confusion, frustration, and ineffectiveness.

Metros are particularly susceptible to this dysfunction because of daily and Sunday print production deadlines. Reporters and editors focus on getting the paper out. More senior folks do so as well while also guiding major features, reporting projects and investigative series, and perhaps longer term thinking about the annual calendar for producing major supplements. Overall, though, senior time and attention is badly out of balance and heavily weighted to the near term while also concentrated mainly on *content* as opposed to audiences, platforms, identifying and closing skill gaps, redesigning key workflows, spurring innovation, partnering with others, building a local ecosystem, coordinating across the news enterprise, managing financial performance — in short, all the things needed to transform the newsroom and get in the game.

Senior newsroom leaders must escape being stuck in the near term and, instead, spend:

- *Much less* time on the immediate and near term, which is always tempting but now must get delegated to audience and platform teams along with other newsroom colleagues.
- *Much more* time on the medium time horizon challenges described above
- *And more time* on the long term in working across the enterprise in areas such as identifying new target audiences, developing revenue opportunities beyond those of individual mini-publisher teams, developing major long term partnerships, assessing next generation technologies and emerging platforms, and increasing the overall profitability of the enterprise.

Collectively, all these shifts in time horizons across the layers of the organization are essential to the enterprise's digital transformation. A major constraint, though, is limited existing leadership capacity and bandwidth. In addition, then, to considering hiring outsiders for leadership roles, your enterprise should:

- Tap the talent, spirit and capacity of individuals to do more in their individual roles as part of evolving a fuller set of skills and perspectives (e.g., learn and practice more of the skills demanded to be a fully skilled and audience focused reporter/producer)
- Form teams and create leadership roles that have wider responsibilities and further out time horizons — audience teams, platform owners and then audience-based and platform-based mini-publisher teams
- Empower these teams and leaders by not getting in their way and, in effect, duplicating their work
- Free up senior leadership capacity to redeploy time, attention and focus to the medium and longer-term needs of the enterprise.

7. Measures of success and tracking progress in closing the gaps

a) Bring together all the elements of success and sustainability in a mini-publisher "P&L scorecard"

The scorecard for a mini-publisher team has three parts: audience growth and value, market growth and share, and financial contribution.

The first two — audience and market performance — are based on earlier Table Stake scorecards: (1) the audience scorecard described in Table Stake #1; and, (2) the platform scorecard found in Table Stake #2. (See Section 7 of these Table Stake chapters.)

The financial portion of the scorecard measures a mini-publisher team's contribution to economic and financial success — the P&L of that team's effort.

This P&L is a managerial rather than strictly financial concept. It's not aimed at complying with financial reporting obligations. Instead, it asks and measures how much cash does the mini-publisher team contribute to the enterprise as a whole — cash that's left over after the costs of the team's efforts are subtracted from the revenues the team generates.

For the mini-publisher scorecard this means counting two types of costs:

- Direct costs (e.g. staff assigned to the team or freelancer piece rate costs)
- Shared costs that can be allocated or attributed to the team's efforts in ways that tie to the real work of the team as opposed to theoretically (for example, rent and benefits link directly while splitting and allocating the salary of the CEO does not).

If costs are controllable by the mini-publisher team and the choices they make, those costs should be allocated to them. Costs over which the team has zero control should not be allocated (again, for example, the CEO salary). Other costs to avoid allocating might include overhead costs for tech support, analytic services contracts, newsroom management, etc.

Similarly, two types of revenue should be attributed to the team's efforts: direct and derived. Direct revenue is earned exclusively from the team's audience, content, and other efforts, such as sponsorship of its content on a shared platform, advertising and sponsorship revenue on an exclusive platform, sale of content to third parties, and events directly related to the team.

Derived revenues are those reasonably attributable to the team's efforts — for example, the team's fair share of advertising on shared platforms based on traffic, digital subscription revenue from shared platforms based on audience loyalty and engagement factors, and splits of event revenue based on pre-agreements tied to level of involvement.

A team's contribution to overall enterprise financial performance derives from comparing the expenses and revenues attributed to the team's work. Mini-publisher teams, and the senior team to whom they report, can use this contribution calculation to track progress against team goals and objectives, identifying what's working versus not working, and defining needed shifts and next steps.

In addition, the senior team should compare and contrast team performance across the entire portfolio of mini-publishing efforts to make and adjust critical choices for investment such as:

- Increasing investment for teams with high and/or fast growing potential
- Holding investment where the current audience is large with good contribution but low growth potential
- Reducing investment where the audience is large but has low value in terms of contribution
- Cutting or dropping investment if the audience is small and has low value in terms of contribution and growth potential.

Shaping the Right Staff Roles and Skills for Your Newsroom

Introduction

Common sense and experience bear out that metro, local and regional news enterprises cannot get into or win the game without **the blend of staff roles and skills required to do the work needed to serve audiences in today's digitally mediated reality**.

The work that must get done today differs dramatically from, say, a decade or so ago. Today's metro, regional and local newsrooms (and their colleagues across the whole enterprise) must have the skills and capabilities to:

1. Serve targeted audiences with targeted content
2. Publish on the platforms used by your targeted audiences
3. Produce and publish continuously to match your audiences' lives
4. Funnel occasional users to habitual and paying loyalists
5. Diversify and grow the ways you earn revenue from the audiences you build
6. Partner to expand your capacity and capabilities at lower and more flexible cost
7. Drive audience growth and profitability from a "mini-publisher" perspective

Building the needed staff roles and capabilities demands that you:

1. **Define what you need** to be in the game/win the game: that is, what specific roles, jobs, skills, behaviors, attitudes and working relationships are needed to succeed at the seven core table stakes.

2. **Identify gaps:** assess the baseline for where you are now versus what you need; that is, what are your shortfalls when you compare your current capabilities to what's required? You need to do this for individuals, for teams (e.g. desks) and for the newsroom and enterprise as a whole.

3. **Close these gaps by:**

    — *Holding folks accountable* — as individuals and as teams — for **results** from learning, practicing and excelling at required skills/talents
    — *Identifying, attracting, hiring, and onboarding new folks* — then holding them accountable for **results** in the same ways as already employed folks
    — *Partnering and/or using independent contractors* — and again holding all accountable for **results**

4. **Focus on performance** — that is, commitments to, and accountability for, performance results — ***as the context for migrating talent toward what is required***.

5. **Monitor and adjust role and skill requirements as the news game evolves** — otherwise, your newsroom will fall in the trap of playing endless catch up.

Are you doing these things? Have you defined the roles, skills and capabilities you need? Have you assessed your current folks against these requirements? Have you specifically identified shortfalls and gaps — for the newsroom as a whole, for teams, and for individuals? Do you have a game plan that blends helping already employed folks to learn needed skills with hiring new folks who have the skills and/or using partnering and independent contracting to get those skills? Do you? Do you have a game plan that's written down and actually used — actually *managed*? Have you connected what success looks like in terms of outcomes and performance results for this game plan? Have you gained commitments to specific and measurable performance results from folks — teams as well as individuals? For example, have you gained traffic and engagement goal commitments from desks/teams and, by extension, individual reporters, editors, producers and so forth? Do you hold folks accountable for those results? Are you providing support and help — data and analytics, training, work shopping, online self-serve guidance and more — to people who have made performance commitments? Are you *actually managing* all this in a rigorous, buttoned-up way? Do you have regular reviews of progress — reviews that fine-tune the game plan based on what's working and what's not working — and also provide everyone — from senior leaders on down — a picture of 'how we're doing' against clearly defined goals?

Are you? Are you doing all this stuff?

If not, then you're not even in the game of getting into the game.

This chapter focuses on how you must hold already employed folks accountable for specific results that arise from learning, practicing and excelling at required skills, behaviors, attitudes and working relationships.

We point briefly to new hires — and to the good news about the sizeable labor pool as well as the importance of onboarding and maximizing the impact of new, already skilled folks — and, by extension, the similar steps for independent contracting. We encourage you to look at Table Stake #6 to identify and take steps to partner to expand capability and capacity. Primarily, though, this chapter reviews what's required to migrate *already employed folks* through the challenges of behavior-and-skill change.

A note on size: The steps to get what's needed vary based on the size of newsrooms. Those of you with, say, 10 or 20 or so folks in the newsroom need to move forward in ways that differ from those of you with, say, 50 or so — and, that, in turn, varies from newsrooms of one or two hundred or more. And the steps you take will differ if your newsroom is unionized. Still, as Robyn Tomlin of Dallas (who has worked in tiny as well as large newsrooms) emphasizes, the principles and objectives driving choices and approaches are the same: namely, the 7 key table stakes.

Regardless of size, your newsroom must:

- Have folks — or partners — with the required skills in the following essential jobs or roles–*reporter, editor as "mini-publisher"*[1]*, digital producer, audience-developer, visual producer, platform owner and developer/coder*. By *job*, we mean a full-time job. By *role*, we mean tasks someone might perform as part of a larger job. So, e.g., in smaller

---

[1]

We encourage you to pick whatever title or phrase you like. If the language of 'mini-publisher' will cause more trouble than it's worth, then choose a different phrase — just so long as the meaning conveyed include responsibilities that, in the print era, were classically owned by publishers: attracting and retaining readers/users, distributing the content, and monetizing.

newsrooms, a front-line editor (a job) might also include duties related to the role of platform manager. *Indeed, as a general matter, and regardless of size, your newsroom gains flexibility and effectiveness by emphasizing roles instead of jobs*.
- Use the discipline built into the talent-management matrix described below to figure out development pathways for folks — *both as individuals and as teams*. If you partner for any needed skills, then you must review and manage those partners (or independent contractors) with this same discipline.
- Make performance commitments and accountability the central focus for training, workshopping, peer-to-peer/colleague-to-colleague, and other development efforts

Help folks take accountability for performance and change

Legacy newspaper enterprises have a **significant number of already employed folks who must learn specific new skills, behaviors, attitudes and working relationships.**

Leading, guiding and managing already employed folks through skill and behavior change differs from hiring and onboarding new folks. Interestingly, you can often take the same individual and get different results in two different contexts:

1. The individual is already employed in a legacy organization facing significant change *versus*
2. The individual gets a job in a new enterprise where most folks have already mastered the new changes.

Individuals have a better track record learning new skills and behaviors in the second situation compared with the first because of culture, ingrained habits, Maslow's hierarchy of needs, and group dynamics. By culture and habits, we mean 'the way we do things around here.' If the 'way we do things around here' in a legacy news organization is print-centric, for example, then folks who are reluctant to learn new skills will be less likely to even try.

In contrast, if the same folks got hired into a digital only news enterprise, their odds of learning new skills go up.

Think about Maslow. There are six levels of need in Maslow; but, for simplicity, they reduce to three core needs:

- **Security:** having a roof over one's head, enough to eat and so forth. In the 21st century, this means having a job. Most folks tenaciously hold on to jobs — and avoid risks that might jeopardize job security. Even in the face of downsizing after downsizing, folks with jobs at stake can trust luck and fate instead of taking the risks to learn and practice new skills, risks they fear will lead to losing their jobs.

- **Affiliation/friendship:** people in legacy news enterprises have relationships with colleagues that they don't want to sacrifice or jeopardize. In a print centric culture, many folks will avoid singling themselves out if doing so might risk their relationships at work.

- **Meaning and purpose:** Not everyone goes to work with a strong commitment of higher purpose. But many journalists do. Indeed, the Knight Foundation funded Knight Temple Table Stakes because metropolitan legacy newspaper organizations have high numbers of journalists who play essential roles in maintaining democracy. This higher purpose, though, might be a shield against change — e.g. journalists might dissuade themselves and colleagues from embracing digital skills by arguing that democracy is ill served when news media pander to audiences instead of, in a well-known phrase, "making audiences eat spinach."

When blended with culture and habits, Maslow's hierarchy of needs increases the odds that reluctant folks take cues from group dynamics that reduce the odds of change. Consider this example from Minneapolis. Shortly after a meeting with one desk introducing new digital requirements and changes, a journalist on the desk drew a newsroom leader aside to say, "Our desk is stuck in a holding pattern because not enough of us buy into all this stuff." In another example from a smaller legacy news enterprise, the Executive Editor dug in his heels and demanded, "Prove to me why audience-first, digital-first approaches are even needed!"

All this points to a major reality in periods of profound change: ***Decisions are essential, but not enough***. The Minneapolis newsroom leaders decided to get in the game of digital news. They *communicated* the decisions clearly and carefully. Yet, when all is said and done, people must take responsibility for their own performance and change. Decisions are key. Imagine if Minneapolis newsroom leaders had not made the decision to change course? Not much if any change would happen.

But the decision itself only frames a possibility of change. Unless and until a critical mass of folks on the desk in this example commit to results and change, the decision has little effect. No one can take responsibility for the performance-and-change of others. Nor can decisions substitute for that.

Decisions have more effect when no fundamental new skills and behaviors are required. Consider the common decision years back to publish zoned editions. Did this decision require skill changes in *lots and lots* of already employed folks in the newsroom? No. Once the decision was made and communicated, zoned editions moved forward in largely productive and predictable ways.

When Minneapolis senior leaders announced, "We've decided and are committed to getting in and winning the game of digital news" — well, as said, that decision was necessary and critical, but not enough. *Real success depended on a critical mass of already employed folks actually learning the necessary skills/etc*.

Plenty is known now about the particular skills, behaviors, attitudes and working relationships required of legacy news organizations. *What's more challenging is how to manage newsroom and enterprises through the period of transformation.* Success requires that you and your colleagues[2]:

- **Keep performance results the primary objective of change. Not change.** Typically 5% to 15% of folks in legacy organizations seek out and embrace change. They often master new skills, behaviors, attitudes and working relationships. Most folks, though, are reluctant or resistant to change. Their hesitancy minimizes the effectiveness of training or other awareness building efforts. Thousands of experiences across journalism and other industries suggest the odds that already employed folks learn and change go way up when folks *commit to specific performance results as opposed to committing to change.* Performance commitments provide focus and motivation, and are measurable. Moreover, performance

---

[2]
These and other principles for driving skill-and-behavior change are described further in *Make Success Measureable* by Douglas K. Smith.

commitments make it more likely learning happens *in the context of the job itself* as opposed to in, say, the training room. Transformation leaders, then, must focus on getting increasing numbers of folks to commit to performance, not to change.

- **Recognize that only individuals can take responsibility for their own performance and change. No one else can do it for them.** Look, if you need to quit smoking, I cannot do that for you. If you talk about learning to play the piano, I cannot do that for you. If you are a journalist in a metro legacy newsroom, I cannot master for you audience engagement, using data and analytics, using social media for sourcing and curating — or myriad other new skills. Nor can specialists do it for you. When specialists do the work for other journalists, the other journalists do not — *do not* — learn those skills.

- **Use teams as crucibles for mastering new skills, behaviors, attitudes and working relationships.** For all but the smallest newsrooms, senior leaders must hold teams accountable for results and let the teams hold individuals accountable. There are exceptions: senior leaders should hold team leaders themselves accountable; and, perhaps, senior leaders should pay attention to particular individuals whose roles and/or potential merit such attention. As further explained in *The Wisdom of Teams* and *The Discipline of Teams*, real teams emerge when small groups commit to shared accountability for performance results. When this happens, group dynamics work in favor of taking risks to master new skills and ways of working instead of the reverse. Teaming, then, increases the odds that individuals take accountability for their own performance and change.

1. Define the talent you need

Today's metro newsrooms (and their colleagues across the whole enterprise) must have the skills and capabilities to:

1. **Serve targeted audiences with targeted content**
2. **Publish on the platforms used by your targeted audiences**
3. **Produce and publish continuously to match your audiences' lives**
4. **Funnel occasional users to habitual and paying loyalists**
5. **Diversify and grow the ways you earn revenue from the audiences you build**
6. **Partner to expand your capacity and capabilities at lower and more flexible cost**
7. **Drive audience growth and profitability from a "mini-publisher" perspective**

Getting there particularly depends on the following key jobs or roles:

- Reporter
- Editor as mini publisher
- Digital producer
- Audience developer
- Visual producer
- Platform owner
- Developer/coder

"Job" here means a full-time job; "role" means the tasks someone might perform as part of a larger job. For example, in smaller newsrooms, a front-line editor (a job) might include duties related to the *role* of platform owner. Here's a guide contrasting traditional jobs with variations on role combinations for today's newsrooms:

TRADITIONAL FUNCTIONAL POSITION	ROLES AND COMBO ROLES FOR AUDIENCE-FOCUSED CONTINUOUS DIGITAL FIRST PUBLISHING
Reporter	• reporter/producer/audience developer ("one-person workflow" capable) • audience team member (for collective audience understanding and collaborative audience development ; see Table Stake #1)
Editor	• producer/editor/audience developer • digital story editor (all elements of the story, not just text) • digital hub "real time" producer/audience developer • digital hub shift editor/manager
Digital producer	• story enhancer (applying advanced skills to select stories) • production skills developer and coach • story form creator (working with audience teams and producer)
Photographer, videographer or graphics designer	• visuals producer/editor/audience developer • visuals skills developer and coach • visual story form developer (working with audience teams, producers and tech developers)
Audience developer	• audience development skills developer and coach • audience development opportunity identifier • audience development innovation/experimentation leader • platform owner (see Table Stake #2)
Tech developer	• story form developer (working with audience teams and producer) • technology awareness coach and advisor (e.g., primers, cautions on breaking and hacking) • audience experience watchdog (e.g. load times, page/screen rendering)

And, by way of example, here are what the four Table Stakes teams defined as requirements for a fully skilled reporter in a 21st century newsroom:

Basic Journalistic Values/Practices

- Fairness, accuracy, verification, spelling, style, grammar, clarity, brevity, speed
- Eyes/ears to the community and target audiences
- Upholds journalism values
- Nose for sniffing out big story/trends
- Attacks stories/problems with goal for positive change
- Basic computer skills
- Other: _____
  (NOTE: 'other' is included to allow for unique situations that vary by newsroom as well as evolution/change in needed skills, etc.)

In Real Life:

- Observing, listening, cultivating and verifying sources, researching, interviewing
- Can report on range of subject matter (not overly narrow)
- Understands community and target audiences as a whole and how coverage plan/effort serves audiences
- Reports on all perspectives in the community to ensure diverse and inclusive points of view
- Other: _____

Virtual:

- Awareness of what other media are doing
- Understands we are not the only players in the game and:
  — Avoids unproductive competition for scoops
  — Aggregates/curates/shares the work of other players
- Understands how to use social media as a reporting tool for sourcing, curating and distribution, including how to mine, verify and incorporate social reporting
- Knows what is trending — on our platforms and others' platforms
- Proactively/routinely considers and uses aggregation/curation as reporting approach
- Other: _____

Audience Engagement Skills

- Understands and can accurately describe the target audience(s) we seek to engage with coverage
- Routinely understands/proposes coverage approaches/angles — from audience point of view — regarding what audience wants/needs and what matters to audience
- Places premium on platform optimization by delivering content when (time of day), where (platforms/sites/devices), and how (size/length/format/etc.) our audiences want it
- Adept at routinely ensuring content is *shareable, findable and explore-able* through:
  — SEO friendly headlines
  — Including links within body of content
  — "Most viewed" lists
  — Using hashtags

- Live chats
- Blogging
- Notifications
- Pushing posts from one platform to others
- Other: _____

- Blogs the beat: real-time postings to guide conversations and engagement with readers/users
- Quickly and insightfully shares what is trending with the target audience
- Can quickly and effectively aggregate/curate and share with audiences on appropriate platforms
- Adept at quickly creating/posting content responsive to buzz worthy/key events (for example, can live-Tweet)
- Recognizes the most interesting and resonant aspects of a story that will connect with our audiences
- Routinely invites/encourages community/audience to create and respond to content including 'talking with readers/users' and not pontificating
- Adept at routinely posting/monitoring/responding to content on platforms used by target audiences, such as:
  - Facebook
  - Twitter
  - LinkedIn
  - Reddit
  - Instagram
  - Snapchat
  - Other: _____
- Has a distinctive, effective voice
- Other: _____

Story Crafting Skills

- Adept at choosing/pitching the stories our enterprise ought to 'own'
- Uses calendar/events schedule as part of coverage plan and pitches
- Routinely considers/suggests how stories can be told in different ways throughout the time the story is being reported (before, during, after)
- Routinely uses best practices/forms/templates for story telling approaches — ones with proven track record of results
- Routinely uses at least 2 or more elements (text, photo, audio, etc.) and is adept at knowing when/why/what is

'best' of the media used: video vs audio vs text vs photo, etc.
- Adept at gallery creation
- Monitors both story developments as well as performance of story (in terms of traffic, engagement, etc) and
    - Keeps others informed
    - Updates when/where/how it makes most sense (including fresh content)/visuals/etc. as well as cross links to original and/or earlier updates)
- If story is 'major,' either on its own or with timely help from others, complements story telling with an array of photography, informational graphics, video, audio and/or data support
- Writing style varies appropriately to platform based on best practices
- Keen eye for producing authoritative and relevant content unique for target audience and tailored to appropriate platform
- Ensures digital assets customized to the platform
- Adept at:
    - Taking (and doing basic edit for different platforms, e.g. mobile) photos on smart phone and posting to social media, embedding in blog post/story or sending to photo desk
    - Taking (and doing basic edit for different platforms) videos on smartphone and posting to social media, embedding in blog post/story, sending to video desk
    - Capturing audio on smartphone and posting to social media, embedding in blog post/story or sending to desk
    - Adding documents to story
- Other: _____

Data/analytics skills

- Always checks/updates the budget/release schedule to ensure others have current and accurate view
- Can do simple A/B testing, e.g. of headlines
- Tags content
- Archives all content into digital asset management system for future use
- Regularly monitors available analytics for patterns of what's working/what's not working with audiences in

terms of story, story forms/templates, media type (photo, video, audio, text, etc.) platform optimization, promotion, etc.
- Regularly views and considers basic analytics of stories with an understanding of sources of traffic, readers' usage patterns, engagement with story and time of day reading
- Uses lessons learned from analytics in pitches/proposals as well as regular team reviews of audience/coverage plans
- Always on top of what's trending on:
  - Our platforms/sites
  - Other's platforms/sites
- Other: _____

Collaboration & Learning Skills

- *Knows* and *timely communicates* when:
  - Can do him/herself
  - Can do but wants someone to check
  - Needs help from others
- Has plan in place to grow/develop specific skills and proactively using this plan
- Regularly takes initiative and personal responsibility for using learning tools available on our enterprise learning platform as well as the Web
- Has interpersonal skills required for effective collaboration and learning
- Regularly participates in and contributes to reviews of best practices, what's working/what's not
- If story — whether routine or 'major' — will perform better with contributions by others who have more specialized skills, engages those folks at the beginning, not end
- Regularly participates in and contributes to team and, when needed, newsroom wide performance reviews (including with biz side)
- Other: _____

Ingrained habits, attitudes, 'will', hopes/fears, and mindset

- Believes in providing targeted content to targeted audiences when, where and how the audience wants/needs

- Driven to cover things that make a difference to our audience's lives — not just being a journalist of record for institutions
- Knows the difference between good traffic and not good traffic
- Thinks/acts/learns what is platform optimal and is not 'platform agnostic'
- Driven to find and connect with the audience vs. believing audience will find content
- Always on deadline vs. focused on end of day print deadlines
- Story centric not text centric
- Releases content when and as audience wants/needs versus print schedule
- Seeks out skill development versus 'waits around to be trained'
- Works hard and collaboratively with biz side to create and monetize valuable audiences versus persists in church/state divides
- Other: _____

Other

- Knows what's legal and not legal to use
- Basic competency with current CMS including how to transfer assets between and among different systems as well as workarounds needed to serve and grow audiences
- Regularly participates in and contributes to review of performance against team's (and newsroom's) value/cost strategy for content
- Other: _____

Please note the inclusion of "other" in each section. Given the pace of technological, demographic, economic and other forces, your newsroom must ask — now and periodically moving forward — if any additional skills, behaviors, beliefs, attitudes or working relationships are required for success.

The teams for Minneapolis, Miami, Dallas and Philadelphia — *having themselves specified what's required of a fully skilled reporter* — also remarked that this job description is daunting. And you may react similarly after reading through it the first time. Look at it a second time and note that much of what's needed for coverage skills as well as collaboration, learning, habits and attitudes are either basic to journalism or basic to curiosity and learning. ***The meat of what's different relates to audience engagement, data and analytics and story crafting in the virtual space of a digitally mediated world.*** And none of those specifics should surprise you: journalists and others have discussed them for nearly a decade now.

Nor do you have to demand that reporters tackle the full list immediately. You can challenge folks to master these in waves. Philadelphia chose to move first on a range of audience engagement and data and analytic skills. The other three newsrooms did so as well. (See below for Philadelphia's digital skills survey and related assessment).

Many other jobs/roles matter to success as well. Here's a list the four teams identified:

- Aggregation editor
- Data journalist
- Photo/video journalists
- Interactive/graphics
- Web designers
- Home page editor
- Newsroom analysts
- Social media editor
- Events planner/coordinator
- Community engagement specialist
- Technology navigator/what's next role
- Partnership manager
- Audience R&D/consumer insights
- Liaison to biz side
- Newsroom Strategist
- Data scientist
- Data warehouse manager/liaison
- Talent Leader
- Technology Architect
- Innovation Leader
- Managing Editor
- Executive Editor

You can and should describe what's required for any of these in ways that are as specific and detailed as the fully skilled reporter.

2. Identify Gaps

Once you've defined the talent and capabilities your newsroom needs, it's essential to compare where you are now versus what is required. Do this at three levels:

- Individuals
- Teams
- Newsroom (or news enterprise) as a whole

Begin by surveying and evaluating individuals with key jobs or roles. For example, Philadelphia used this questionnaire to establish a baseline of current versus required skills:

Digital Skills Questionnaire

With all the changes in our newsroom, we know it is important that all our journalists have the competitive skills needed to thrive in a digital environment. We want to provide opportunities for everyone here to grow their skills through training, workshops and documented best practices.

In order to do this, we need your help. Please complete the following survey to help us identify where to focus our training and education efforts.

Questions? Please feel free to reach out to Erica, Michael, Ellen or Kelly.

Part 1: What does a journalist in 2016 need to know?

Think big-picture here. If you were giving advice to a journalism student about the skills required of modern journalists, what do you think that student needs to know? There are some suggestions listed here, but feel free to add your own.

In 2016, all journalists should know how to ... *

_ Write a web headline.
_ Add links to a story on the website.
_ Add photos to a story on the website.
_ Tweet

- Post on Facebook.
- Verify the authenticity of a source on social media.
- Identify when a topic is trending on social media and worthy of coverage.
- Make a correction to a story on the website.
- Use tools like Slack to communicate with other staffers.
- Moderate comments on the website.
- Other:

* This is a required question

Part 2: How comfortable are you with digital skills?

Now, think about your personal experiences here at PMN. This section will help us identify opportunities for training and skills workshops.

I can ... *

- Write a web headline.
- Add links to a story on Philly.com.
- Add photos to a story on Philly.com
- Tweet on your personal Twitter handle.
- Post a story on your own Facebook page.
- Verify the authenticity of a source on social media.
- Identify when a topic is trending on social media and worthy of coverage.
- Make a correction to a story on Philly.com
- Use tools like Slack to communicate with other staffers.
- Moderate comments on Philly.com.

I would like more training on how to ... *

- Write a web headline.
- Add links to a story on Philly.com.
- Add photos to a story on Philly.com
- Tweet on your personal Twitter handle.
- Post a story on your own Facebook page.
- Verify the authenticity of a source on social media.
- Identify when a topic is trending on social media and worthy of coverage.

- Make a correction to a story on Philly.com
- Use tools like Slack to communicate with other staffers.
- Moderate comments on Philly.com.
- I don't feel that I need any more training.

Part 3: Open Forum (OPTIONAL)

Did we miss anything? When it comes to training, education, skills workshops, what do you want us to know?
What should we know about digital skills at PMN?

Your answer:

Your name:

In addition to asking journalists to describe/rate themselves, Philadelphia also asked others to evaluate folks in the newsroom and then scored folks against the requirements. By establishing this baseline, Philly could describe gaps for the individuals, for the teams, and for the newsroom as a whole.

3. Close the gaps

There are three pathways to close talent and skill gaps in your newsroom:

- **Holding already employed folks accountable** — as individuals and teams — for learning, practicing and excelling at performance results related to the required skills/talents

- **Identifying, attracting, hiring, and onboarding new folks** — then holding them accountable in the same ways you do already employed folks

- **Partnering and/or using independent contractors** — and again holding all accountable for results

Imagine, then, headline writing. It is table stakes for reporters to get good at the headlines that drive traffic and engagement because:

- **Content must be findable, shareable and exploreable.** Headlines determine find-ability (search) and share-ability (social).

- **Internet speed requires reporters do this themselves.** When others write headlines for reporters, it takes two steps instead of one. It's slower. And slowness means missed traffic and engagement.

- **Audience-first strategy demands adopting and responding to the audience's perspective.** The first thing audiences see are headlines. When reporters pitch headlines, they get good at succinctly describing the story in terms of why the audience cares. If someone else is doing this for the reporter, then that reporter does not understand the connection between the story and the audience.

This is a skill and attitude shift for print reporters because (1) headlines that work in print differ from headlines that work in digital; (2) print reporters were not always responsible for headlines; and, (3) print headlines came as the last step when today they come first.

Consider the 'headline rodeo' at the Dallas Morning News. Each morning the folks in Dallas gather to decide which stories to emphasize through: (1) discussing a series of proposed headlines crafted to convey the essence of proposed stories; (2) workshopping those headlines to make them better; and, (3) reviewing/debriefing how previous headlines actually performed.

In Dallas, it is table stakes for reporters to be good not only at headlines that are findable/searchable and shareable but also headlines that distill the essence of a story from an audience-first perspective. Philadelphia also has a version of a headline rodeo. And they expect reporters to grasp an additional nuance: the difference that *sometimes* exists between web headlines (search engine optimization) versus promotional headlines that are not related to search algorithms. As Erica Palin of Philly pointed out in a note to her newsroom colleagues:

> - **"Web headline** = the headline that appears on your story on Philly.com and will show up on Facebook and Twitter when someone shares your story. *This is the headline that Google scrapes and looks at for keywords and SEO. Once this headline is live on Philly.com, we shouldn't change it (unless there's a spelling or fact error).* Reporters should write this — with guidance and help from assigning editors/copy editors.
>
> - **Promo headline** = the headline that appears on the homepage and section fronts. Sometimes this is the same as the web headline, *but not always. This is written by producers and can change throughout the day.* Google does not read this headline for SEO purposes."

In the days of print, neither reporters nor others worried about such distinctions.

With headline-related skills and attitudes in mind, consider reporter X in your newsroom. Here are the key steps you must take:

- Does Reporter X already know how to use headlines to drive traffic and engagement as well as pitch stories?
- If yes, great! Encourage X to keep getting better — and seriously consider asking X to work with others in or beyond X's team because peer-to-peer help is powerful.
- If no, X has a skill gap to close.
- Is Reporter X trying?
    - If yes, great! Just make sure X commits to specific traffic and engagement performance results that benefit from X's efforts
    - If not, what actions might increase the odds that Reporter X is motivated to try?
- If Reporter X has a gap and is trying, how can you use Reporter X's commitment to headline *performance results* as a condition and context for providing help? For example, how might you make X's commitment to

specific results the 'price' X pays for the opportunity to attend training and workshops, or get help from a digital specialist or peer?

Such questions determine where — in this illustration with regard to headline skills — Reporter X is positioned in a talent management matrix:

Talent management matrix — individual

		Abililty/attitude (skill/will)		
Current behavior		Gets it	Doesn't get it but might	Doesn't get it/ Won't get it
	Doing it now			
	Trying			
	Not trying			

Consider any "Reporter X" in your newsroom. Think of 'it' (e.g. 'gets it') as headline writing. Where would you place X on this matrix? Now use this version of the talent management matrix to identify actions you must take:

Talent management matrix — actions

		Abililty/attitude (skill/will)		
		Gets it	Doesn't get it but might	Doesn't get it/ Won't get it
Current behavior	**Doing it now**	• Make champions and coaches • Provide greater opportunities		
	Trying	• Get them to commit to performance goals that demand the skill in question • Provide skill development help	• Get commitments to performance results that demand the skill in question • Provide skill development help • Keep assessing	• Won't make it • Is there 'highest and best' use in non-digital efforts? • Counsel out
	Not trying	• Gain commitments to performance results • Set expectations and timeframes • Keep assessing	• Make commitments to performance the "price" of gaining skill development help • Set expectations and timeframes • Keep assessing	• Manage out • Find other "best use" if job protected

The essential step is getting Reporter X to commit to performance results that depend on X getting better at headlines — as opposed, say, to attending headline training.

The folks in Miami demanded that all reporters increase traffic by 7.5% — and then increased the odds of success by providing skills training to help reporters succeed. So did Dallas (though they used 10% as well as performance increases in a specially tailored engagement index).

Who is responsible for managing talent — for managing and guiding the transition of folks who must learn new skills such as headline writing? The answer:

- *First and foremost, each individual is responsible for her/his own performance and change.* No one can do this for them. If Reporter X wishes to get good at headlines, then Reporter X must take responsibility for doing so.

- *Second, teams must take responsibility for the skills of individual team members.* Minneapolis' newsroom has roughly 250 folks. Senior newsroom leaders cannot keep tabs on so many individuals. Teams need to do that.
- *Senior leaders must keep tabs on the teams* — and use the talent management matrix to guide them. Senior leaders might pay attention to particular individuals such as team leaders and folks who can influence overall performance results and/or change momentum either positively or negatively.

Teams should use the talent management matrix to position, then migrate, *individuals* to the upper left box. Senior leaders should use the matrix to position, and then migrate *teams* to the upper left box. Here's an illustration for the team view of the matrix:

Talent management matrix — teams

		Abililty/attitude (skill/will)		
		Gets it	Doesn't get it but might	Doesn't get it/ Won't get it
Current behavior	Doing it now	Breaking News Team		
	Trying		Sports Team / Arts Team	
	Not trying			

The 'it' in the matrix varies depending on jobs, roles, skills, attitudes and working relationships. For example, in Philadelphia, the 'it' included writing web headlines, adding links to a story on the website, adding photos to a story on the website, tweeting, posting on Facebook, verifying the authenticity of a source on social media, identifying when a topic is trending on social media and worthy of coverage, making a correction to a story on the website, using tools like Slack to communicate with other staffers, and moderating comments on the website.

In addition to using the talent matrix to guide already employed folks, you can also use it to consider additional options for closing gaps: hiring new folks and/or partnering with others, including independent contractors.

There's good news in this. Consider the skill differences among digital natives (people who have grown up from childhood with digital technology), digital emigrants (people who have embraced digital technology as adults), and digital nevers (people who don't get it and won't get it). Today, there are millions more digital natives and digital emigrants than, say, in 2002 or 2005. Your newsroom has more opportunity than ever before to identify, attract, hire and onboard folks with key skills. Even in the face of tight budgets, Philadelphia, Minneapolis, Miami and Dallas took advantage of the growing labor supply of digital natives and digital emigrants to fill digital producer, audience developer, coder/developer and platform owner jobs and roles.

They also learned that what happens *after* such folks are hired matters a lot. In particular, metro newsrooms must overcome:

- **Digital divide:** In the autumn of 2015 (just at the beginning of the Table Stakes effort), folks with digital skills *in all four* newsrooms were frustrated about isolation and being "after thoughts." These concerns arose from print-centric culture and practices. It was commonplace for a significant story to be all but fully complete before the digitally skilled folks were asked to get involved. Instead, folks lamented that stories would be done, then "thrown over the wall" with the request to "make it work on digital."

- **Print-driven meetings and choices:** Prior to the Table Stakes efforts, the daily meeting flows were print-focused and habits such as 'hold that story for Sunday' marginalized folks with digital skills.

- **Do it for them (not with them):** Digital specialists spent nearly all their time doing digital work *for* others instead of *with* others. Consequently, skills were not getting acquired or practiced by most folks in the newsroom.

- **Boredom and lost opportunity:** People with significant skills — whether audience developers or coders or others — were not being challenged enough. They joined their metros with a deep sense of mission and wanted to make a difference. But, too often, senior leaders and others were not asking them to make much difference at all. Few were specifically asking digital experts to lead and/or contribute to the major transformative efforts critical to getting metro newsrooms into the 21st century.

4. Use performance commitments to drive skill and behavior change

Performance is the primary objective of change, not change. Don't ask folks to commit to attending headline or tweeting training. Instead, get folks to commit to specific performance results that depend on excellent headline writing or tweeting.

Here are four approaches to increase the odds folks make performance commitments:

- **Hierarchy:** Bosses can and should demand specific performance results from subordinates.

- **Volunteers:** Early adopters and other volunteers often embrace change. That's great! But you need volunteers to commit to specific performance results, not to change.

- **Teams:** When teams commit to specific performance results, the individuals on those teams contribute to success or, over time, single themselves out as bad fits for the teams

- **Exchange:** Think for a moment of Weight Watchers. In exchange for specific weight loss goals (and money), Weight Watchers provide customers support and guidance of various sorts. You can do the same thing. In exchange for providing training, workshops, coaching and other resources and help, you can demand a 'price' — namely, individual and/or team commitments to specific performance results.

[3]

For more on SMART goals, see *Make Success Measurable* by Douglas K. Smith

Specific performance results should be SMART *outcomes, not activities*. Activities are such things as 'I commit to go to training." SMART outcomes describe results or impacts that are[3]:

- Specific
- Measureable
- Aggressive yet achievable
- Relevant to the work at hand
- Time-bound

Folks who commit to specific performance outcomes are more likely to take advantage of help. To increase their odds of success, you and your colleagues should also recognize that different folks learn differently.

For example, Joy Mayer and her team at University of Missouri, asked journalists to describe their preferred learning approaches. Here's what was reported[4]:

[4]

"We asked journalists: How do you fit in time to learn about industry information?" Mayer, October 6, 2016

- Short text (like blog posts): 73 percent
- In-person events: 59.5 percent
- Social conversation (like Q&As): 45.9 percent
- Podcasts: 43.2 percent
- Long text (like reports or white papers): 35.1 percent
- Short videos: 35.1 percent
- Long videos (like webinars): 32.4 percent
- Games or quizzes: 2.7 percent

You and your colleagues should consider these and any other approaches. Indeed, think about the Table Stakes requirement to be audience-first. Well, when it comes to mastering the skills, attitudes, behaviors and working relationships mandated to be in today's news and information game, journalists (and business side colleagues) are the audience for any effort aimed to help bridge gaps. The first requirement is to get these folks to commit to performance, not change. Once those performance commitments are in place, though, pay attention to your audience — your colleagues with skill gaps — and tailor help in ways that they need and want.

5. Monitor and adjust talent requirements as the news game evolves

The game of 21st century news and information is dynamic. It moves fast. Things change. For example, some folks now argue that, because the home page matters a lot less than previously, newsrooms should consider eliminating a home page editor. Another example: notwithstanding the relentless pace of change, too few newsrooms have a technology navigator — whether as job or role –someone who monitors developments and pragmatically forces conversations and decisions about what technology and tools ought to be adopted versus experimented with versus monitored further.

Senior leaders must regularly step back to evaluate the shifts happening. For any particular shift (illustration: rapid advances in virtual reality and augmented reality), leaders must ask:

- How might this new development help us better reach and serve audiences, provide superior content and/or experiences, improve our economics or otherwise make positive differences for us?
- What specific performance gains might we achieve if we were to adopt, partner and/or otherwise get good at this new thing? What are the associated costs and risks (including risks to such things as trust and brand)?
- How confident are we? How much certainty versus uncertainty is there to key questions such as: (1) "Is there a market for this?" (2) "Do we believe there is such a market?" (3) "Is the technology for this proven?" (4) "Do we have the capabilities required for this?"
- How might we best move forward? Adopt and roll out something immediately to the whole newsroom? Experiment? Buy or partner?
- How would we know success? That is, what SMART outcome-based goals should we commit to achieving as part of moving forward?

Depending on the size of your enterprise, your best path forward could shift among the three main paths of behavior/skill change of already employed folks versus new hires versus buying/partnering. Regardless of the pathway or blend of pathways selected, you must use the disciplines of performance-driven talent migration described in this chapter to succeed.

Winning: Execution and Innovation

This report spells out the Table Stakes required for metro, local and regional news enterprises to be in the game of news and information in 2017 moving forward. Table stakes[1] is a term from poker: the table stakes are what you must ante up to get a seat at the table. If you go to Vegas, Atlantic City or even a friendly Thursday night game with friends, you *must* ante up the $10, $50, $100 or whatever minimum, or else you don't get to play.

This concept applies to markets and networks: competitors cannot be in the game if they lack the minimum capabilities and resources demanded. For quite a long time, for example, carbon paper was table stakes for companies competing for the business of customers who needed to have copies of documents. Following the advent of Xerox (and then others), carbon paper was no longer table stakes. A range of other copying technologies emerged to take its place.

You don't, of course, sit down at a $25 poker game to lose your $25. You want to win. And that means playing your hand to win — which, in the markets and networks analogy, means folks in your news enterprise *must figure out how to differentiate yourselves from others in ways that win*.

Okay. So how does your metro, local or regional news enterprise win?

What's the winning playbook?

No one knows the *full* answer.

This differs from two or three decades ago. Imagine that, in the 1980s or 90s, the owner of *Big City Metro* interviewed you for publisher and asked, "How will you ensure *Big City Metro* wins?"

You knew the entire answer.

1

As indicated earlier, you and your colleagues may not like the term table stakes. That's fine. Pick something else. Just make sure the meaning is the same: what your legacy newspaper enterprise must do to be viable in 2017 and beyond?

The playbook for winning was clear. As publisher, you would expect circulation to sell and service as many newspaper subscriptions as possible, optimize revenues through varying subscription offers, and focus on renewal rates. Circulation and distribution would coordinate in ways that kept subscriber complaints to a minimum. You'd also work closely with the printing plant(s) to ensure they operated efficiently and, from time to time, upgraded equipment to take advantage of technology developments. You'd keep on top of distribution's single copy sales arrangements as well as their routes and costs. You'd help the operations folks tangle with the editorial folks about when, how and why to have late closes. And, of course, you'd spend time working with your ad sales folks generating revenues from advertising, classifieds and couponing, inserts and so forth. Finally, you'd expect the Executive Editor and colleagues to provide readers the very best journalism possible.

You knew what to do to win. All you and your colleagues needed to do was *implement. Execute. Operate.*

In the 1980s and 90s, if you executed well, you won. Interestingly, even if you operated in mediocre ways, you won because *Big City Metro* had oligopolistic or monopolistic market power. In a sense, you couldn't lose. You could only do more or less well based on how effectively you and your colleagues implemented the playbook. There were risks and uncertainties — but you knew what they were and how to analyze them. For example, you knew how to analyze and market test whether zoned editions would lead to better coverage, different and/or more advertising, more subscribers, higher subscription rates and/or better retention rates. You knew how to analyze the risks of adding another printing plant, or investing in an upgrade of printing technology.

You might get the choices wrong. Or, you might make the right choice but then implement poorly. You could lose money — or, more likely, *make less money*. But you really couldn't mess up so badly that *Big City Metro* would go out of business.

Today, you and your colleagues *know* **part** *of the playbook* — the seven core table stakes:

1. **Serve targeted audiences with targeted content**
2. **Publish on the platforms used by your targeted audiences**
3. **Produce and publish continuously to match your audiences' lives**

4. **Funnel occasional users to habitual and paying loyalists**
5. **Diversify and grow the ways you earn revenue from the audiences you build**
6. **Partner to expand your capacity and capabilities at lower and more flexible cost**
7. **Drive audience growth and profitability from a "mini-publisher" perspective**

These — and the related work, workflows, roles, skills, technology and tools — are what you must implement, execute and operate.

Consider, for example, the imperative to get as many people and enterprises as possible to pay for content that they value — for example, through digital subscriptions. The odds of success go way up when you and your colleagues get really good at providing targeted content with value to your selected audiences, and publishing that content to meet the needs of those audiences on the platforms the audiences use when they use them — all while you folks also get good at funneling random, occasional users in those audiences into loyal, paying customers.

What's different today, though, is this: *even when you implement the table stakes well, you might fall short. You might not win.*

Why?

Because today abounds with unfamiliar risks and uncertainties that you and your colleagues do not fully understand yet still must act upon. For example:

- Will (enough) consumers who have lost the habit of paying for content reverse course?
- Will (too many) advertisers who have the data-driven, analytical means to precisely target their efforts as well as myriad alternative ways of reaching audiences keep reducing CPMs and/or even abandon local news enterprises?
- Will major, established vendors of content management and related systems adjust their offerings and economics in ways that dramatically lower costs and increase flexibility and innovation?
- Will the costs of technology, data and analytics become insurmountable for local news enterprises?

- Will the pace of technological change outstrip metro, regional and local news enterprises' financial and human capacity to keep up?
- Will single topic/single audience digital players use scale and reach to strip out (too many) local consumers?
- Will the decline in *newspaper* revenues deprive your enterprise of the cash needed for innovation?
- Will a private equity or other financial buyer acquire your enterprise to profit not from journalism but rather a blend of cost reduction and financial engineering?
- Will your owners and/or senior executives have the courage to *risk losing cash and capital* on unproven experiments and strategies?
- Will a critical mass of folks *across your enterprise* have the courage — and discipline — to risk jobs and livelihoods by changing how you *work together in specific ways* that no one, in advance, knows for sure will work?
- Will you, your colleagues and your enterprise's owner(s) have the courage to reimagine the purposes and value of local journalism, and how to work with local audiences and communities to make such purposes and value real?

No one knows how these uncertainties will work out. Yet, to win, you and your colleagues must risk time, effort and money to tackle the issues and questions notwithstanding that *you don't know how things will turn out — even if you implement and execute brilliantly.*

To win today, then — unlike during the 1980s and 1990s — **you must innovate**.

Innovation means risk and uncertainty. It means the possibility of failure.

The poker analogy is apt: you might ante up the needed stakes, and do your best to play your hand — yet still lose. Unlike the 1980s and 1990s, you might go out of business. Or, perhaps worse, limp forward almost zombie like while squandering your best opportunities for innovation — or while your owners strip out whatever cash keeps them from selling or closing you outright[2].

You must take risks that have the possibility of failure. Not failure to learn -- that is unacceptable. But failure in the sense that you dedicate time, skill, effort and money and come up short.

[2]

The Rise Of A New Media Baron And The Emerging Threat Of News Deserts by Penelope Abernathy (2016)

Consider some innovation risks taken by participants in Knight Temple effort:

- Dallas' experiment with obsessions
- Miami's use of "Inc's"
- Philadelphia's effort to use data to create shared understanding of valuable audiences in the newsroom and marketing/ad sales
- Minneapolis's creation of a story form wiki

All four groups gained value and insights from these efforts. Still, as of the end of 2016, it was not clear just how much these innovations would spell the difference between just being in the game versus winning the game.

What Winning Looks Like

The Table Stakes are part of the winning playbook — but not all of it.

Figuring out the rest demands innovation — identifying, experimenting and learning whether *possible approaches* work.

Innovation is most likely to succeed if you know what you're seeking to accomplish. For example, when the computer scientists at Xerox PARC embarked on experiments that would lead to personal distributed computing, they started with a question: how can we convert computers from machines that calculate into machines that also communicate? How might we recreate the pencil, paper and telephone in the form of a computer[3]?

To them, winning looked like making computers into communication machines.

Here's what winning *looks like* for you and your colleagues:

- **Geography once again is a source of competitive advantage.** Today, geography is a source of competitive disadvantage. It's an anchor weighing you down. You cannot win the scale and reach game against competitors who are not stuck within a geographic footprint. There are exceptions. If you have a brand that travels well, you can and should explore specific products and services whose customer base is not geographically

3

See *Fumbling The Future* by Douglas K. Smith

confined. *Miami Herald* and *El Nuevo Herald* would be wise to embark on strategies grounded in Miami's status as the "capital of Latin America." But, be careful about this. It's unusual for metro, local or regional legacy news brands to have Miami's opportunities.

You must reverse what has happened over the past couple of decades. *You must find ways to make geography a competitive advantage.* That means identifying, experimenting, learning and expanding on *as many ways as possible* to convert your local presence, information and knowledge, convening authority, data, and relationships into products and services that big scale players cannot match no matter how much data they have, no matter how inexpensively they can operate, and no matter how powerfully they are branded.

- **You create substantial local value that is not an undifferentiated commodity.** You must create and deliver unique, not easily replicated value. In market economics, commodities are fungible: a ton of sand, for example, is a ton of sand. Competitors in fungible commodity industries work hard to use price, service, information and other things to differentiate their offerings. Your enterprise must avoid "news as an undifferentiated commodity" because you cannot win a commodity battle. Identifying and delivering *local benefits to local audiences* is key to de-commodifying what you do.

- **Your enterprise purposes go beyond providing content.** Content matters — a lot! Especially content that adds local, differentiated and not-easy-to-replicate value because it helps local audiences and enterprises navigate, survive and thrive locally. But content is not likely to be enough. You and your colleagues are more likely to win if, in addition to content, *your purposes also extend to fostering experiences, connectedness, conversations, convening and community problem solving.* Local audiences, for example, gain more value when your journalism initiates and sustains *conversations* as opposed to one-time reports (even one-time, major and insightful investigative or enterprise reports).

  Technology that is always on, always searchable, always social has altered when and how folks seek answers to the problems in their lives. Imagine a family buying a home for the first time. They have school age kids. They must find an affordable home in a safe area that has good schools and within reasonable commutes from the parents' jobs. A metro news enterprise's 2014 investigative report into local unaffordable housing, 2013 report on the crisis of leadership in the local school board, and 2015 toxic paint article — however amazing — do not serve this family very well. *An ongoing conversation that is persistently updated and connects the dots across schools, housing, crime and more serve them better.*

The disruptive forces that have destroyed the oligopoly or monopoly market position of your metro, local and regional news enterprise also have transformed how people live and enterprises operate in localities. **These forces have emptied out what "local" means and how it is experienced — and left a range of serious problems in their wake.** Many folks yearn to connect with others, to experience some form of community — of 'we' together. Your news enterprise's odds of winning go up when you *purposefully* choose to respond to these needs — both because the need is so markedly unfulfilled and because scale players like Facebook, Google, the *Washington Post* and others cannot efficiently and effectively serve such needs *in every locality on the planet*.

- **You weave together what happens in real and virtual life with what is local and social in as many ways as possible.** Imagine a study that records where and how people in your metro or local area spend their time. How much of each 24 hours do people spend in virtual as opposed to physical reality — where virtual means connected to technology (including radio and TV and not just the Web)? This blend of virtual and real is where you must compete to win by creating and delivering value in local experiences, connectedness, problem solving, conversations and convening — as well as content. Recall the 2016 viral phenomenon of Pokemon Go. It operated simultaneously in the physical and virtual worlds. It was social. And it was *local*.

- **You have many brands, products, services, revenue streams and business models — not just a few.**
  "What's *the* new business model?" is among the most asked questions about news over the past decade or so. And, *it's the wrong question*.

  Metro, local and regional legacy newspaper enterprises have lost their oligopoly/monopoly market power. No *business* model, however sophisticated, can replicate the profitability that comes with oligopoly or monopoly economic and market power. Facebook does not mint money because of its advertising dominated business model. It mints money because it has oligopolistic control over distribution.

  A better version of the question, then, is "In what ways might your metro, local or regional news enterprise regain the oligopoly and/or monopoly market power you have lost?"

  The answers lie in figuring out how to make what you do *indispensible* to those you serve and *un-replicable* by potential competitors. When and as you do that, you'll regain the pricing power of yesterday's print economics.

  Another version of the question simply adds an "S" at the end of business model. Instead of asking, "What's *the* new business model?" — and boxing yourselves into the delusion of a monolithic, single answer — ask this: "What *portfolio* of profitable business-to-consumer and business-to-business productS, serviceS, brandS, business modelS and revenue streamS can sustain us and those we serve as we navigate the profound changes afoot?"

- **Local audiences and enterprises pay you for the value you create in many ways not just a few.**
  Funneling lots of people and enterprises into paying you for content is essential to winning. But it's likely not enough to win. You need lots and lots — not just a few — ways for folks and organizations to pay you for what you do. You need as many revenue streams as possible — for example, subscriptions, memberships, eCommerce, ticket sales, one-time sales of products, fees for services and more. Yes, you have to avoid unwieldy complexity. And you have to make sure the economics of any particular product or service are profitable and sustainable. But you will not win if you get stuck in the

classic two-cylinder engine of newspaper profitability: subscriptions and advertising.

Winning also means that private, nonprofit and governmental enterprises pay you in many ways — not just a few — for access, data, technology and other services. Yes, these include advertising and sponsorship — and in many forms (e.g. native ads). Winning, though, goes beyond advertising and sponsorship to include monetizing data, licensing technology, providing digital marketing and other services, partnering in eCommerce and more.

- **Your enterprise costs are lower, more flexible and variable, and shared.** Neither you nor your colleagues nor your shareholders/owners will win if your enterprise strategy relentlessly reduces costs to stay ahead of declining revenues. Your owners can profit this way. They *can* take cash out of the business. And you and your colleagues might hold onto your jobs for some time to come. Eventually, though, your news enterprise will fail.

    Winning demands changing how you think about and incur costs. For example, you must lower your average cost of content while simultaneously increasing its value to those you serve. You need to migrate away from costly print and print related distribution. You need to make your costs as variable and flexible as possible — for example, through using independent contractors and aggregation, licensing instead of building technology and tools, shifting at least some folks' compensation to include incentives, outsourcing work to others and so forth. And for reasons spelled out in Table Stake #6 about partnering, you must figure out how to share costs and risks if you are to increase the odds of staying technologically relevant while simultaneously lowering the costs of risk taking.

Innovation Gaps

Gap: The need for innovation versus capacity for innovation: Compare your enterprise's cash and people capacity for innovation against what is needed:

- **Cash:** Working with the CFO, CEO and others, identify *how much cash you can and will dedicate* each year to innovation, experimentation, change and risk taking. Just go ahead and do this. Get a number! As you're doing this, remember: This is cash you folks are willing to bet on innovations that might fall short. If you do not have a budget line called "innovation," then it is likely the answer to this question is "zero" — we are unwilling to lose any cash on bets that might not work out.

- **People:** Identify the key people throughout the enterprise who are best suited to pursue innovation, risk taking and experimentation. With the list in hand, ask/answer "How much time and attention are we prepared to have these folks dedicate to innovation?" Avoid the delusion of percentages like 2% of their time. Instead use increments not less than 10%. Add up all the available time and attention and you'll have a people budget for innovation. (Pay attention to functional expertise. For example, in addition to the enterprise's total time and attention budget for innovation, how much is available from, say, technology folks?)

Put together a **full list of innovations** required to (1) experiment with new products, services and audience-first approaches, (2) have what's needed in terms of technology and tools, (3) skill up the workforce (through training as well as new hires), and (4) any other opportunities as well (e.g. an acquisition, a shift in strategic vendors, entering into a new form of business such as events marketing — and so forth).

Estimate the cash and people time required to pursue these opportunities. Compare that to what you identified as available — and you'll have a good enough picture of any **gaps in innovation capacity.**

Gap: Innovation disciplines

Take this quiz and discuss it, remembering that "Yes" responses indicate gaps:

	YES	NO
We rarely, if ever, establish specific goals prior to embarking on any innovation or change.		
We rarely, if ever, describe specific learning objectives prior to embarking on any innovation or change.		
We do not have an innovation budget of money and people's time/effort.		
We fail to distinguish our levels of confidence and certainty prior to embarking on any innovation or change; that is, while we sometimes discuss assumptions, we fail to name those we are most worried about versus those we are most confident about.		
We do not specifically ask or discuss just how confident we are about having the capabilities and capacities required for innovations and changes at hand.		
We neither ask nor answer just how confident we are that a market exists for possible new products or services.		
We do not have well-established criteria for comparing and choosing among different possible innovations.		
We neither have an individual executive nor a team or committee responsible and accountable for managing innovation and change.		
We often pursue innovations strictly within the newsroom or strictly on the business side — as opposed to the entire enterprise working together.		
Not that many people in our enterprise understand the difference between continuous improvement versus fundamental innovation — or why they matter.		
We are not as adept as we should be at failing fast and failing cheap in order to convert uncertainties into go/no go choices for moving forward with innovations.		
We don't have a portfolio of innovations underway that we manage on a persistent basis.		
TOTAL		

Actions To Take To Close The Gaps

There is no recipe that guarantees your metro, local or regional will win. Still, there are steps you can take to build and practice **the disciplines of innovation** from which winning approaches can emerge. These include:

1. **Distinguish continuous improvement from fundamental innovation**
2. **Establish a budget for fundamental innovation — and use criteria for choosing among ideas competing for those resources**
3. **Embrace fast following**
4. **Look again at Table Stake #6: figure out how to partner with other metros on fundamental innovation and fast following**
5. **Put an executive, or more likely, a team in charge of enterprise wide innovation**

1. Distinguish continuous improvement from fundamental innovation

All news enterprises must continuously get better at what they do. Consider, for example, the headline rodeo at Dallas Morning News. Each morning, folks gather and use headlines as the basis for choosing stories to emphasize. But, they do more than that. They brainstorm and discuss how they might better craft headlines to generate better results. They also review results for previous story headlines — and tease out lessons about what worked well, what didn't work well, and why.

This is what continuous improvement looks like. *It is focused on performance results and learning: learning from continuously doing the work at hand in new and different ways every day.* In well-managed enterprises, everyone seeks to improve continuously — every day — in the work they do. This discipline for continuous improvement includes:

- **Setting clear performance goals:** set specific performance goals that folks are expected to achieve through continuous improvement — that is, getting better at what they do every day (Example: Desk X commits to growing traffic and engagement by 5% each month.)

- **Articulate learning objectives:** expect people to identify and articulate what they are trying to learn — what hypotheses they are trying to test. Then pay attention to — and debrief and learn from — what works, what doesn't work and why (Example: Over the next few months, Desk X will experiment and learn about the impact of "two or more story elements" — visual, traffic, audio, etc. — on traffic and engagement.)

- **Be clear on the resources needed:** provide folks the time and space — and in some cases cash — needed to practice continuous improvement (Example: Those of us on Desk X will experiment with 'two or more story elements' at least one-third of the time, seek out visual, audience and other specialists to help us, and spend at least an hour a week debriefing and learning what works.)

The nature of risks and uncertainties distinguish continuous improvement from fundamental innovation. For example, contrast Dallas' headline rodeo with Philadelphia's effort to use data as a bridge to better understand and act on what the newsroom and ad sales see as valuable users. Philadelphia's effort was more fundamental than that of Dallas because the Philly folks had to:

- **Figure out if the technology existed to even make the innovation possible:** The data and analytical formats used by marketing differed from those used in the newsroom. In addition, getting to shared data and analytical approaches demanded partnering with third parties in entirely new ways.

- **Shape and grow significant new capabilities:** Newsroom and advertising marketing and sales folks all had to learn new skills, behaviors, attitudes and ways of working together. Content creators had to figure out how to make use of the insights from the data bridge in ways that supported high quality journalism. Ad sales folks had to learn how to shift from selling spaces for ads to selling audiences.

- **Learn if the effort would be attractive to advertisers:** Philadelphia was confident that advertisers would pay more for attractive audiences. Still, they had to find out if this would happen.

- **Deal with internal questions, skepticism and/or lack of confidence about whether the effort was worthwhile:** Innovations of this magnitude inevitably involve fundamental shifts in 'how we do things around here' — which in turn trigger anxieties about whether the time, effort and money involved will be worth it.

This Philly effort went well beyond getting better every day at what folks did. And the discipline — what it takes to get good at fundamental innovation — is more extensive than continuous improvement because it:

- **Involves more serious risks and uncertainties.** If Dallas folks tweak a headline and get it wrong, the story will not do so well. If Philadelphia cannot get third parties to devote the time and attention to build a useful data and analytic bridge, neither users, the newsroom, advertisers nor ad sales folks will even get the chance to see if they can make a positive difference.

- **Can quickly get expensive.** Time, money and valued relationships (e.g. with the third parties) can get costly fast in the Philadelphia situation whereas the headline rodeo in Dallas only redirects how existing resources are used instead of risking more of those resources.

- **Takes longer.** The time it takes to learn whether a Dallas headline makes a difference to traffic and engagement is a day or less. Philadelphia's data bridge innovation was still underway nearly a year after it began.

Fundamental innovation and continuous improvement each benefit from setting clear performance goals, articulating learning objectives and being clear on the needed resources. In addition, though, the discipline of fundamental innovation demands:

- **Distinguishing assumptions from knowledge.**
  Common sense and experience indicates that proposed changes in strategy or innovation involve assumptions. For example, the Philadelphia data bridge assumes that information can be assembled that is rich and actionable enough to lead to results. Research by Columbia Business School Professor Rita McGrath[4] indicates that assumptions like this one — assumptions that inevitably get articulated at the beginning of major efforts — are *all but forgotten within six weeks of the start* of such projects. Six weeks. For a set of cultural and habitual reasons, folks involved in innovation across all industries somehow, someway come to believe and act as if the articulation of assumptions turns the assumption into reality.

  To avoid this, folks in your news enterprise must distinguish assumptions (things that must work yet about which you have relatively little confidence) from knowledge (things that must work and about which you are reasonably to fully confident).

  Writing these down — and monitoring instead of forgetting them — is a key element in the discipline of fundamental innovation. Consider using this 4 point scale that was used in Table Stakes (as well as other programs such as Sulzberger that deploy Doug Smith's challenge-centric, performance-and-accountability approach™):

  1. Pure gut, just a hunch, hopeful thinking
  2. A few insights, some evidence, many remaining questions
  3. Mounting evidence, a small number of remaining questions
  4. Extensive evidence and known facts, real certainty/knowledge

  For example, the Philly data bridge team confidently believed advertisers would pay for qualified and more attractive audiences. They monitored this confidence — and only grew more confident as a result. In contrast, though, the team had *a lot of questions and uncertainty* about whether (1) the needed technology would work; (2) the advertiser information would be rich and actionable enough to yield results; and, (3) enough value would happen soon enough to keep the effort going. By

[4]

For more on Professor McGrath's important work, see *Discovery Driven Growth* by McGrath and MacMillan (Harvard Business School Press, 2009), and *The End Of Competitive Advantage* by McGrath (Harvard Business School Press, 2013).

writing down these assumptions, testing and learning about them, and monitoring what emerged, the team avoided the traps of forgetting the assumptions and/or magically converting them into 'facts' to be relied upon.

- **Paying attention to the cost — not rate — of failure:** Professor McGrath exhorts folks involved in fundamental innovation to *fail fast, fail cheap in converting assumptions into knowledge* — in the above scale, converting 1s and 2s into 3s and 4s. She has a file of costly failures (to make it into her file, a company has to have lost at least a billion dollars on an innovation that failed). In one example, executives at an industrial chemical company imagined using their chemical know how to enter and dominate the field of women's fashion. Industrial chemicals and women's fashion: what do you think? Chemical compounds are essential to fibers and threads. Still, it's not the most obvious connection; this innovation for the chemical company depended on many profound uncertainties. Yet, instead of cataloguing — then quickly and cheaply testing — the core assumptions, the company managed to invest more than a billion dollars before dropping the idea. Put differently, the chemical company fell into the trap well characterized by the famous line from the movie *Field of Dreams*: build it and they shall come.

- **Defining — and using — phases and "traffic lights" to manage/monitor progress of fundamental innovations:** Because the time horizons for fundamental innovations can stretch over several months or longer, it's wise to define a series of phases with varying degrees of expectations and permitted resources and risk taking. The risks, resources and expectations for the first phase of any fundamental innovation are much more circumscribed than, say, the last phase when an enterprise is seriously considering rolling out something new. Separating these phases are "traffic lights": a formal evaluation point where innovations get reviewed and either approved for the next phase's greater risks, resources and expectations (a green light), rejected and stopped (red light) or returned to the previous phase for one more try (yellow light).

You must define the number of phases plus expectations and allowable resources and risks for each phase. Three or four phases usually suffice. And, within each phase, you must define what are the expectations for what is to be accomplished. For example, phase 1 expectations might include failing fast and failing cheap at the most critical assumptions (the 1s and 2s in the scale mentioned above). Teams pursuing a fundamental innovation in phase 1 might be given limited resources and also told not to take any significant risks that could affect the brand. In this case, at the end of phase 1, only teams that had converted 1s and 2s into enough knowledge and confidence would be permitted to move to phase 2 (that is, given a green light).

2. Establish a budget for fundamental innovation — and use criteria to choose among ideas competing for those resources

Because of deteriorating economics, it is understandable that metro, local and regional legacy newspaper enterprises tend not to budget money, time and effort for possible innovations that could fail. It's hard, though, to imagine how such enterprises will win in the absence of taking such risks.

Instead, your news enterprise ought to establish a pool of money and a set budget of people's time and attention — and explicitly dedicate these resources to experimenting with fundamentally new and different ways of adding value to your markets and local communities. Once you've done so, it's essential to (1) spell out criteria for which innovations to pursue; and, (2) make sure to only compare 'apples to apples' when you do this: that is, do not choose between continuous improvement possibilities versus fundamental innovation possibilities.

3. Embrace fast following

Metro, local and regional news enterprises must set aside budgets for fundamental innovation. Still, such budgets will be too limited to conceive and test the entire range and number of fundamental innovations likely required for success in the dynamic and changing landscape of news, information, technology and more that so convulse the industry.

As a consequence, your news enterprise must embrace what is called *fast following*: monitoring innovations that emerge with an eye on quickly 'following' — quickly using innovation disciplines to test whether and how what works elsewhere will or might work in your market. It is critical to use criteria for selecting innovations to follow/test — and to use the core disciplines of cataloguing and monitoring assumptions versus knowledge, failing fast and cheap for key assumptions, and using phases and gates to manage innovations that will take time to get right.

4. Look again at Table Stake #6: Partner to expand your capacity and capabilities at lower and more flexible cost

Geographically bound markets, difficult and challenging economics, highly dynamic shifts in technology and socio-demographic behaviors, the huge range and number of possibilities to test, and limited resources for fundamental innovation — all of these reinforce why your news enterprise must consider partnering as part of your approach to fundamental innovation. The corporate chains in news media have an advantage here. For example, among their criteria for what innovations to pursue, they can (should) require "if this innovation is successful, it is replicable in some to many of our other news enterprises."

Independently owned news enterprises must figure out how to collaborate — among themselves and with others — toward the same end because no single news enterprise on its own has the time or resources to test all of the innovations that are likely needed to find a path to winning.

5. Put a team in charge of enterprise wide innovation

Senior leaders must ask a team to take charge of managing innovation. This team's charter might include oversight of continuous improvement as well as fundamental innovation.

This team probably ought to be no greater than 5 or 6 folks who come from the newsroom, digital strategy, marketing/publisher, technology and product management.

Your news enterprise's senior management group should:

- Define the team's charter while also setting specific expectations about (1) performance outcomes and learning objectives; (2) the budget of money and people resources the team should use; and, (3) the team's authority to use partnering approaches.
- Expect the team to define the disciplines, process (e.g. phases and traffic lights) and criteria for choosing among possible innovations and managing progress
- Establish periodic reviews (for example, once every two to four months) when the team shares with senior management the portfolio of efforts underway; progress updates on what's moving forward versus what's being stopped or put on pause; how much of the budget has been used versus what remains; and, how the company's innovation efforts are doing against performance and learning goals.

The team should use the charter as well as processes and criteria established to identify and choose among innovative ideas and approaches — ones that should explicitly call for fast following, home grown innovations and partnering. In particular, the innovation team should:

- Brainstorm (with selected others) as complete a list as possible of innovation and change opportunities/challenges necessary to win;
- For each possible innovation or change, identify:
    — The people/team who will pursue the innovation in question
    — The estimated required cost (money, time) to pursue

- The uncertainties (hi/lo for technology, capability, market readiness and internal confidence about market)
- The other risks involved (e.g. brand risk)
- Whether partnering is a preferred approach; and, if so, how that will get done
* Establish criteria for selecting which innovations and changes to pursue now versus later
* Make choices and get going.

With the initial choices about which innovations to pursue in hand, the team then should:

* Ask teams pursuing selected innovations to define the performance results as well as learning objectives they seek (the learning objectives must connect to converting any sources of uncertainty into clarity and certainty)
* Choose the most appropriate disciplines for these teams to use among:
    - Continuous improvement: establishing and pursuing performance and skill improvements in the context of 'just doing our jobs'
    - Fundamental innovation: using a 'phases and traffic lights' approach to riskier and more uncertain innovations
* Establish periodic review sessions in which progress and lessons learned are monitored — and choices get made to add other innovation and change efforts as the needed resources to do so emerge
* Periodically (and persistently) going back to the first step above: that is, brainstorm as complete a list as possible of innovation and change opportunities/challenges necessary to get to — indeed, beyond — table stakes (including those arising from fast following and, if such collaboration exists, those being done with partners)

Tracking Progress

Each particular innovation — just as each continuous innovation effort (see examples above about "Desk X") — has its own scorecard — it's own set of outcome-defined performance results plus learning objectives. And, your news enterprise's team running innovation and continuous improvement must monitor, update and act upon those objectives.

Having said that, we'll conclude this chapter by repeating what success looks like for winning news enterprises (at least as of mid 2017). At least a couple times a year (if not more often), your news enterprise ought to assess how you're doing against these markers of success — and, if you have gaps, how you'll close them:

- We have made geography a source of competitive advantage and profitability.
- We routinely create substantial local value in ways that others cannot replicate.
- Our enterprise purposes go beyond providing content and also include fostering experiences, connectedness, conversations, convening and community problem solving.
- Our newsroom weaves together in as many ways as possible what our targeted audiences experience in real and virtual life with what is for those audiences also local and social.
- Our news enterprise has many brands, products, services, revenue streams and business models — not just a few.
- Our local audiences and enterprises pay us for the value we create in many ways not just a few.
- Our enterprise costs are lower, more flexible and variable, and shared.

Notes

Notes

About the Initiative

The Knight-Lenfest Newsroom Initiative is designed to help major metropolitan daily news organizations accelerate their shift to digital from print, evolving their practices to reach new audiences and better engage their communities. Launched in 2015 at Temple University's School of Media and Communications as the Knight-Temple Table Stakes project, it expanded beyond the original four newsrooms in 2017 when the John S. and James L. Knight Foundation was joined by The Lenfest Institute for Journalism in supporting the initiative.

Made in the USA
Middletown, DE
08 May 2019